A Century of Violence in Soviet Russia

A CENTURY OF
VIOLENCE IN
SOVIET RUSSIA

ALEXANDER N. YAKOVLEV

Translated from the Russian by Anthony Austin

Foreword by Paul Hollander

Yale University Press

New Haven and London

The more representatives of the reactionary clergy
we manage to shoot, the better.
— V. ULIANOV (LENIN)

Originally published in Russian under the title *Krestosev*. Copyright © 2000 by Vagrius and
A. N. Yakovlev.

Designed by James J. Johnson and set in Sabon Roman types by The Composing Room of
Michigan, Inc.

Printed in the United States of America by R. R. Donnelley & Sons, Harrisonburg, Virginia.

Library of Congress Cataloging-in-Publication Data

IAkovlev, A. N. (Aleksandr Nikolaevich), 1923–
 [Krestosev. English]
 A century of violence in Soviet Russia / Alexander N. Yakovlev; translated from the
 Russian by Anthony Austin ; foreword by Paul Hollander.
   p. cm.
 Includes bibliographical references and index.
 ISBN 0-300-08760-8 (alk. paper)

 1. Communism—Soviet Union—History. 2. Soviet Union—Politics and government.
3. Political purges—Soviet Union—History. I. Austin, Anthony. II. Hollander, Paul, 1932–
III. Title.
HX311.5 .I3513 2002
947.084—dc21   2002022991

A catalogue record for this book is available from the British Library.

The paper in this book meets the guidelines for permanence and durability of the Committee
on Production Guidelines for Book Longevity of the Council on Library Resources.

10 9 8 7 6 5 4 3 2 1

Contents

Foreword

Alexander Yakovlev's name is largely unknown to the American public, although he was a major political figure during perestroika, a key adviser to Gorbachev, and a high-ranking official in the Soviet political hierarchy for most of his adult life.

Born in 1923, Yakovlev came from a poor peasant family; his father had four years of education and was the first chairman of the local collective farm. His mother was an illiterate, "downtrodden peasant woman and a religious believer to the end of her days." Yakovlev became a Party member in 1943. He worked in the Central Committee of the Party between 1953 and 1973 in positions connected with ideology and propaganda and became head of the Party's propaganda department in 1969. He was ambassador to Canada from 1973 to 1983; in 1983 he was appointed director of the Institute of International Economy and Relations. Under Gorbachev he was restored in 1985 to his position as head of the Party's propaganda department, and in 1986 he became secretary of the Central Committee in charge of ideological matters. In 1987 he was appointed to the Politburo.

Yakovlev has published another important book in English, *The Fate of Marxism in Russia,* a pathbreaking study that examines the link between Marxism and the political practices and institutions of the Soviet Union and other "actually existing" Communist systems.[1]

A Century of Violence in Soviet Russia provides a remarkable range and amount of information despite its compactness, enumerating and illuminating the major phases, trends, and events associated with the repressive policies of the Soviet system. Like the earlier, more theoretical work, it amounts to an exploration and summation of what went wrong with what used to be called, charitably, "the Soviet experiment." But unlike the other volume, *A Century of Violence* focuses on specific institutional and moral failures and the human costs the system exacted; it identifies the groups and strata of the population that suffered most. As such, it may be compared to *The Black Book of Communism*, which attempted to document and examine the crimes not only of the Soviet Union but of all other existing or extinct Communist states.[2] There are, however, important differences. None of the contributors to *The Black Book* were ever Communist officials, let alone high-ranking ones, and, due to its scope, *The Black Book* could not be as detailed and thorough as the work here introduced.

Readers accustomed to dispassionate, scholarly analyses of political phenomena and traumatic historical events should be warned: this is not a detached, bland discussion wrapped in neutral social scientific terminology—it is an emotionally charged expression of deeply felt pain and moral indignation, which accumulated during a lifetime of witnessing the suffering, misery, and mendaciousness inflicted by the Soviet system. Doubtless Yakovlev's personal pain was intensified, even in retrospect, by the fact that he himself devoted much of his life to that system.

While there are many critiques of Communist systems by authors of different backgrounds and nationalities, what makes this volume unusual is the biography and stature of its author. It is hard to think of any other Communist official of comparable rank and distinction who so explicitly, sweepingly, and powerfully repudiated the system he was a part of, who was as much an insider and a product of the system as Alexander Yakovlev. Only Milovan Djilas occupies a comparable position: he was similarly highly placed (in the Yugoslav Communist ruling elite) and his indictment of Soviet-style Communism is notable for its depth and scope.[3] Trotsky, too, renounced the Soviet regime in its Stalinist incarnation, but he remained a Marxist and even a Leninist, and his critiques of the Soviet system are less far-reaching than Yakovlev's. Unlike other insider critics of Communist systems, Yakovlev did not defect, nor was he exiled. He still lives in Russia, devoting much of his life since the collapse of the Soviet system to the fate of its victims in his capacity as head of the Commission on the Rehabilitation of Victims of Political Repression.

While for most readers Yakovlev's insider position and perspective will immeasurably add to the authenticity of this book, there will probably be some for whom the intensity of his disillusionment and moral passion will cast doubt on the credibility of his message. For them, the demise of the Soviet Union has had the unhappy result of rendering the United States the only superpower. They are even more likely to be disturbed by Yakovlev's unqualified rejection of Marxism and not just the Soviet system. In their eyes it is a grave transgression to link Marxist theory to the policies and practices of a Communist system such as the Soviet Union used to be. Yakovlev has no doubt of such a linkage, as he also made clear in his earlier book.

Yakovlev's critiques of the Soviet system will not be easy to discredit. He is neither a pampered Western intellectual in search of a cause nor a defector who can be accused of having been bought off by Western lucre. It will be interesting to see the response of those who find it hard to stomach his conviction that Marxism, too, bears significant responsibility for the human toll exacted by Communist systems.

Yakovlev ranks as a major historical figure on several grounds. In the first place, he made crucial contributions to the political changes associated with Gorbachev, to the liberalization of the Soviet system that hastened its end. He was also a key contributor to the intellectual and spiritual ferment that led to perestroika and glasnost, promoting the quiet and gradual evolution that preceded Gorbachev's reforms and providing their intellectual foundations. Known as "the father of glasnost," he belonged to the small group of Party intellectuals who (as another close associate of Gorbachev, Anatoly Chernyaev, puts it) "were in many ways the ambassadors to Gorbachev of a larger liberal intelligentsia, one whose humanist, 'Westernizing' philosophical and practical orientation had been developing for over two decades. . . . [They were] collectively described as 'Children of the 20th Congress,' reformist thinkers who kept alive the unfulfilled hopes of Khrushchev's 'thaw' for broader liberalization of Soviet society and integration with the international community."[4] Yakovlev was also among those who tried to keep Gorbachev on a steady course of reform and to bolster his liberal-democratic policies against the resistance of the nomenklatura and his own fluctuating political impulses.

Yakovlev has been unique among former Soviet officials and ideologues in confronting the relationship between Marxism and the debilitating flaws of the Soviet system. *The Fate of Marxism in Russia* is the major expression of that effort in English, but the reader will find references to the same theme in this volume.

Among his other contributions, Yakovlev has devoted a great deal of his time since the early 1990s to documenting and rehabilitating the victims of Soviet Communism and has remained a voice of critical conscience in the post-Communist period. In the course of these activities he has acquired many detractors at both ends of the political spectrum. In recent years he has been among the most outspoken critics of the many serious deformations of Russian public life and politics associated with old-style Communism, right-wing nationalism, and anti-Semitism. He understands keenly the deep roots of the historical pathologies that the Soviet system represented and that made the transition to a political democracy and civil society difficult:

> The land of Rus accepted Christianity from Constantinople in A.D. 988. Characteristics of Byzantine rule of that era—baseness, cowardliness, venality, treachery, overcentralization, apotheosis of the ruler's personality—dominate in Russia's social and political life to this day. In the twelfth century the various fragmented Russian principalities . . . were conquered by the Mongols. Asian traditions and customs, with their disregard for the individual and for human rights and their cult of might, violence, despotic power, and lawlessness became part of the Russian people's way of life.
>
> The tragedy of Russia lay first and foremost in this: that for a thousand years it was ruled by men and not by laws. . . . They ruled ineptly, bloodily. The people existed for the government, not the government for the people. Russia avoided classical slavery. But it has not yet emerged from feudalism; it is still enslaved by an official imperial ideol-

ogy, the essence of which is that the state is everything and the individual nothing.

These circumstances presumably also help account for what Yakovlev does not hesitate to call the "slave psychology" of the Russian people, which remains a major obstacle to the genuine liberalization of the society and its economic reconstruction. Thus Yakovlev connects both the pre-Soviet and Soviet past and the post-Communist present, and his reflections on recent developments are pessimistic.

A Century of Violence is an impassioned, bitter, and emotional indictment of the Soviet system from its earliest days and a methodical and detailed inventory of its misdeeds. Yakovlev has no illusions about the "purity" of the early Soviet goals and policies allegedly promoted by Lenin or, for that matter, about the personality of Lenin, whom he regards as having been as evil and unscrupulous as Stalin. ("Stalin did not think up anything that was not there under Lenin: executions, hostage taking, concentration camps, and all the rest.") This is a major departure from the conventional wisdom that has long prevailed among Western academic specialists, who detect significant discontinuities between the policies and personalities of these two figures.

A survey, in effect, of the worst repressions of Soviet history from Lenin to perestroika, *A Century of Violence* contains a wealth of information, including case histories of victimization, based both on Yakovlev's personal experience and on his privileged access to archival sources. Yakovlev systematically probes the policies and individuals behind these repressions, whose victims included children and adolescents, Mensheviks, Social Revolutionaries, Anarchists, and other socialists (early allies of the Bolsheviks), the peasants, the intelligentsia, the clergy, the nationalities and Jews, former prisoners of war (in World War II), and civilians taken to Germany as forced laborers. Yakovlev holds the Soviet system responsible for the deaths of at least sixty million Soviet citizens. He is particularly strong in his coverage of the repression of the intelligentsia, touching on many famous groups and individuals, including those silenced, exiled, or imprisoned in the 1920s; the "Trotskyist terrorist" writers in Leningrad in 1937; Pasternak, Daniel, Sinyavsky, Brodsky, and Solzhenitsyn.

Another strength of the volume is its treatment of the ethnic-national policies and repressions directed at the Ukrainians, Volga Germans, Kalmyks, Crimean Tatars, Ingush, and others and its detailed discussion—particularly relevant today—of the mistreatment of the Chechens.

While many of the major events and policies discussed in this volume are known, at least in their general outlines, many others are likely to be unfamiliar, even to specialists. As early as 1918, for instance, there was labor unrest in Motovilikha, a village in Perm province, where "the workers demanded a stop to special food privileges for Soviet government and Party workers, an end to summary executions, guarantees of freedom of speech and assembly." Yakovlev also brings to light Lenin's predilection for hostage taking as a means of consolidating the system; the mistreatment of close to half a million Soviet prisoners of war returned after the Soviet-Finnish war; the communications between Romain Rolland (the pro-Soviet French writer) and Stalin about the punishment of children and adolescents; Meyerhold's complaint to Molotov about his treatment in prison; the numerous intrigues and denunciations among various writers and artists; the persecution of theater companies and moviemakers in the 1930s; the fate of the Korean minority; the huge number of Soviet workers severely punished simply for being late for work; the alleged organizations of Jewish bourgeois nationalists in the Stalin Works in Moscow and at the Kuznetsk metallurgical complex; the preparations to deport Jews at the time of the "doctors' plot" before Stalin's death; the suppression of the 1962 food riots in Novocherkassk. Yakovlev also demolishes the myth, widespread in the West, of Yuri Andropov's liberal credentials. It may also surprise some readers that Yakovlev regards the early twentieth century as the brightest, most promising era of Russian history.

Yakovlev's revelations and graphic descriptions of the many misdeeds of the system are only one noteworthy aspect of this book. Another is what we learn about the transformation of his own beliefs and attitudes, how and why he became profoundly critical of the system he helped legitimize and keep in power for decades.

The case of Yakovlev illuminates the process of political disillusionment in our times. It raises the intriguing question of what it takes to reject a political system and its legitimizing ideas for a man raised in, fully committed to, and well rewarded by it, a high-ranking member of the political elite who spent much of his life in the rarefied heights of the nomenklatura. Even more significant and unusual is that this sweeping, unconditional rejection of the system comes from a man with a long and deep involvement with official doctrine, with ideology, and with the task of convincing the population of the virtues and legitimacy of the system. In an interview in 1994 he linked his disaffection precisely to his involvement with ideology: "The main thing that changed my worldview was the fact that my ideology was my business. . . . I took the work seriously. And gradually, step by step, more and more often, it nauseated me. Then I went back again to the primary sources. . . . When you get older faith alone is not enough, you want to look more deeply. And as soon as you begin to analyze what you believe it begins to crack."[5]

Three sets of experiences played a major role in the undermining of Yakovlev's beliefs and commitment to the system. The first was acquired during World War II, in which he served and sustained serious injuries, the second was Khrushchev's historic revelations during the 20th Party Congress in 1956, and the third was his demotion in 1972 as the result of an article he wrote criticizing Russian nationalism and anti-Semitism.

His doubts and disillusionment during World War II were stimulated by the inhumane treatment of former Soviet POWs: "A serviceman taken prisoner was regarded as having committed a premeditated crime. . . . Soldiers and commanding officers who had broken out of encirclement were treated as potential traitors and spies. . . . When, at the beginning of 1942, a group of us young officers arrived at the Volkhov front . . . we saw this practice take place under frontline conditions." Soviet soldiers were supposed to fight to the death regardless of the circumstances. There was also apprehension on the part of the authorities that exposure to life outside the Soviet Union, even for prisoners of war or slave laborers, might have implanted attitudes that would erode unquestioning loyalty to the system. Sometimes former Red Army officers who had been liberated from prison camps or had broken out of encirclement were assigned to "assault battalions," which "were employed in situations where it was almost impossible to stay alive." It is hardly surprising that such experiences gradually undermined Yakovlev's political faith; what is more surprising is that they did not have a similar impact on many others and did not impair their capacity to work for the regime.

Another particularly disturbing experience was Yakovlev's witnessing the return of Soviet POWs from Germany:

> I remember the Vspolye train station in Yaroslavl a year after the war, the rumor that a train would be passing through with some of our soldiers . . . from German prisoner of war camps. I was still on crutches, but I went with the others . . . to watch. Railway cars, small windows with iron bars; thin, pale, bewildered faces at the windows. And on the platform, women weeping and wailing . . . running back and forth between the cars looking for their husbands, brothers, sweethearts. . . .
>
> The people on the platform . . . couldn't understand why these boys from the Nazi camps were being transported like criminals to the Urals and Siberia. I remember the tortured faces, the total incomprehension, theirs and mine.

The second major blow to Yakovlev's loyalties and beliefs (as to those of many others of his generation) was Khrushchev's famous speech at the 20th Party Congress in February 1956. Yakovlev was present and what he heard, he says, "plunged me into the deepest dejection, if not despair. Everything seemed unreal, even that I was sitting there in the Kremlin hearing words that were destroying everything I had lived by, shattering the past, rending the soul. Everything crumbled, never to be made whole again." Nevertheless, Yakovlev remained a highly placed functionary for decades to come, leading what must have been a difficult inner life:

> I had been honest in my previous faith, and I was equally honest in rejecting it. I came to detest Stalin, . . . who had deceived me so cruelly and trampled on my romantic dreams. From then on I devoted myself to searching out a way to put an end to this inhuman system. . . . All this took the form of hope, not action. . . .
>
> I lived a double life of agonizing dissimulation. I conformed, I pretended, trying all the while not to lose my bearings and disgrace myself. No longer interested in working for the Central Committee, I looked for an out and found one. . . . I sensed a need to reeducate myself, to reread everything I'd read before, go back to original sources—Marx, Engels, Lenin, the German philosophers, the French socialists, the British economists, all the fountainheads of my outlook on the world.

Even before the 20th Congress, Khrushchev made public statements disclosing the rampant mismanagement of the economy; these
Yakovlev "jotted down" and found distressing. To wit:

> We've been squandering the accumulated capital of the people's trust
> in the Party. We can't go on endlessly exploiting the people's trust. . . .
> We've become like priests and preachers: we promise a kingdom in
> heaven, but in the here and now there are no potatoes. Only our long-
> suffering Russian people would put up with something like that. . . . We
> are not priests, we are Communists, and we must give them this happi-
> ness here on earth.
> When I was a worker, there was no socialism, but there were pota-
> toes, and now we have built socialism and there are no potatoes.

The third set of experiences that helped change his worldview was
set in motion in 1968 in Prague, where he was sent to oversee Soviet
journalists covering the Soviet invasion. At the time he was deputy
head of the propaganda department of the CPSU Central Committee, and this was a vital assignment. Officially the dispatch of troops
was described as friendly assistance, but Yakovlev was shocked by
what he found. "I saw gallows with effigies of Soviet soldiers hanging there. . . . People were shouting 'Fascists, Fascists.'" Yakovlev
has summed up the experience as "an important school for me. . . . It
had a great sobering effect."[6]

As to the article that led to his demotion as head of the Party's propaganda department (and to his exile to Canada as ambassador), he
recalls: "No sooner had I written an article in 1972 on the dangers of
chauvinism, nationalism, and anti-Semitism in the USSR—hung out
the dirty laundry, as it were—than I was removed from all Party
work. Moreover, I remain labeled to this day as a 'Russophobe' and
a leader of 'kike-masons' and supplied with . . . different surnames—
Epshtein, Yankelevich, Yakobson." In other words, Yakovlev continues to pay a price for defying both the elements in the old Soviet
hierarchy and the anti-Semitic groups and attitudes that have resur-
faced over the past decade.

In Yakovlev's summation, the most serious damage (and the hardest to repair) has been to what Trotsky called the "human raw material." Political reform, institutional change, free elections, and new
laws are welcome and essential, but they will not create a stable,

democratic, and decent society unless the basic attitudes and values of the people change, or those of a critical number of people change. Yakovlev writes: "The Bolshevik regime is guilty not only of the deaths of millions of people and the tragic consequences for their families, not only of creating an atmosphere of total fear and lies, but of a crime against conscience, of producing its notorious 'new historic community of people' distorted by malice, doublethink, suspiciousness, and pretense. Lenin and Stalin and their henchmen . . . destroyed the nation's gene pool, . . . undermining the potential for the flowering of science and culture."

This is indispensable reading for anybody who wants to grasp the nature of the Soviet system, the full range of its crimes against its people, the sources of its collapse, and the grave problems it left behind.

PAUL HOLLANDER

Abbreviations

AKhU	Administrative-Economic Department
CC	Central Committee
CEC	Central Executive Committee
CPSU	Communist Party of the Soviet Union
FSB	Federal Security Service
KGB	Committee on State Security
MGB	Ministry of State Security
MVD	Ministry of Internal Affairs
NKVD	People's Commissariat of Internal Affairs
OGPU	United State Political Administration
PSR	Party of Socialist Revolutionaries
RKP	Russian Communist Party
RKP(b)	Russian Communist Party (of the Bolsheviks)
RSDRP	Russian Social Democratic Workers Party
RSFSR	Russian Soviet Federated Socialist Republic
SNK	Council of People's Commissars
SR	Socialist Revolutionaries
TsKK	Central Control Commission
VChK-OGPU	All-Union Extraordinary Commission-United State Political Administration
VKP(b)	All-Union Communist Party (of the Bolsheviks)
VTsIK	All-Union Central Executive Committee

THE SOWING OF CROSSES

Sleeves rolled up, axe in hand, they lopped off heads. . . . They packed them off by freight like cattle: so many bulls, so many cows, so many lambs. . . . If the nation only knew their hands dripped with innocent blood, it would have met them not with applause but with stones.

— MARSHAL G. K. ZHUKOV

LATE IN LIFE, as fate would have it, I was called upon to take part in my country's progress toward freedom. It fell to me to assume the awesome burden of heading a commission—initially under the Politburo of the Central Committee (CC) of the Communist Party of the Soviet Union (CPSU) and subsequently under the office of the president of Russia—on the rehabilitation of victims of the political repression of our past.

The task has been a weary one. To descend step by step down seventy years of Bolshevik rule into a dungeon strewn with human bones and reeking of dried blood is to see your faith in humankind dissolve.

Papers are not destroyed; people are. More and more of the bloodstained documents pile up on my desk. From the archives of the president and of the Lubyanka, headquarters of the KGB. If only the files would burn up and the men and women return to life! But they will not return. And the timeless chronicles of endless suffering go on casting their pitiless flames. Nothing I have ever read comes close to the horror of these semiliterate compositions of the secret police and these covert denunciations of informants, or "well-wishers." I ought to be used to them by now. I'm not. Too much gets in the way: pity, bitterness, indignation, disillusionment.

When you are young you don't know much, you brim with romantic ideas, everyone seems kind and decent, and you blindly believe everything your elders say, never thinking that people can lie, deceive, and be hypocrites.

Then the doubts, the terrible doubts. They creep up slowly. For me, they began to seep in very early, in the years of World War II, which I hate with all my heart: it killed millions of young men my age and left me disabled. I remember the constant requests from headquarters for more names of those who had distinguished themselves in battle, and for the name of at least one coward. And the commander of a mortar unit in the forest dugout next to ours who kept asking us to confirm direct hits—putting a couple of tin cups of raw spirits our way in return.

Heroism and lies marched in step. And no matter how much praise our generals heaped on us combatants after the war—for our heroism, our patriotism, and so on—my own memory of the war, especially at night, is of a jumble of mud, blood, lice, drunken hysterical attacks, and dead comrades.

In the postwar years my doubts increased. I remember the Vspolye train station in Yaroslavl a year after the war, the rumor that a train would be passing through with some of our soldiers and officers from German prisoner of war camps. I was still on crutches, but I went with the others from the city to watch. Railway cars, small windows with iron bars; thin, pale, bewildered faces at the windows. And on the platform, women weeping and wailing. Tossed out through the bars, rolled-up scraps of paper with the names and addresses of relatives and appeals to let them know that so-and-so was alive. And the women running back and forth between the cars looking for their husbands, brothers, sweethearts, or just acquaintances, friends. The guards didn't dare push back the deafening crowd, but after that the trains came through at night.

The people on the platform waited and waited. They couldn't understand why these boys from the Nazi camps were being transported like criminals to the Urals and Siberia. I remember the tortured faces, the total incomprehension, theirs and mine, as to what was going on. And yet they shouted some, they cried their fill, and it was over. What kept us from seeing things clearly was our elation over the defeat of the Nazis and our enduring faith in Stalin's righteousness. It took a long time, unfortunately, for people to realize that those liberated soldiers would meet their end in concentration camps and prisons, having been tricked aboard the trains by their executioners, who feared them.

Later, looking into the circumstances of this crime against our Soviet war prisoners, I often recalled that ghastly, ominous scene at the Vspolye train station in Yaroslavl.

With the 20th Congress of the CPSU the country arrived at a threshold. After that came the floundering and the reversals—up and down, left and right, freeze and thaw, hope and disappointment. The outlook changed with every shift in public sentiment. Slowly the nation faced up to the truth. No one who had not lost touch with reality could fail to see that the Bolshevik system was plunging headlong toward bankruptcy and was incapable of bringing us anything but new disasters.

Not many of those who heard Khrushchev's "secret speech" at the congress are still alive. The report's scope and substance—and the danger it posed to the establishment—were such that it was not published in our country until some thirty years later, in the time of perestroika.

I was among those at that Party congress.

But even before that, while on an official trip to the Primorsky district, I heard Nikita Khrushchev speak to some local Party activists in the economic field. He was on his way back from China. In his speech and his answers he touched on this and that. He flew into a rage, shouted, and threatened drastic action when the captains of some fishing vessels reported on the disgraceful state of the fishing industry. They'd fill their fishing nets four or five times but often weren't able to offload their catch for lack of processing equipment on shore. So they'd throw the fish back in the sea. And this would be repeated season after season.

So there's our planned economy for you, Khrushchev fumed. Spotting Mikoyan in the audience, he dressed him down on the spot, and he phoned Malenkov in Moscow with orders to buy new processing equipment—special vessels, as I recall, from Denmark. He glowed with energy. The captains were ecstatic. Later, back in Moscow, I inquired into what had been done on his instructions. The answer: absolutely nothing.

Khrushchev was deeply suspicious of China's leaders. He wouldn't have put it past them to strive for domination of the world Communist movement, make territorial claims against the USSR, and seek rapprochement with the United States.

All this was worrisome—the mismanagement inside the country, the possibility of a falling-out with China. But what really astonished me were his unflattering comments on the Stalin era. I jotted down some of his words at the time, and I still have them. This is what Khrushchev said, long before the 20th Congress of the CPSU:

> We've been squandering the accumulated capital of the people's trust in the Party. We can't go on endlessly exploiting the people's trust. We Communists, all of us, must be like bees in nurturing the people's trust.
>
> We've become like priests and preachers: we promise a kingdom in heaven, but in the here and now there are no potatoes. Only our long-suffering Russian people would put up with something like that, but we can't go on banking on their patience. We are not priests, we are Communists, and we must give them this happiness here on earth.
>
> When I was a worker, there was no socialism, but there were potatoes, and now we have built socialism and there are no potatoes.

Returning to Moscow I didn't dare relate any of this to my coworkers, except maybe to whisper to one or two of my friends.

I'd been with the CC only a year and a half. I still saw things through naive eyes, believing that everything that was going on, or almost everything, was founded on truth and justice. And now to hear words like these from the head of the Party and government! Little did I know that in a mere eighteen months the country would be rocked by Khrushchev's speech at the 20th Congress.

The speech—"On the Personality Cult and Its Consequences"—was delivered on 25 February 1956, the last day of the session, although it was not on the agenda. It told of the villainies and crimes Stalin committed against the Soviet people, and it proclaimed the advent of a new era in our country's history and in the world's. What I heard plunged me into the deepest dejection, if not despair. Everything seemed unreal, even that I was sitting there in the Kremlin hearing words that were destroying everything I'd lived by, shattering the past, rending the soul. Everything crumbled, never to be made whole again.

I was up in the balcony. The hall below was sunk in silence. Not a chair creaked, not a cough or a whisper could be heard. No one looked at anyone else; those in attendance were too overcome either by the unexpected or by the fear that seemed to have taken permanent root in the psychology of so-called Soviet Man and in the very core of his being. And all the while Khrushchev kept piling fact on fact, one more horrifying than the other. He spoke at length, emotionally, departing now and then from his text; clearly he was overwrought. I was so bewildered I don't remember if there was any applause; I think not. We left with bowed heads. The shock had been indescribably severe, especially since this was the first time we'd been told officially of the crimes of Stalin himself. No one said anything. Now and then I detected a muffled "Mmm . . . yes . . . yes. . . ."

I was crushed, not knowing in whom to believe—in Stalin, with whose name generation after generation had linked their lives and hopes, or in the new chief, who spoke with such passion and conviction of the crimes of his teacher, under whom he had served so loyally and unquestioningly for so long. To believe the new leader was not easy—one had to leap over oceans of faith in the old. But to dismiss everything I'd heard was impossible: I knew that for Khrushchev to lie about Stalin would have been political suicide. I sensed that Khrushchev was telling the truth, but it was a truth I was afraid of.

Something similar had happened to me once when I was a child. In 1937 one of the grooms on our kolkhoz and one of our team leaders were arrested. I asked my father why. He warned me sternly never to ask anyone about it.

And now my fledgling doubts and a raft of tormenting considerations gnawed at me. I began to lose interest in my work; sometimes I'd become apathetic about everything that was going on. At the same time I became much more attentive to the speeches of our higher-ups, only now from a critical standpoint, finding them full of mawkish nonsense, pretense, and outright lies. Gradually, my trust in our leaders' words unraveled; I began to look more closely about me, and the prevailing careerism, unscrupulousness, bootlicking, and intrigue grew more and more evident. These were bitter discoveries indeed.

I tried to sort things out. In the first place, why did Khrushchev's words have such a devastating effect on me? What played the decisive role? Did the shining star of faith come crashing down on our sinful land? Or was I simply experiencing the provincial naïveté of my convictions? Or the wounded response of one cheated and betrayed? Or something else, mysterious, unknown, hidden even from myself?

One realization I acquired for the rest of my life: any social system based on bloodletting has to be swept off the face of the earth, for it preaches the demonic religion of evil.

I had been honest in my previous faith, and I was equally honest in rejecting it. I came to detest Stalin, this monster who had deceived me so cruelly and trampled on my romantic dreams. From then on I devoted myself to searching out a way to put an end to this inhuman system; the trick was not to err in the choice of a new one. All this took the form of hope, not action, but of one thing I was sure even then—this new way must be strictly nonviolent if it was to lead to freedom.

I lived a double life of agonizing dissimulation. I conformed, I pretended, trying all the while not to lose my bearings and disgrace myself. No longer interested in working for the Central Committee, I looked for an out and found one, more by feel than by plan. I sensed a need to reeducate myself, to reread everything I'd read before, go back to original sources—Marx, Engels, Lenin, the German philosophers, the French socialists, the British economists, all the fountainheads of my outlook on the world.

Right after the 20th Congress I asked my superiors to assign me to study in the Academy of Social Sciences attached to the CC. They turned me down twice. On my third try they approved—on condition that I enroll in the department of the history of the CPSU. Only after innumerable interviews was I able to bring them around. The academy simply couldn't understand why I didn't want to study in the department of the history of the CPSU, natural as that would have been for a CC staffer like me, and a historian to boot. But after the 20th Congress I simply couldn't wade into those muddy waters. I chose the department of international relations instead.

I studied feverishly, I read copiously, I took examinations and wrote term papers. I got straight As. Only once did I get a B, in political economy, for refusing to delete from my paper a paragraph asserting that neither from a scientific nor from a practical standpoint was the total destitution of the working class under capitalism remotely possible. Professor Lapin, the kindest of men, tried to persuade me to drop the paragraph, but I held out and he had to lower my grade. He was scared.

I'm grateful to the academy, very grateful. It had a stable, creative atmosphere. I'm often asked when exactly I became aware of a turning point in my thinking, when it was I began really to reexamine my views on Marxism. I can't be all that precise—these things don't happen from one day to the next; the process is long and tortuous. But it was at the academy, while immersed in studying primary sources, that I became fully conscious of the hollowness and unreality of Marxism-Leninism, its inhumanity and artificiality, its inherent contradictions, its demagogy and fraudulent prognostications. This recognition and others did much to heal the wounds left by the 20th Congress. I began to acknowledge that Khrushchev was right, although I still didn't understand why he had chosen to take a swipe, in effect, at the very ideological foundations of the new society. And the deeper I explored the theoretical rantings of the Marxist classics, the more clearly I saw the reasons for the dead end at which the country had arrived.

I also began to understand how developments in Russia had been determined by another aspect of Marxism. As a practical-minded heir to Marx's utopian visions and as a master at translating all kinds of theoretical schemes into political prose, Lenin had extracted from Marx's highly contradictory projects only those elements that answered to his main purpose—the seizure of power.

I have written about this phase of my life, with its waverings and its insights, in an earlier book, *Obval* (Collapse, published in English as *The Fate of Marxism in Russia*). Here I'd like to mention another circumstance that has long puzzled those who were not privy to the political games of the time.

Khrushchev's speech, as I've noted, remained an official secret for the next three decades. A few weeks after the congress someone put it out to the West, but it remained hidden from the Soviet people, and for a very simple reason: the leadership didn't want the idea of de-Stalinization to go beyond the Party elite, fearing its explosive danger to the system.

I remember the protracted arguments that arose after the CC's 1957 decree on the personality cult. The struggle was over every word, every formulation, to protect the existing system and leave untouched the fundamental postulates of an ideology convenient for the authorities and brutal for everyone else. Despite the impact of the 20th Congress, the habit of ignoring illegality and oppression and glossing over Stalin's crimes reasserted itself even then.

The top Party leadership issued a flood of threats against any Party member who dared to say anything new in the field of social sciences or to interpret Khrushchev's speech in a personal way. Particularly sensitive was the problem of the mass arrests.

All this went on before my eyes and lives on in my memory.

Soon after the 20th Congress the Politburo circularized the Party with letters demanding a more intensive struggle against anti-Party and anti-Soviet tendencies, with special reference to those members who had been harping on the arrests. These letters show how soon after the congress the Party apparatus embarked on a determined campaign to undermine its decisions.

As early as April 1956, a little more than a month after the session, the Central Committee addressed a confidential letter to all Party members warning against criticism that went beyond the authorized limits. The problem was that those rising to speak at meetings were naming not only Stalin but others with him on the CC Presidium as having shared responsibility for the arrests. Summarizing the letter, that town crier of Stalinism *Pravda* called for a campaign against all "demagogues" and "rotten elements" who criticized the Party's policies under the guise of addressing the personality cult and the mass arrests.

The letter didn't have the intended effect. As I recall, it seemed to dissolve and drown in a round of new discussions, which, as the leaders saw it, took a dangerous form. Recognizing the turn of events, the CC came out with a second letter in July 1956 announcing the prosecution of certain Communist figures and the disbanding of the Party organization at the thermotechnical laboratory of the Academy of Sciences of the USSR—all this for the airing of "incorrect" views on the decisions of the 20th Congress.

But even the second letter didn't help. Bit by bit, despite the Party's fulminations, the spontaneous appeal of de-Stalinization eluded the control of the Party committees and took hold of the people, starting with the educated classes and with writers most of all.

This democratic movement grew not only in the Soviet Union but in the countries of Central and Southeastern Europe. In October 1956 the popular revolt in Hungary broke out. To suppress it the Soviet Union sent in troops. And the threat of military intervention was present in Poland as well.

The events in Hungary threw the Presidium of the CC of the CPSU into total panic. On 19 December 1956 it was decided to send yet another letter to all Party organizations "on the intensification of the Party organizations' political work with the masses and on the blocking of attacks by anti-Soviet, hostile elements." The material for the Presidium was prepared by a commission headed by Brezhnev and composed of Malenkov, Aristov, Belyayev, Serov, and Rudenko.

The letter was purely Stalinist in spirit, crude and full of threats; a sense of fear clearly showed through. It concluded with these words:

> The CC of the CPSU cannot emphasizes too strongly that there can be no question as to how to deal with the enemy rabble. In its attitude toward anti-Soviet elements the dictatorship of the proletariat must be merciless. All Communists working in the public prosecutor's office, the courts, and the national security services must be alert in guarding the interests of our socialist state, must be vigilant in combating the intrigues of hostile elements, and must take timely measures in accordance with Soviet law against all criminal activities.

A wave of arrests and sentencings rolled over the country, sweeping both Party and non-Party workers into prison for "slandering the Soviet system" and for "revisionism." In the first few months of 1957 alone, hundreds of people were indicted. For believing Khrushchev and taking a stand on the side of reform, thousands were thrown into concentration camps.

The CC of the CPSU stiffened its control over all ideological, artistic, and scientific institutions and over the mass media. A series of decrees strongly condemned the line taken by newspapers and magazines influenced by Khrushchev's speech. The practice of the mid-1950s demonstrated once again that violence and repression remained the instruments the Party leadership used to strengthen its grip.

From what I was told by friends in the inner circle, I know that the CC leadership was in a highly agitated state, admonishing Party workers to tighten the reins and redouble their vigilance. But there was no real unity even in the apparat.

In Khrushchev's memoirs certain passages give some inkling of how he regarded the thrust of events after Stalin's death and the 20th Congress. He writes: "[We] were unable to break with the past, we couldn't summon up the courage, the will, to part the curtain and look behind it. To see what hid behind the outward show of Stalin's time. . . . We were paralyzed, it would seem, by our service under Stalin, still not free of his power."

Nothing could be truer. The head of the CC's scientific department, Sergei Trapeznikov, once asked me what I thought would happen to Marxism when we were dead. If the CC of the CPSU continued to underestimate the dangers ahead, he predicted, Marxism, under the pressure of hostile revisionist forces, might cease being a revolutionary teaching and become an opportunistic device. He is the author of an amusing observation, the cause of much laughter in Moscow. It appears in his book on the agrarian question and it reads: "The wolf pack of revisionists has woven a hornet's nest."

The question remains: Why did Khrushchev shift the course of de-Stalinization?

The main reason, it seems to me, is that after speaking the truth about Stalin's crimes he was alarmed by the consequences of his historic action, which began to lead to public debate on the nature of the system itself. Nor could he forget his own guilt. About this, more later.

I regard Khrushchev's speech as a heroic deed because it is to him personally that we owe the following achievements: first and foremost, the freeing of millions of people from the gulag, the unraveling of the Stalin cult, and the return of entire peoples from exile; second, the deliverance of the peasantry from a state of serfdom, from the burden of crushing taxes, and from confinement to virtual rural pales without the identity papers that would permit them to move—plus the enactment of uniform labor laws; and third, a quest for mutual understanding and cooperation with other countries that produced the first rifts in the Iron Curtain.

History loves paradox. To start with, Khrushchev buried Stalin in the literal sense: he was chairman of the funeral committee. Then he buried Stalin historically, at the 20th Congress. At Stalin's funeral he had Malenkov, Beria, and Molotov deliver their eulogies in that order—by prior arrangement. Two or three hours before Stalin's death the top command had reapportioned the dictator's power: Malenkov was to be chairman of the Council of Ministers, Beria and Molotov first deputy chairmen. As for Khrushchev, he was put in charge of the CC of the CPSU, which henceforth was to limit itself to questions of ideology and personnel, with no economic role.

What dyed-in-the-wool schemers they were, and how badly they miscalculated, imagining that Khrushchev would be content to remain the triumvirate's puppet! Admittedly, it would have been difficult for them not to misjudge him at that point. This, after all, was the same Khrushchev who at Stalin's bidding, at the dacha in Volynsk, had danced the gopak, puffing and streaming with sweat, as everyone around him laughed and clapped their hands. Stalin laughed so hard tears rolled down his cheeks. A buffoonish performance. But the notion that Khrushchev would dance just as obediently to the new leaders' tune was soon to be dispelled.

A word about the plenary session of the CC of the CPSU of June 1957, a year after the 20th Congress. It was clear then—and it is even clearer now—that this was a decisive moment in the country's history. By that time, Khrushchev had made major concessions to the orthodox Stalinists in the Politburo. Recovering from their initial shock, they plotted their revenge. The crisis within the Politburo drew to a head.

I was still studying in the Academy of Social Sciences, but even we graduate students got wind that Khrushchev was about to be deposed. The question as to who would move against him, those favoring de-Stalinization or those opposing it, remained unclear up to the plenum's final days. Moscow lived on rumors. In the academy we had other things on our minds: spring, examinations. Besides, we were tired of politics. Only the day before we had buried Stalin, we had cried a bit—some of us, not all. Then there had been the repercussions. Beria shot. That was fine. Malenkov dismissed. Fine, too. Then the 20th Congress. Even better. And now some other kind of squabble. Enough was enough.

The CC Presidium was convened. Its members had barely taken their places when trouble began for Khrushchev. (No record was kept of that meeting; what happened there was recounted by participants at the subsequent CC plenum.) A majority demanded that the meeting be conducted by the chairman of the Council of Ministers, Nikolai Bulganin.

The Presidium sat for four days. The upshot was that a majority—Bulganin, Voroshilov (chairman of the Supreme Soviet), Molotov and Kaganovich (first deputy chairmen of the Council of Ministers), Malenkov, Pervukhin, and Saburov (the council's deputy chairmen)—voted seven to four to relieve Khrushchev of his post. The threat of a return to Stalinism and a new wave of arrests now hung over the country.

The situation was plainly critical. And it was at this point that Khrushchev proved himself a skillful organizer and a brave man. On his orders, Ivan Serov, the head of the Committee on State Security (KGB), requisitioned a number of air force transport planes to fly some of the more influential first Party secretaries, all CC members, from the provinces to Moscow. They intervened vigorously with the Presidium. Scared, the anti-Khrushchev faction backtracked. The question of dismissing Khrushchev was stricken from the agenda, and a plenary session of the CC was called.

The extraordinary CC plenum convened on 22 June and met for seven days. No time limit was set on the speeches. On that score, Khrushchev's game was fairly obvious. The floor was given first to his unquestioned supporters, in the hope that they would create a favorable atmosphere on his behalf and that what followed wouldn't matter. Evidently, he was apprehensive that his opponents might have supporters, perhaps among their personal friends. Presiding over the plenum, Suslov was meticulous in stage-managing the debate. In the end, no one spoke against Khrushchev; the nomenklatura was used to rallying around whoever seemed strongest at the time.

Why do I rehearse this plenum in such detail? Because the political differences it dramatized were grounded in Stalinism and its attendant crimes. In plotting Khrushchev's removal the Stalinists had planned to take their revenge, just as in our day, in demanding Boris Yeltsin's dismissal, the Stalinists in the Communist Party of the Russian Federation sought to restore the past. The tactics were the same.

The first to speak was Marshal Zhukov. He produced documents that accused Molotov, Kaganovich, and Malenkov of principal responsibility for the arrest and execution of political workers within and without the Party. (In a later chapter I will go into this more fully.) Yet in saving Khrushchev with his forthright and candid address, Zhukov signed his own political death warrant; the reprisals against him came as early as October of that year. Denouncing the members of the so-called anti-Party group, Zhukov went on to call for a thorough investigation of the mass arrests and for punishment of all guilty parties. He demanded that the offenses be treated not as political but as criminal in nature. The Party dinosaurs, however, were far more cautious. The paragraph of the resolution accusing Malenkov, Kaganovich, and Molotov of personal responsibility for the mass arrests was adopted in secret session and was not published in the newspapers. The proposal by CC member Sheremetiev that the documents cited by Zhukov be laid out in a letter for restricted circulation was rejected. The fear was of further disclosure; the decision was that of the criminals themselves.

Fundamentally, the responsibility for the genocide—or, rather, democide—that took place in Russia and the entire Soviet Union rests on the ideology of Bolshevism, in the form it took within various Communist organizations under different names. With the close participation of Bronstein (Trotsky), Rosenfeld (Kamenev), Alfelbaum (Zinoviev), and Dzerzhinsky, these crimes were committed under the direct supervision of Ulianov (Lenin) and Dzhugashvili (Stalin).

Vladimir Ilyich Ulianov (Lenin): Chairman of the first Soviet government after the violent seizure of power in 1917. Exponent of mass terror, violence, the dictatorship of the proletariat, class struggle, and other inhuman concepts. Organizer of the fratricidal Russian civil war and the concentration camps, including camps for children. Incessant in his demands for arrests and capital punishment by bullet or rope. Personally responsible for the deaths of millions of Russian citizens. By every norm of international law, posthumously indictable for crimes against humanity.

Iosif Vissarionovich Dzhugashvili (Stalin): Organizer of mass arrests of millions of innocent victims. Architect of the gulag system for totally destroying human life. Carried on with Lenin's criminal project for wholesale extermination of peasants, the intelligentsia, the clergy, and all other "alien class elements." Inventor of a whole category of "enemies of the people" subject to annihilation along with their families. Directly responsible for the country's unpreparedness for war with Nazi Germany and the resultant deaths of almost thirty million people. Shares responsibility with Lenin for the division of the peoples of Russia into hostile camps, producing a state of constant civil war. Organizer of the democide of the Russian and other peoples of the USSR. By every norm of international law, posthumously indictable for crimes against humanity.

Besides Lenin and Stalin, the principal ideologues and directors of this program of mass murder spanning the years from the late 1920s to the early 1960s were Beria, Molotov, Kaganovich, Zhdanov, Voroshilov, Khrushchev, Mikoyan, Malenkov, Andreyev, Suslov, Kossior, Bulganin, Yagoda, Yezhov, Abakumov, Vyshinsky, and Ulrikh.

Vyacheslav Mikhailovich Skryabin (Molotov): Chairman of the Council of People's Commissars of the USSR from 1930 to 1941. Bears the main responsibility for the extermination of members of the apparat, many of whom were arrested and shot at his personal initiative. Of the twenty-eight people composing the Council of People's Commissars at the beginning of 1938, twenty were done away with. Only Mikoyan, Voroshilov, Kaganovich, Andreyev, Litvinov, and Molotov himself were left alive. The six-month period from October 1936 to March 1937 saw the arrest of almost two thousand political workers of the people's commissariats of the USSR, not counting the staffs of the Commissariats of Defense and Internal and Foreign Affairs. Stalin was always spurring Molotov on. In a letter to him Stalin recommended a "thorough purge" of the People's Commissariat of Finance and the State Bank, for which "it will be necessary to execute two or three dozen saboteurs within these apparats, including a dozen cashiers of one sort or another." On occasion, when the People's Commissariat of Internal Affairs (NKVD) would submit a list of those for whom it recommended prison sentences, Molotov would write the letters *VMN*, meaning capital punishment, next to some of the names. The emendations were enough to cause these persons to be shot.

In 1949 Molotov approved the arrest of a number of Soviet citizens and foreigners accused on falsified evidence of espionage and anti-Soviet activities.

Lazar Moiseyevich Kaganovich: His entire political career is one of punitive action. Known for the results of his actions during the collectivization period in the Ukraine, the Voronezh oblast, the northern Caucasus, and western Siberia. Played a particularly sinister role during the mass arrests of 1935–39. As early as 1933, at the January plenum of the CC and the Central Control Commission (TsKK) of the All-Union Communist Party (of the Bolsheviks)—VKP(b)—he declared angrily, "We don't shoot enough people." With his approval, thousands of workers in the railroad system and in heavy industry were arrested and sentenced to death or long-term imprisonment. The cases of railroad workers arrested in 1937–39 as "enemies of the people" on orders signed by him personally extend to a full five volumes. To whip up mass arrests on a wider scale Kaganovich made special trips to the Chelyabinsk, Yaroslavl, and Ivanov oblasts and to the Donbass.

Andrei Aleksandrovich Zhdanov: For a long time, served in effect as second secretary of the CC of the VKP(b). Directly responsible for many of the mass arrests. In September 1936, in a telegram from the south, he and Stalin jointly demanded an increase in the number of arrests. At their urging, Yezhov was made head of the NKVD. In the period before the war, more than 68,000 people were arrested in Leningrad on Zhdanov's initiative. To oversee and expand the scale of mass arrests, Zhdanov paid visits to the Bashkir, Tatar, and Orenburg Party organizations. In the Orenburg oblast alone, 3,655 persons were arrested in the six months between April and September 1937, and half of them were sentenced to death. Yet on arriving in Orenburg at the beginning of September, Zhdanov found this number inadequate, and it was increased by 598. After the Party purges carried out by Zhdanov on the spot, another 232 persons were arrested in Tataria and another 342 in Bashkiria. Almost all were shot.

Zhdanov played an active role in the vicious treatment of the secretaries of the CC of the Komsomol in 1938. Speaking for the Politburo, he described them as "traitors to the motherland, terrorists, spies, Fascists, politically rotten enemies of the people pursuing hostile policies within the Komsomol"—in short, as a "counterrevolutionary band."

Wholly on Zhdanov's conscience rest the ideological pogroms

carried out in the fields of literature, motion pictures, theater, and music in 1946–48. He was, as well, one of the organizers of the meeting in August 1948 of the V. I. Lenin All-Union Academy of Agricultural Sciences at which dissenting scientists were brought into line with state orthodoxy. In a memorandum to Stalin of July 10, he laid down the proposals that led to the persecution of a large group of biologists.

Kliment Yefremovich Voroshilov: Authorized the elimination of the top officers and political workers of the Red Army. The purge in the 1930s eliminated 3 of the army's 5 marshals, 15 of the 16 army commanders, 60 of the 67 corps commanders, 136 out of 199 division commanders, all 4 of the navy's top flag officers, all 6 of its first-ranking flag officers, and 6 of its 15 second-ranking flag officers. All 17 of the army's first- and second-ranking commissars were shot, along with 25 of the 29 commissars at the corps level. Voroshilov's tenure as people's commissar of defense saw the arrest, in 1936–40 alone, of more than 36,000 middle- and top-level Red Army officers. The files of the Federal Security Service (FSB) contain more than 300 cases of prominent army commanders arrested at Voroshilov's behest. As World War II approached, the country's armed forces were, for all intents and purposes, decapitated.

Nikita Sergeyevich Khrushchev: There is documentary evidence of mass arrests organized by Khrushchev in the prewar period in Moscow, the Moscow oblast, and the Ukraine. On occasion, he himself sent in written proposals for the arrest of leading workers of the Moscow Soviet and the Moscow Party oblast committee. In 1936–37 alone, 55,741 persons were arrested in Moscow. In January 1938 Khrushchev was made Party leader for the Ukraine. More than 106,000 persons were arrested in the Ukraine that year, 12,000 the following year, and 50,000 in 1940.

Anastas Ivanovich Mikoyan: Authorized the arrest of hundreds of workers in the People's Commissariats of Food Supply and of Foreign Trade. Mikoyan not only approved the arrests but initiated some of them. Thus, in a letter to Yezhov of 15 July 1937, he recommended the arrest of members of the All-Union Scientific Research Institute for the fisheries industry and oceanography. He made similar proposals in regard to staff members of Vneshtorg, the foreign trade organization. In the fall of 1937 Mikoyan went to Armenia to purge the Party and government there of "enemies of the people." As a result, thousands perished. Mikoyan and Yezhov spoke at the plenum on the Bukharin case held by the CC of the VKP(b) in February and March 1937.

Georgy Maksimilianovich Malenkov: Directly involved in most of the actions taken by the NKVD against leading figures in Moscow and in the provinces. Often made trips in order to carry out mass arrests on the spot. Thus, in 1937, he and Yezhov went to Belorussia, where they oversaw a virtual massacre. For the same purpose he paid visits to the Tula, Yaroslavl, Saratov, Omsk, and Tambov oblasts, as well as to Tataria. Malenkov would often be present at the interrogation and torture of suspects. That was how he and Beria trumped up the case of the "counterrevolutionary organization" in Armenia. Malenkov's criminal role in the fabrication of the so-called Leningrad case is well established.

Andrei Andreyevich Andreyev: As a member of the Politburo and the Secretariat of the CC of the VKP(b), he took a personal part in mass arrests within the Party organizations of the Central Asian republics, including Uzbekistan and Tadjikistan, as well as those in the Povolzhie area and in the northern Caucasus. His trips led to the execution, approved by Stalin, Molotov, and others, of 430 leading Party workers in the Saratov oblast, 440 in Uzbekistan, and 344 in Tadjikistan.

Mikhail Andreyevich Suslov: Took part in mass arrests while a secretary of the Rostov Party oblast committee. On becoming first secretary of the Ordzhonikidze Party district committee, he not only emphatically objected to the release of a number of innocent people convicted on false charges but insisted on additional arrests. In July 1939 an NKVD commission reported to Beria that Suslov was dissatisfied with the work of the NKVD's local office, calling it "complaisant." Suslov personally submitted a list of people he thought should be arrested; his suggestion was followed. As chairman of the CC Bureau of the VKP(b) for Lithuania, he was directly responsible for the deportation of thousands of people from the Baltic states. Suslov orchestrated the persecution of many prominent members of the Soviet artistic and scientific intelligentsia, as well as the action taken against the Jewish Anti-Fascist Committee.

A word about Mikhail Ivanovich Kalinin. Pathetic and spineless,

Kalinin is a special case. As chairman of the Central Executive Committee (CEC) of the USSR, he signed the decree of 1 December 1934 drawn up by Stalin and Yenukidze mandating "the introduction of changes in the operative criminal-procedural codes of the Soviet republics." Henceforth the authorities could take legal action without giving the accused a chance to be heard and to appeal. The decree provided, too, for capital punishment. Between 1931 and 1946, as head of a CEC commission for the review of court cases and of sentencing in particular, Kalinin pandered to the rule of lawlessness and mass terror: not a single appeal for clemency was approved. Like Molotov, he slavishly submitted to his wife's imprisonment on concocted political charges.

These were our leaders. They all deserve to be tried for crimes against humanity.

Another comment is in order. There are still some people who credit the myth that these mass repressions were the work only of Stalin and his underlings; in Lenin's time, they claim, it was different. Others maintain that the measures taken in Lenin's day were random or necessitated by specific events. Alas, these assertions are not borne out by the facts. The truth is that in his punitive operations Stalin did not think up anything that was not there under Lenin: executions, hostage taking, concentration camps, and all the rest.

As early as January 1918, only two months after his counterrevolutionary coup, Lenin would write approvingly: "In one place, they will jail ten or so moneybags, a dozen crooks, a half dozen workers who shirk their duties (in the same sloppy way as many typesetters in Petersburg do, especially in the Party's printing shops). In another place, they will make them clean out the toilets. In a third, the people will keep an eye on them as *harmful* until they reform. In a fourth, *one out of ten* of those guilty of parasitism will be shot on the spot. In a fifth, they will think up a combination of various measures" (italics mine).

"One out of ten": a fateful formula. Later it would commend itself to Hitler, as when the SS would shoot their Soviet civilian hostages. The style is the same. There is much that is similar in the actions of nonhuman beings.

After the assassination on 21 June 1918 of Volodarsky, head of the Petrograd Cheka (secret police), Lenin wrote to Zinoviev: "Just today we in the CC heard that the workers in Petersburg wanted to respond to the murder of Volodarsky with mass terror and that you (not you personally, but those in the Petersburg Central and Party Committees) restrained them. I emphatically protest! We compromise ourselves . . . we are *holding back* the perfectly proper revolutionary initiative of the masses. This is im-pos-sible! The terrorists will think we're dishrags. We are at war to the death. *We must spur on the energy and mass character of the terror* against the counter-revolutionaries, especially in Petersburg, whose example will be *decisive*" (italics mine).

Lenin's call for spurring on the "mass character of the terror" indeed produced action on a mass scale. In response to the assassination of Uritsky, another head of the Petrograd Cheka, five hundred hostages were shot. On 9 August 1918 Lenin sent two telegrams, one more monstrous than the other. To Fyodorov in Nizhny Novgorod: "We must make every effort, form a triumvirate of dictators (you, Markin, and someone else), *impose mass terror immediately,* shoot and deport hundreds of prostitutes who have been getting soldiers, former officers, and so on drunk. Not a minute's delay. . . . We must take all-out action: mass searches, executions for concealing weapons, mass deportation of Mensheviks and the unreliable." The same day, to Bosh in Penza: "Essential to organize stronger bodyguard of handpicked reliable people, *launch merciless mass terror* against kulaks, priests, and White Guards. Suspicious individuals to be locked up in concentration camp outside city." The next day, also to Penza:

To comrades Kurayev, Bosh, Minkin, and other Penza Communists. Comrades! Uprising of five districts of kulakdom must be *mercilessly* suppressed. This demanded by interests of entire revolution, since "final conflict" with kulaks going on everywhere. Need model for action.

1. Hang (by all means hang, so *people will see*) no fewer than 100 known kulaks, fat cats, bloodsuckers.

2. Publish their names.

3. Take *all* their grain.

4. Select hostages in accordance with yesterday's telegram. Do it so that for hundreds of miles around people will see and tremble. . . .

Confirm telegram received and *acted on.*

Yours, Lenin.

P.S. Find tougher people.

What is most tragic and despicable in our story is that the "tougher people" were found in abundance.

More instructions from the chief. To the Executive Committee in Livny: "Essential . . . to confiscate all the grain and property of the rebellious kulaks, *hang* the instigators among the kulaks, mobilize and arm the poor under reliable leaders from our ranks, take hostages from among the rich and hold them until every last bit of grain is removed from their districts. . . . To finish off Yudenich (literally finish off, do him in) is hellishly important. If the offensive has begun, can we not mobilize some 20,000 more Petersburg workers, plus 10,000 or so bourgeois, place some machine guns behind them, *shoot several hundred* and bring some real mass pressure against Yudenich" (italics mine).

And it's not just Lenin, although his personal role in the murder of millions of Russian citizens, especially during the civil war, is self-evident. Essentially it's the system he began to create. A system based on the ideology of violence.

When, in the severe cold of January 1924, a team of workers with spades and crowbars were digging the foundation for the Lenin mausoleum, they punctured a sewage pipe. The breach froze over. In the spring the mausoleum was flooded with sewage. Hearing of this, Patriarch Tikhon said, "The relics got the holy oil they deserved." The patriarch had it right.

The taking of human life is the most ancient of sins. The twentieth century has created neo-Cainism. Democide. The annihilation of a people, of whole peoples. A new branch of industry—democidal, nonstop assembly-line, murderous. In Auschwitz, for belonging to one of the "inferior races." In the prisons and camps of the gulag, for "class inferiority."

Neo-Cainism: damns by "race" and damns by class. You can be Einstein himself, but if you're a Jew, into the gas chamber with you. You can be a Vavilov or a Gumilyov—having a mind of your own means punishment. For Vavilov, lengthy torture by starvation; for Gumilyov, a bullet.

Lenin, Stalin, Hitler—the troika that created neo-Cainism. The worst criminals of the century. The century of Cain, the century that saw Russia ruined, her thousand-year-old model of development cast aside. She used to be a country of peasants—she became a country of the lumpen, the vulgar and uprooted. She used to be Russian Orthodox—she became atheistic. She used to press forward—she began to lag behind. To the marrow of her bones she was injected with the deadly poison of lumpenism. Justly she has been held in contempt. For what should she be respected? For sloth, for boozing, for envying her neighbors' prosperity, for sponging off others? There is nothing the Russian people aren't capable of. They can produce a Pushkin, a Gogol, a Tsyolkovsky, a Vernadsky. They're good at everything, but especially at drinking and at drunken bouts of laziness. He may be penniless, your Russian, but he won't work up a sweat. There may be money lying trampled on the ground, but he's too lazy to bend down and pick it up. As for those who aren't lazy, there's no life for them in Russia. One day it's revolution, another day it's robbery by those in power.

Only for repentance is there no courage, no conscience, no time.

Gone is Orthodox Russia. Vanished. Everything smashed, the temples wrecked by the lumpen cattle. Everything dissolved in lies. The mind clouded, the soul coarsened. In place of truth, the devil's lie is enthroned, for truth, by lumpen reasoning, is bad for people: it hurts the eyes and grates on the ears. Truth is harmful, so power lives on lies.

In the course of two revolutions—in 1905 and February 1917—Russia had become first a constitutional monarchy and then a democratic republic. The counterrevolution of October 1917 threw the country into backwardness, and the Stalinist collectivization and industrialization that followed took it even further back—into medieval inquisition.

Stalin and the other Bolsheviks lied in saying that the Russia of Tolstoy and Stolypin lagged behind the West by a hundred years. It was catching up. It wasn't that Russia was lagging, it was that the Bolsheviks broke its legs, bashed out its brains, and turned it backwards. By means of a total inquisition, the flower of the nation was blighted: aristocrats, merchants, officers, professors, and others (or, in Lenin's words, that whole "intelligentsia shit") categorized like witches by degrees of guilt. A seventy-year witch trial. A concentration camp by the name of Socialism.

Have you forgotten how it was in that "land of joy"? You bought a bottle of vodka—happiness; a piece of sausage—even better; a pair of women's boots or a refrigerator—an occasion for wild drunken parties. There was no relief from the lines for tainted meat and rotten potatoes—nor from the informers in one's midst and from the denunciatory debates within Party and trade union committees as to who . . . and how . . . and with whose wife. Marshal Zhukov and the theatrical director Georgy Tovstonogov had their bedrooms bugged. Our masters had an inquisitive turn of mind, a thirst for knowledge.

Reform in the USSR and in Russia turned out to be a difficult process politically and economically, and even more so psychologically. In trying to reform the country we, and here I include myself, underestimated a great deal—above all, the psychological condition of the society, which turned out to be more inert, indifferent, and dependent than we had imagined. To this day, many people pin their hopes on some great man, some idol, and dream of slavery and "stronger" leaders. There you are: the "riddle" of the Russian soul. In actual fact, nothing more than a slave psychology.

Of course, nothing on earth is that simple. Millions of people spent their entire lives under this system studying, working, raising children, knowing sorrows and joys. It is hard for them to accept the thought that their lives flew by senselessly, in vain. But that is the lot of all generations as they approach the end. When life ebbs, melancholy settles in the soul.

Youth as we remember it is always beautiful, to the point of heartache and tears. Everything around is wonderful, sunny, full of love and hope.

The declining generation can and must be understood. It does not want to break with the past. Especially hateful is the thought that instead of a promise of a tranquil old age, one must worry about getting enough money for a funeral.

Everything that happened after October 1917 adds up to a fantastic drama embroiling an entire country and all its peoples. An unbroken sequence of suffering on the part of some and crime on the part of others. And yet the totalitarian regime was far from being all there was of life; Bolshevism was only one aspect of existence, however repellent. The times demand an honest answer to the main question: How was it that at the whim of a small group of criminals in power millions of innocent people were annihilated, and more millions were doomed to endless suffering as social outcasts, victims of an inhuman state machine?

One reason, of course, was that the Russian people, exhausted by a thousand years of poverty and continual humiliation, were befuddled and thrown off by promises of an instant earthly paradise, grew deaf to their doubts, and placed their faith in the lie. The main thing was to achieve a better life, no matter what the cost. Infinitely vile, the Marxist-Leninist lumpen ideology played on that faith.

And that trait is still with us. Has there been an end to voluntary informing on others? Today it is done not only through anonymous letters but openly, on television, in the newspapers, from the rostrums of mass demonstrations, and by the use of compromising material. Is there less thievery, less giving and taking of bribes? Less lying and hypocrisy? Do we not hear calls for retribution, trial, and death for those who rose up against Bolshevism? Aren't over a hundred frankly Fascist newspapers published in our country? Aren't anti-Semitic leaflets plastered on our walls? Don't many of our judges and prosecutors, with years of faithful service to Bolshevik lawlessness behind them, give active support to a creeping restoration, extending legal sanction to the anticonstitutional actions of our Nazis?

The practice of mass arrests has inflicted an incalculable loss on all the peoples of Russia, drained society of its lifeblood, and determined its moral collapse. During the seventy years of Bolshevism the forms of repression altered but the causes and nature of the despotism remained unchanged. The regime and its top leaders were ready to commit any crime against humanity to entrench their monopoly on power, ideology, and property and to create a submissive herd, albeit with the psychology of "people on the barricades."

And today's Bolsheviks (our current Communists, national patriots, and other Russophobe, antipatriotic groups) are still capable of curtailing the country's democratic development and throwing it back into the cesspool. I am convinced that only a consistent de-Bolshevization of the state and the society can save our people from final ruin, both physical and spiritual.

The twentieth century has come to an end. For Russia, it was the most terrible, the bloodiest century, shot through with hatred and intolerance. It would appear to be time to come to our senses, repent, ask forgiveness of the still-living survivors of the concentration camps, kneel before the graves of the millions of people who were shot or who died of hunger, and realize, at long last, that we lived in a criminal state, helping it to enslave us—all of us together and each of us separately.

Basically, it was the awakening of 1956 that led to the perestroika of 1985, the era of reformation—late in coming, but here. We who lived through these times will no doubt have to return more than once to that tangled labyrinth of public and personal relationships to analyze what happened, take pride in what was achieved, and repent of our sins and errors.

The gulag harvest of crosses . . . limitless in space, though recent in time. The biggest cemetery on earth, as well as in history. Neglected, overgrown, befouled by denunciations, polluted by radioactive and chemical waste, desecrated again and again by mindless simpletons with portraits of Lenin and Stalin. The graveyard of human hopes. An eternal seal of infamy on our hapless land.

SOCIALLY DANGEROUS CHILDREN

IT IS in the name of the children that history today judges the evil of Bolshevism. There can be no pardoning crimes against children. There can be no pardoning what emanates from Yezhov's Order No. 00486 of 15 August 1937. Here are some of its clauses. I quote from the original; its style is its own:

Preparing for operation. This begins with a thorough check of every family slated for repression. Additional compromising material is collected. On the basis of that the following is compiled:

a. a general report on the family;

b. a separate brief report on children over 15 who are socially dangerous and capable of anti-Soviet actions;

c. a separate list of the names of children under 15 of preschool and school ages.

The reports are reviewed by the People's Commissariats of Internal Affairs of the republics and by the heads of the oblast and district offices of the People's Commissariat of Internal Affairs (NKVD).

The latter:

a. authorize the arrest and search of wives of traitors to the motherland;

b. decide on measures to be taken in regard to the children of the arrested wives.

Carrying out arrests and searches. Wives in a state of legal or de facto marriage to a person convicted are subject to arrest from the moment of his arrest.

Wives who are divorced from the convicted person at the moment of his arrest are subject to arrest if involved in the counterrevolutionary actions of the convicted, concealing him, knowing of his counterrevolutionary actions but failing to inform the authorities.

After the arrest and search, the arrested wives of the convicted are sent to prison in convoys. Simultaneously, the children are removed in accordance with the procedure set out below.

Procedure for recording cases. Investigations are opened for every arrested wife and every socially dangerous child over 15. These investigations are forwarded for review by the Special Council of the NKVD of the USSR.

Review of cases and penalties. The Special Council reviews the cases of the wives of traitors to the motherland and of children over 15 who are socially dangerous and capable of anti-Soviet actions.

The socially dangerous children of the convicted, depending on their ages, the degree of danger, and the likelihood of reform, are subject to imprisonment in the camps or reform labor colonies of the NKVD or in the special-regime orphanages of the People's Commissariats of Education of the republics.

Procedure for carrying out sentences. The convicted socially dangerous children are taken to the camps, reform labor colonies, or special-regime orphanages of the People's Commissariats of Education of the republics in accordance with the personal orders of the gulag of the NKVD with respect to the first and second institutions, and of the Administrative-Economic Department (AKhU) of the NKVD of the USSR with respect to the third institution.

Placement of children of the convicted. All other categories of children left orphaned after the convictions are to be placed as follows:

a. children between the ages of 1 to 1½ and 3, in the orphanages and nurseries of the People's Commissariats of Health in the convicted persons' places of settlement;

b. children between the ages of 3 and 15, in orphanages of the People's Commissariats of Education of other republics, districts, and oblasts (in accordance with the established order of distribution), but outside of Moscow, Leningrad, Kiev, Tbilisi, and Minsk and not in the maritime or border cities.

Cases of children over 15 to be decided on an individual basis. Infants are to be sent with their convicted mothers to concentration camps, where, upon reaching the age of 1 to 1½, they are to be turned over to the orphanages and nurseries of the People's Commissariats of Health of the republics.

In the event of relatives (not repressed) wishing to accept the orphans as their full dependents, no objections are to be raised.

Preparations for receiving and dispatching children. In every city involved in the operation, special measures establish reception and dispatch centers where the children will be taken immediately after their mothers' arrest and from which the children will then be sent on to orphanages.

The heads of the NKVD offices and of the centers where the orphanages of the People's Commissariats of Education are located, together with their managers or representatives of the Oblast Departments of Eduction (OBLONO), check the personnel of the orphanages and discharge all politically unstable, anti-Soviet, and decadent people. Those discharged are replaced by trustworthy, politically reliable staffs capable of the work of educating and bringing up the arriving children.

Procedure for sending children to orphanages. At the reception and dispatch center the children are received by the manager or head of the center and by a specially selected expert of the State Security Service (UGB).

Each accepted child is registered in a special book, and his or her documents are sealed in a separate envelope.

The children are then divided into groups, depending on where they are to be sent, and taken in groups by specially selected workers to the orphanages of the People's Commissariats of Education, where they are handed over with their documents to the manager on his personal signature.

Children under 3 are handed over personally to the managers of the orphanages or nurseries of the People's Commissariats of Health on their personal signatures. The birth certificate is handed over with the child.

Supervision of children of the convicted. Supervision of the political attitudes of children of the convicted, and of their education and upbringing, is assigned to the People's Commissariats of Internal Affairs of the republics and to the heads of the district and oblast offices of the NKVD.[1]

I reread these Yezhov-Stalinist compositions and once again I fall into bewilderment and uncertainty: Might not all this be a fabrication, a forgery? Could these bloodthirsty cadences really have been the work of heads of state with children of their own? One of two things must be true: either they, writing in blood, were insane or I, reading, have myself gone mad.

Alas, it all took place, and not that long ago. That is why rage can be the only response to those who march up and down our land braying that Stalin "didn't go far enough" and left his purifying mission unfinished. Although they're right in a way—he annihilated only sixty to seventy million people. He didn't have time for all of them. He departed for hell, to report to the devil.

May the Lord preserve our grandchildren and great-grandchildren from the lot of those on whom the Communist regime pinned the label "children of enemies of the people." Official documents had a special abbreviation for them, ChSIR, for "member of the family of a traitor to the motherland." It was the burdensome cross these children were to bear all their lives.

Children are children. They are always in need of their elders' care. Naturally, in a formal sense, it was not the children who were put on trial before these "troikas," or three-man revolutionary tribunals, and these "special councils" but their parents. It was the parents and not the helpless minors who were sentenced to be shot or sent to prison camps and special settlements or into exile. But the tragedy of parents and children is indivisible. At all the train stops and way stations of their lives, along their whole road of suffering, humiliation, and abuse, the children had it worst. The Leninist-Stalinist machine of political repression uprooted millions of the young from their families and left them face to face with their torturers, deprived them of everything—of their parental homes and even of their names, which in the orphanages where the NKVD placed them they often forgot—and robbed them of a future. It is frightening to think of all this—and even more insufferable to admit that it happened.

Today, many of the children of the concentration camps are getting on in years. They are war veterans, pensioners. Their parents did not live long enough to see the changes leading to a democratic Russia. And the time is not far off when these former "Stalinist orphans" will be the only surviving witnesses to the tragic events and crimes of the fascist regime. And then they, too, will be gone.

The Commission on the Rehabilitation of Victims of Political Repression, which reports to the president of Russia and which I head, has quite a few letters from the young prisoners of the past. They write that to this day they dream of the horrors of the gulag, to this day they search for their parents. They live and remember. Their memories are their lifelong cross.

Here is one such recollection, written by Viktor Ivanovich Pankov of the Tiumen oblast: "I was five when our family was deported as kulaks in 1930. Our family consisted of seven people. We were exiled to Tobolsk. Then they assigned us to the newly organized Sovietsky village beyond the swamps 70 kilometers west of Tobolsk. We lived in barracks. A lot of the exiled kulaks, especially the children and old people, died of hunger and cold. We didn't know what it was like to have a childhood or to be young. We starved, we lived on scraps of leaves and moss, we wore bast shoes and homemade clothes."[2]

A litmus test for any government, however it may disguise itself, is its treatment of children. Yes, the Soviet Union had its sunny Artek youth camp as an advertisement for happy childhood; it had its Young Pioneers and its trips to summer camps at discounted prices. But it also had its gulag concentration camps, and its itineraries for those exiled to Siberia, and its travel papers from the agency of Yagoda, Yezhov, and Beria.

Repressive action against children is the lowest depth of the inhumanity of Bolshevik fascism. Nothing is more despicable than a government that wars on the young with all its punitive might.

The Bolsheviks came up with the unique and all-embracing concept of "childhood in disgrace," embodied in multiple directives of the Politburo of the Party CC, personal orders by Lenin and Stalin, legislative acts adopted at the highest levels of government, and advisories and instructions by the NKVD on living arrangements for children of "traitors to the motherland," including constant surveillance of their behavior. The program established mobile centers for receiving and dispatching new arrivals, special orphanages and nurseries, and camps and settlements. The children had to forget who they were, where they came from, who and where their parents were.

It was barefaced hypocrisy for Stalin to say that the son does not answer for the father. The lie originated not in 1937 but right after the Bolsheviks came to power. If we were to turn to the very first names in the ledger of murdered children, we would have to begin with the execution on the night of 16–17 June 1918 of Czar Nicholas II and his family in the Ipatiev House in Yekaterinburg. Shot together with the czar, as we know, were Czarina Aleksandra Fyodorovna and their children—Olga, Tatiana, Maria, Anastasia, and the czarevich, Aleksei, who wasn't quite fourteen.

Lenin's government gave its approval for the execution of the czar and his family. It would go on to approve countless other shootings. Told by Sverdlov of the execution of the czarist family, Trotsky asked, "Who decided?" Sverdlov replied, "We here decided. Ilyich thought we couldn't leave them as a living banner, especially in these difficult circumstances."[3]

In later years, in fate's grim revenge, the children of Nicholas II were followed by the children of those who Sverdlov said "decided." Two sons of Mikhail Ryutin, a son of Grigory Zinoviev, and two sons of Lev Kamenev were shot; Trotsky's own sons were killed; two sons of Yu. Piatakov disappeared without a trace. The fathers were accessories to Lenin's and Stalin's crimes and reaped what they had sowed.

The harvest was ominous: mass terror, concentration camps, hostages, with mothers, wives, and children shot because their sons, husbands, and fathers refused to cooperate with the adventurers in power. The number of hostages runs into the thousands. As early as 1918, on orders from the Petrograd Cheka, 500 hostages were shot.[4] Shot the following year, also in Petrograd, were the relatives (including the children) of officers of the Eighty-sixth Infantry Regiment who had gone over to the Whites. In May 1920 the newspapers told of the execution in Elizavetgrad of the elderly mother and four daughters, ages three to seven, of an officer who had refused to serve the proletarian regime. Arkhangelsk, where the Cheka shot children of twelve to sixteen, was known in 1920 as the "city of the dead." Between 1918 and 1922 the Bolsheviks frequently held children hostage in their struggle against peasants attempting to resist the regime's agrarian policy. The fall of 1918 saw the creation of concentration camps whose prisoners at first were largely hostages, including women with infants, taken as relatives of the "rebels."

The minutes of the meeting of 27 June 1921 of the commission on the maintenance of child hostages in concentration camps in Tambov province notes a sizable influx of minors, including infants, into the "concentration field camps," and it speaks of the inadequacy of these camps for long-term support of children and the resultant intestinal and respiratory diseases. The commission recommends that children fifteen and under be held separately from grown-ups in special facilities, within camp boundaries when possible. In extreme cases, with the concurrence of the local branches of particular departments, the children could be placed in structures adjoining the camps, "under mandatory security guard."[5] Documents show that even after the campaign for "thinning out" the concentration camps in July 1921, the camps in Tambov province still held more than 450 hostages ages one to ten.[6]

The well-known theoretician of anarchism Prince Kropotkin is quite fair in his verdict on that sanguinary "invention" of the Bolsheviks, taking children as hostages. In a letter to Lenin in December 1920, he called the Bolshevik leaders' use of hostages, no less than their resort to mass executions, unworthy of men undertaking the construction of a new society. The prince thought his voice would be heard. But Lenin scrawled on the letter: "To the archive . . ."

An appeal to the authorities on the subject of hostages came from Tikhon, the patriarch of Moscow and All Russia, who admonished, "We shudder to think that such things are possible, when in the course of hostilities one camp defends its ranks with wives and children taken hostage from the opposing camp. We shudder at the barbarity of our times."

Experts have estimated that the number of kulak households decimated in the 1930s and 1940s in the country as a whole reached almost seven million. With peasant families consisting on the average of five to seven people, half of them underage, we can imagine the magnitude of the regime's crimes against children. Most of the peasant families were deported en masse to special settlements or labor settlements in remote regions of the country (dubbed "kulak exile" or "labor exile"). Millions of people were hauled and herded to the north and to the east like cattle. A letter to M. Kalinin on the deportation of families from the Ukraine and Kursk had this to say: "They were packed off into the terrible cold—infants, pregnant women piled in cattle cars on top of one another, and right there women gave birth (could there be a worse indignity); then they were thrown out of the cars like dogs and put in churches and dirty, cold sheds, lice-ridden, freezing and hungry, and here they are, thousands of them, left to the mercy of fate, like dogs no one wants to notice."

Stuck in ungodly holes unfit for human habitation, the "specially resettled" were doomed to a slow death. The more zealous overseers had graves dug in advance, in full sight of those for whom they were intended. A document describing conditions in the special settlement of Bushuika in the Aldan region was submitted to the Commission on the Specially Resettled set up by the Politburo in 1931 for administering the program for "deportation and resettlement of kulaks." The commission included Andreyev, Yagoda, and Postyshev. The paper reported that the settlement consisted of 3,306 people, 1,415 of them children fourteen or under. The food was so vile that 184 children under five died over a period of eight months. There was an epidemic of typhoid and typhus. A memorandum observes drily that mortality was highest in June (81 deaths) and July (99). As for medical help during the epidemic, there was none. The so-called orphanage, where most of the children lived isolated from their parents, was nothing more than a barracks with a double row of wooden bunks.

In all such places of exile people succumbed by the thousands to disease, starvation, and hard labor. Infant mortality was especially high. In a memorandum of 26 October 1931 to Ya. Rudzutak, chairman of the TsKK of the VKP(b), G. Yagoda notes the high incidence of illness and death among the resettled. The monthly death toll accounts for 1.3 percent of the exiles in northern Kazakhstan and 0.8 percent in the Narym district. A particularly large proportion of the dead are very young. Here the monthly fatalities among children under three add up to 8 to 12 percent, and in Magnitogorsk even higher—up to 15 percent. One customary feature of "kulak exile" was the homeless state of many of the children. At the end of 1934, in the labor settlements of the "Western Forest" alone, there were 2,850 of these *besprizorniki*, waifs whose parents had died or had escaped.

Let me cite a few more chilling letters on the tragic fate of these young "members of peasant households" who fell victim to the regime. This from Maria Bazikh: "On 12 April 1939 they arrested my husband. . . . On 14 May I was sent away in a convoy. They didn't let us bring anything. Took us naked and barefoot, hungry, with small children. Off to Narym, and me with six little ones and another one eight months along. To the north, to the Narym district in the Novy Vosyugan region, down the Vosyugan River on barges. Loaded us off in the swamps. There were no buildings. In that place, children and grownups died like flies from hunger and cold. My own children died there. Why, and who will answer that question?" Of the fate of her family Anastasia Lavrovskaya writes: "Our family of

nine (my eldest sister got married and wasn't rounded up) was exiled. . . . We lived in the special settlement of Kopanka, then in
Kosolbanka. Between 1931 and 1934 the family was virtually wiped
out; my father died in 1931, then five of my sisters and brothers. In
1933 they took me away from my ailing mother and put me in an
orphanage in the city of Verkhoputiye. My entire family died of
hunger. That would have been my fate, too, if they hadn't taken me
to the orphanage. I still cannot understand why, for what sins, my
relatives perished—only because they had their own farm and could
feed themselves? This is so crazy, so unfair."

No less tragic was the fate of children of arrested peasant families
who were subjected to the "third category of dekulakization," without confiscation of property. As a member of the Andokhin family,
arrested in the 1930s, tells it:

In February 1932 my parents . . . and our entire family were dekulakized—expelled from the agrarian commune, deprived of voting rights,
thrown out of our house, left with no means of subsistence. We weren't
exiled, although my father repeatedly asked the authorities to send us,
along with the other kulaks, to a special settlement. There we would
have had the right to work and earn some money and thus had some
kind of life. But I repeat, our family was not exiled.

Apparently it was part of some kind of class struggle, making the victims stay where they were, to be jeered at, hounded, and terrorized by
the local inhabitants and by the authorities. . . .

Our family, our huge family, had nowhere to live, nothing to eat, no
place to work. . . . We scraped along until spring; with the thaw we dug
a pit in the courtyard, and the whole family lived in this pit.

In the spring of 1932 we were given a plan for sowing grain. Obvi-
ously, the man who gave us the plan knew very well that it would not be
followed, not because we didn't want to but because there were no draft
animals, there was no plow, there were no seeds.

That autumn, for failing to follow the plan for delivering bread to the
state, Father was sentenced to 2½ years in prison. And earlier the same
autumn, our mother was sentenced to 10 years because, with the permission of one of the team leaders, she had gathered five pounds (that's
what the sentence said) of ears of grain on a field for grazing cattle.

The local activists made deliberate efforts to wipe out the whole fam-
ily. We realized that very clearly in the course of our hard, wretched life.
They took away from us the alms the small children got begging "for
Christ's sake," they took away any instrument that could be used to

earn anything. . . . We weren't allowed in school, and, hungry and in rags, we weren't eager to attend. After the dekulakization none of us were able to finish even the elementary classes.[7]

Letters like these run into the thousands.

The end of the 1930s saw a sharp increase in juvenile crime. In December 1934 the Politburo set up a commission on homeless children, with Kalinin as chairman. There could have been no worse hypocrisy, for once again the blame was laid on the children themselves. Once again, criminal legislation affecting children was hardened.

Among the factors contributing to this hardening, in my view, was a letter of 19 March 1935 from the people's commissar for defense, Voroshilov, to Stalin, Molotov, and Kalinin. Voroshilov's letter of "outrage" was prompted by the report in the Moscow press of a knife attack by a nine-year-old boy on the son of the Moscow deputy prosecutor, a man named Koblents. In his letter to Stalin, Voroshilov enclosed a newspaper clipping that, in his words, illustrated "on the one hand, the monstrous forms assumed by adolescent hooliganism here in Moscow and, on the other hand, the well-nigh complacent attitude of the courts (reducing sentences by half, and so on)." Voroshilov was nonplussed: why not have such miscreants shot? As if responding to Voroshilov's request, on 8 April 1935 the newspapers published a decree of the CEC and the Council of People's Commissars (SNK) of the USSR, dated April 7: "On Steps to Combat Criminality among Juveniles." "Juveniles age twelve and over," the order read, "are to be tried in criminal court and subject to the full range of criminal penalties."[8]

For the local authorities, the question was whether the "full range" included the death penalty. Until then, the death penalty had not applied to children and teenagers under eighteen. The answer came in a secret clarification by the Politburo on 20 April 1935. It was intended for the courts and the prosecutors' offices, and it confirmed that the forms of criminal punishment provided for in the first paragraph of the decree included the death penalty (execution). In other words, judges could have twelve-year-olds shot.

The children of so-called enemies of the people were commonly used to put pressure on those arrested. How this was done is recounted in documents and in the memoirs of the children themselves, many of whom are no longer alive.

Petya Yakir, the son of Commander Yakir, was arrested in 1937, when he was fourteen. A photograph shows a boy in a cap and a jacket over a white shirt buttoned to the neck. "You are accused," he was told, "of organizing an anarchist mounted band designed to operate in the rear of the Red Army during the coming war, as well as of propagating the anarchist ideas of Bakunin-Karelin-Kropotkin among pupils in school." A young boy . . . and a mounted band positioned behind the Red Army during the coming war?

Today it sounds like lurid nonsense, a figment of psychotic imaginations, but at the time, during the Stalinist years, fantasies like it had tragic consequences. Petya—you really can't call him by anything but his youthful diminutive—wasn't shot; he was imprisoned in Astrakhan, about which he was to write in his book, *A Childhood in Prison.*

At age sixteen he took part in a hunger strike with his cellmates and was one of four who were yanked out of the cell for reprisals aimed at finding the instigator. He writes:

> I endeavored to explain that no one had instigated anything; the conditions in the cells were quite simply unbearable. I was struck a second time, and when this evoked no response, I was dragged into an adjacent room to the sound of the governor [warden—*Trans.*] shouting: "The jacket'll loosen his tongue all right."
>
> In the next room I was thrust into a canvas jacket, which was longer than I was tall and had long sleeves. Then they threw me face downwards on the floor, put my hands behind my back and tied the sleeve ends together. After this they tied these ends to the hem of the jacket and fastened the knot to a rope, which passed through a pulley hanging from the ceiling. Then they began to hoist me upwards in short jerks, kicking me in the ribs as they did so. First of all my body bent and my stomach remained on the ground. The pain was excruciating. When I was pulled clear of the floor, I lost consciousness. . . . The hoisting procedure was repeated twice more.[9]

The law providing for capital punishment for children caused shudders even among those in the West who, regrettably, were supportive of the so-called experiment in socialist construction. In the 1930s the illusions of "friends of the land of the Soviets" gradually began to dissipate. These friends couldn't understand why the Soviet leaders were persecuting mere children.

Quite a few Western writers, among them Henri Barbusse, Bernard Shaw, and Leon Feuchtwanger, visited the Soviet Union. They wanted to see things with their own eyes. At Gorky's invitation, Romain Rolland came to the USSR in the summer of 1935, and on 28 June he was received by Stalin in the Kremlin. They had a conversation, which Rolland prolonged, in a fashion, in his letters to Stalin. In a letter dated 28 December 1935, he observes that among some French intellectuals—professors, teachers, honest members of the petit bourgeoisie—feeling toward the USSR has cooled. "They are troubled and confused at not being able to obtain answers to many disturbing questions," the writer confides to Stalin. Among these disturbing questions, the letter singles out "the law on punishment of children twelve and over." Romain Rolland goes on:

> I foresaw the emotions this would arouse in Western countries. These emotions have exceeded all my expectations. The most awful rumors are spreading. I had to write a dozen letters to various friends to reassure them. Their anxiety was not allayed, and the wave of protests is growing. All this plays into the hands of enemies of the USSR. A very well known and, unfortunately, respected dignitary of the church is giving a series of lectures in the provinces of Belgium and France in which he goes so far as to allege that, under this year's statute of 7 April, twelve-year-old children can be sentenced to death for "religious obstinacy." This demands an answer. I can't provide it in the words of our conversation: my mouth is stopped. But one way or another, an answer is essential. Without revealing the real motives for this law, is there no way of quashing these shameful, slanderous rumors? And above all, it should be stated (as you asserted to me at the end of June) that to this day not a single child has been executed![10]

Rolland had raised the question of the law in his talk with Stalin, telling him that "the text of this law is not well enough known. And even when it is known, it gives rise to serious doubts. One gets the impression that these children are threatened with the death penalty!" Stalin didn't evade answering but tried to portray his actions as a preventive and necessary measure: "This decree has purely pedagogical significance. We needed it in order to frighten not so much the delinquent children as those who organize this juvenile delinquency. . . . In the USSR there are still quite a number of people of former times

who have lost their bearings—gendarmes, policemen, czarist officials, their children, their relatives. These people are not used to
working; they are embittered and provide fertile soil for crime."[11] As
for confirming to the world that despite the repressive law not a single child had been put to death—that request in the French writer's
letter remained unanswered.

Nor did Stalin answer a letter from Rolland on another question.
When Rolland learned of the arrest of a fellow writer, Aleksandr
Arosyev, chairman of the All-Union Society for Cultural Relations
with Foreign Countries (VOKS), who had accompanied him to the
Kremlin in 1935, he wrote to Stalin in August 1937 raising the ques-
tion of Arosyev's children: "One of them is only three. They have no
relatives in Moscow. Arosyev and his wife both have heart trouble.
Be so kind as to let them know their children are being taken care
of."[12] The children were being taken care of—by the "tutors" of the
NKVD.

The second half of the 1930s has rightly been called the time of
the "great terror." But it would be even more accurate, in my view, to
call it the time of the "witch-hunt after children."

On 15 June 1937 Yezhov confirmed a set of instructions for an
operation designed to exile from Moscow, Leningrad, Kiev, Rostov,
Taganrog, Sochi, and its environs the families of Trotskyists, rightists, leftists, and those expelled from the VKP(b). The members of
the last group were to be exiled together with their families. The operation was to be carried out from 25 June to 25 August 1937.[13]

On 3 July the instructions were amended. The local offices of the
NKVD were told to submit lists of the families of people sentenced
after 1 December 1934 by the military collegium of the Supreme
Court, as well as of the families of socially dangerous persons sentenced by the special collegia of the courts. These families, numbering 6,000 to 7,000 people, would soon "be sentenced and would
have to be isolated under specially strict conditions."[14]

On 5 July, having reviewed the "NKVD question," the Politburo
accepted the proposal "for internment in camps, for five to eight
years, of all wives of convicted traitors to the motherland and members of rightist-Trotskyist espionage-diversionary organizations."
Decided at the same time was the fate of their children. The NKVD
was told to "place the children in the existing network of orphanages

and secret boarding schools of the People's Commissariats of Education of the republics."[15]

On 15 August an "Operative Order" appeared over Yezhov's signature with precise instructions on the arrest of wives and the separation of children from their parents. The preamble stated: "On receipt of this order, begin arresting wives of traitors to the motherland and members of rightist-Trotskyist espionage-diversionary organizations convicted by military collegia and military tribunals of the first and second categories from 1 August 1936 on." Detailed instructions follow on preparing for the operation, arresting wives and searching their apartments, preparing cases, selecting punitive measures, and executing sentences. Several sections have to do with children; the document deals in part with resettling the children of convicted parents, making arrangements at the distribution centers (these indeed existed in those years), keeping children of enemies of the people under surveillance, and so on.

In short, we have before us a bulky document ungrammatical but abundantly specific about where to take the wives and children and to whom to give the orphaned 1½-year-olds. The tormentors' epithets resound loudly and clearly: socially dangerous children, convicted socially dangerous children, special-regime orphanages of the People's Commissariats of Education, special-duty squads of the gulag of the NKVD and the AKhU of the NKVD for socially dangerous children . . .

It's as though one were dealing with the collection of scrap metal and not the fate of little children. It defies belief that the men who wrote these instructions were once children themselves and had children of their own. How demented, brutish, and debased must one be not to hear the children wail? How low must one sink to give tongue to the jackal's boast that in the land of the Soviets the young have the happiest childhood on earth?

Preserved in the archives of the NKVD are hundreds of letters, bits of evidence, and notes by the agencies' own "inspectors" attesting to the outrages perpetrated in the orphanages for children of enemies of the people: "In a number of orphanages there is a hostile attitude toward children of the arrested amounting at times to sheer abuse. . . . [In] many orphanages the children of the arrested are called Trotskyists and are persecuted like enemies." Another letter:

"In the Fyodorovsky orphanage in the Kustanaisky oblast of the Kazakh SSR . . . the children of the arrested persons Kruchin and Stepanov were raped by adult inmates. The cafeteria of an orphanage with 212 children has only 12 spoons and 20 plates. The bedroom has one mattress for three persons. The children sleep with their clothes and shoes on."[16]

The security agents paid close attention to the attitudes of the children and the arrested parents. One of the NKVD's directives has this to say: "In the Nizhny-Isetsky orphanage in the Sverdlov oblast, the inmates Tukhachevsky, Gamarnik, Uborevich, and Shteinbriuk demonstrate counterrevolutionary, defeatist, and terrorist attitudes. To conceal their counterrevolutionary actions they have joined the Komsomol. Said group of children demonstrates terrorist intentions against leaders of the Party and the government to avenge their parents. In the Cheremkhovsky orphanage in the Irkutsk oblast, the inmates Stepanov, Grunde, Kazakov, and Osipenko have been arrested by the authorities of the NKVD for anti-Soviet statements."[17]

It wasn't only within the walls of the orphanages that the security agencies enforced such iron control over the "isolated children." The NKVD of the USSR laid down these rules in a circular dated 20 May 1938:

> Children of arrested parents are not to be released from orphanages (as overage or upon completion of courses) without special instructions from the AKhU of the NKVD of the USSR. . . . In regard to children of arrested parents over fifteen years of age who have been given work or assigned to further study, the administration of the NKVD is to report in writing to the AKhU of the NKVD of the USSR. . . . Said contingent of children of arrested parents is to be placed under agency surveillance to ensure timely exposure and to put a stop to anti-Soviet, terrorist attitudes and actions. . . . Socially dangerous children exhibiting anti-Soviet attitudes and actions must be handed over to the courts on general grounds and sent to camps by special-duty squads of the gulag of the NKVD.[18]

Even as World War II raged and the country's fate hung in the balance, the mechanism of repression remained unchanged. Indeed, it was tightened on the pretext that these were critical times. In its Order No. 270 of 16 August 1941, Supreme Command Headquarters ruled that commanders and political workers who surrendered to the enemy and were taken prisoner were to be "regarded as malicious deserters whose families are subject to arrest." Toward the end of May 1942, the People's Commissariat of Internal Affairs and the chief prosecutor of the USSR gave orders for "expanding the repression of families of traitors to the motherland."[19]

During the war the Nazis hustled children in one direction, to Germany, while the Stalinists sent them in the other, to Central Asia, Kazakhstan, the east. The children of Volga Germans, Poles, Chechens, Kalmyks, Ingush, Karachayevs, Balkars, Crimean Tatars, Bulgarians, Greeks, Armenians, Turko-Meskhetins, Kurds, Khemshils—and, after the war, Estonians, Latvians, Lithuanians—were consigned to the far regions. By April 1945 there were as many as 34,700 Karachayev children under sixteen within the borders of Kazakhstan, Kirgizia, and Uzbekistan. Some 46,000 children were brought to Uzbekistan from Georgia. During their first years in their new locations, the annual mortality rate among the resettled climbed as high as 27 percent, and most of the dead were children.

The land groaned with human suffering, but the authorities grew more and more rabid. After a visit to Kazakhstan, the future minister of internal affairs, S. Kruglov, recommended that all resettled children left without supervision not be placed in the orphanages of the educational system and instead be sent to the labor colonies of the NKVD.

The bitter cup of exile was drunk to the dregs by the Kalmyk poet D. Kugultinov. Put to work bookkeeping, he was told one day to make an inventory of the nursery of the Norilsky concentration camp. As he recalls it: "I crossed the threshold: children. A horde of children of five or six in little padded cotton jackets and pants with numbers on the back and chest, like prisoners. The numbers were their mothers'. The children were used to seeing only women around, but they'd heard that there were papas, men. And so they ran up to me crying, 'Papa, Papachka, why did you take so long?' There's nothing more terrible than children with numbers. And inside the barracks, the catchphrase 'Thanks to Comrade Stalin for our happy childhood.'" I saw something similar when I went to Magadan for the dedication of a monument by Ernst Neizvestny to victims of the Stalinist regime. Even at this solemn gathering some went so far as to shout insulting remarks about the onetime prisoners. To this day these former trusties, investigators, and camp commanders cannot resign themselves to being deprived of their allotment of human flesh.

In Magadan there is a museum of the repression era and a gallery of the prisoners' artworks. What amazed me in the museum were the posters with devastating messages such as "To the Party's and government's concern for us we shall respond with Stakhanovite labor." The canvases and drawings in the gallery reflected two different outlooks. Some of the works were in dark, gloomy tones. People pushing carts, spades in hand. Faces grimy with coal dust. Eyes of infinite sadness and despair. Other pictures astonished me with their joyousness. Forests and thickets, flowers, boys and girls in white shirts and sweaters. Children at play. These works spoke plainly of longing for the past and hope for the future.

The war against Fascism came to an end, the world exalted the murderer Stalin, but he himself had not yet rounded out his war against the Soviet people. He continued to send the wives and children of enemies of the people into exile from Leningrad, Moscow, the Ukraine, the Baltic states, and other areas. The millstones of the criminal regime continued to turn overtime, grinding up the lives of new generations.

People were cast out by the system without even being told for how long. Under the Decree of the Presidium of the Supreme Soviet of the USSR of 26 November 1948, the status of the specially resettled was extended indefinitely, their right to return to their original homes denied. And still, children suffered. A joint directive of the Ministry of Internal Affairs (MVD) and the Chief Prosecutor's Office ruled on 16 May 1949 that children of the resettled living in special settlements with their exiled parents or other relatives were to be counted as permanent exiles upon reaching the age of sixteen. Even children were robbed of the hope of returning to their homes.

In 1949 the minister of internal affairs, S. Kruglov, reported to Stalin that his agency had intensified its controls over the resettled and the exiled, especially in regard to labor and surveillance. He also reported that there were 2,562,830 exiled and specially resettled persons on the MVD's lists. It had been four years since the end of the war. Five years later, in March 1954—a whole year after Stalin's death—the Ministry of Internal Affairs reported to Malenkov and

Khrushchev that, according to its records, the number of specially resettled stood at 2,819,776, including 884,057 children under sixteen.

Behold the empire of the gravediggers in its prime!

The years pass. With perestroika, the government's war against its own people came to an end. The "orphans of the state" had grown up, grown old. Not all of them lived to see the day they had waited for, the day the backbone of Bolshevism shattered. When you meet these people and talk to them, you can't help marveling at how brave they were, how they managed not to grow callous and come to abominate everything around them.

And yet, in dealing with the victims of political repression, our lawmakers for some reason distinguish between parents and children. The parents were repressed, the argument goes, but the children only suffered in consequence. This concept has been adopted legislatively and determines the payments made to retirees and the disabled. Children of arrested parents do not receive compensatory supplements to their pensions. I don't want to argue with lawyers. Perhaps, from a strictly formal point of view, one could say that it was the parents, not the children, who were put on trial—that the repression was not directed against the children themselves. But then what does one call those measures that applied directly to "socially dangerous children"? What does one say about the hundreds of thousands of children who were in the concentration camps with their parents? And the children of parents who were shot—does one say they were not repressed, either?

We are still unimaginably far from escaping our barbarity. To this day the country proliferates with monuments to Lenin and streets named after him; many a local government leader has Lenin's portrait hanging in his office; hundreds of Bolshevik and frankly Fascist newspapers are being published; monstrous speeches defending Stalin and attacking the victims of the evil regime are delivered in the Duma. Let me cite as examples a few pronouncements by Vladimir Zhirinovsky touching on the Stalinist repressions. Take his remarks to the parliamentary majority during the Duma's debate of 4–5 February 1998 on the government budget: "You voted to give 500 million [rubles] to the very people who destroyed the country—the repressed, the people who wrecked our lives. From 1991 on they've been muddying the waters, and in your 1998 budget you give them 500 million. Let's strike from the budget this clause about help to the so-called repressed. We haven't had any repressions for a long time now." Addressing the finance minister, he continues:

Give us proof: Who was the money given to in 1997? What is this Fund for Political Repression? We can't have this. The people, the Russian people, also suffered repressions. Let's get to the point: This 500 million, who will it go to this year, or who did it go to last year? Looks like 300 went to the dissidents, 150 to some homeless bums, and 50 you gave to some ethnic region.

. . . I'm categorically against all these victims of repression—there aren't any such victims of repression. All of Russia was repressed for the whole twentieth century. If you're speaking of a few thousand old-timers who spent their lives shouting anti-Soviet slogans, destroyed our country, and won out in 1991, we shouldn't give them anything but instead take back right away everything that should be taken back. That is our party's fundamental position. You're giving money to those who destroyed the Soviet Union. People like Rybakov and his kind. And if you still don't understand, then back to prison with you so you'll get it.

And further on:

Comrade Stalin, the head of our state, didn't resettle people for no reason. When the KGB reported to him that thousands of Kalmyks had organized into brigades and were making raids on the Red Army and killing thousands of Soviet soldiers—then those of them who were left alive were indeed resettled, and they're alive to this day. They're pushing eighty and they're still living. And where they weren't resettled, they died of that horrendous life that you, you perestroika freaks, handed us. The Crimean Tatars—why were they resettled? They turned over to the Germans all the partisan units in the Crimea.

I don't even want to comment on these ravings. Can it really be that the Russian people will never pull themselves out of the gutter into which politicians burdened neither by conscience nor by feeling for their homeland dragged them in 1917? Once again we exclaim over the past and ask ourselves, "Was it possible?" And off we go again like a herd of cattle stampeding toward the slaughterhouse. We Russians have a very short memory. Perhaps because too much sorrow has befallen us, the road of suffering has been inordinately long.

FELLOW TRAVELERS

THE FATE OF Russian social democracy has been infinitely tragic. It lacked the wisdom to discern in Bolshevism the destructive force that was to demolish the democratic republic born in February 1917 and to fling Russia into the backwater of historical development. More than that, nearly every socialist-oriented party helped the Bolsheviks in their criminal seizure of power. The price the socialists paid for their mistake was unconscionably high.

Having carried out their counterrevolutionary coup of October 1917 and seized power, all with a show of social-democratic slogans, the Bolshevik adventurers were quick to realize that they could stay in power only through the harshest dictatorship—in conformance with the Marxist axiom that violence is the midwife of history.

Without a moment's hesitation, Lenin cast aside the democratic program worked out as a compromise with Plekhanov back in 1903 and embarked on his betrayal of the social-democratic movement. As early as the summer of 1918 the Bolsheviks unabashedly shed the last of their social-democratic trappings and took on the name of the Communist Party, separating themselves emphatically from the socialist movements of Russia and the West.

In the first phase, when their resources were not all that impressive and the socialist groupings retained considerable influence, the

Bolsheviks adopted the tactic of discrediting the socialists. This work was entrusted to the Party's potent propaganda machine, which had seized power. Moreover, Lenin's circle actively exploited the endless squabbling among the Mensheviks, Socialist Revolutionaries (SRs), Anarchists, and other socialist parties, as well as their naive and incredibly blind hopes that the Bolsheviks would come around to reason.

The policy of eliminating the socialists proceeded in stages. The basic—and in time the only—instrument for achieving this end was the secret police, the All-Union Extraordinary Commission–United State Political Administration (VChK-OGPU), backed unfailingly by the CC of the Communist Party. The initial task was to remove the socialists from positions of influence and force them out of the Soviets through machinations of one kind or another. In the process, and again with various forms of chicanery—charges of nonexistent conspiracies, mock trials, staged meetings of "repentant" socialists, and so forth—ways were found to compromise these parties in the eyes of the public.

In view, however, of the Bolsheviks' purported ideological similarity to the other parties—especially the Menshevik Russian Social Democratic Workers Party (RSDRP), which swore by the dogma of Karl Marx—and in view of the extensive and long-standing personal and familial relationships among the various adherents, the years of joint underground revolutionary activity, the traditional popularity of the socialists with the democratic elements in the country, and, finally, the socialists' great international prestige, the ruling Communists were compelled to maneuver in suppressing their sometime brothers in revolutionary adventurism and to back off temporarily on arrests. In other words, getting rid of their revolutionary allies presented, at first, a somewhat delicate problem. That was doubtless why the principal socialist parties—the Left and Right SRs, the Mensheviks, the SR-Maximalists—managed just barely to prolong their existence until the end of the civil war.

In the post-October period there were eleven socialist parties and anarchist organizations, not counting those of a nationalist type (Jewish, Ukrainian, etc.), operating at various times on Russian territory. As early as 1917, their membership exceeded 1.5 million. In the first half of the 1920s they were virtually stifled, although as a school of social thought the non-Bolshevik brand of socialism disappeared in Russia only during the "great terror" of the late 1930s and the beginning of the 1940s, concurrently with the murder of its chief ideologues and leaders.

The persecution of the socialists began with the strangling of the socialist press. As Maxim Gorky wrote in the newspaper *Novaya Zhizn* (New Life) in November 1917, "Lenin, Trotsky, and their followers were already afflicted by the rotten poison of power, as shown by their disgraceful attitude toward freedom of speech and of the individual and the whole sum of those rights for which democracy had struggled." Indeed, negotiations on creating a government coalition "ranging from the Bolsheviks to the populist socialists" were still in progress when, on 9 November, the Lenin government "suspended" publication of the populist socialist newspaper *Narodnoye Slovo* (The People's Word). The harassment of the newspaper of the Mensheviks-Oborontsev, *Den* (The Day), began later that month. The paper was closed down six times, reappearing each time under a different name, but in May 1918 its operations were halted for good.

Toward the end of January 1918, a new law, "Provisional Regulations on the Publishing of Periodical and Nonperiodical Publications in Petrograd," stated that newspapers of a "clearly counterrevolutionary" nature could be shut and their editorial staffs arrested.[1] In January–February 1918 alone, just two months after the counterrevolutionary coup, almost seventy newspapers were closed down in Petrograd and Moscow. It was enough for a publication to express the slightest doubt about any Bolshevik decision for it to be branded as counterrevolutionary.

The hounding of the Menshevik newspaper *Vperyod* (Forward) in March–April 1918 brought protests from the workers in a number of industrial plants in Moscow—Postavshchik, Ludvig i Smit, the central city power station, and others. The workers passed a resolution calling the newspaper of the Social Democratic Mensheviks "the defender of the real interests of the working class against Bolshevik power." On 13 May the Mensheviks received permission to reopen the paper under a new name, *Vsegda Vperyod* (Ever Forward), but the very next day, by order of the Cheka, the newspaper was closed down again.[2]

The authorities' view of what made a paper counterrevolutionary is made clear by the circumstances surrounding the closure of the Menshevik publication *Novy Luch* (The New Ray of Light). The paper was suppressed for reporting on workers' meetings at the Obukhov and Putilovsky plants that called for an end to "commissarocracy" and for the convening of a Constituent Assembly. The provincial authorities did not lag far behind the center. In the first months of 1918 they cracked down on the Menshevik newspaper *Golos Naroda* (The People's Voice) in Tula, the paper *Zhizn* (Life) in Saratov, and others. By that summer, virtually the entire Social Democratic press was proscribed.

The problem of freedom of the press was solved simply and for a long time to come. The new "freedom" was in force until 1985, when the first stirrings of reform prepared the way for glasnost.

Unfortunately, the socialist parties were mired in antagonism, bickering constantly, often over trifles. Even in the prisons and concentration camps and in exile, the socialists avoided contact with members of parties other than their own and intrigued among themselves. The secret police skillfully exploited the myriad differences—from disagreements on programs and tactics to accumulated grievances and suspicions—within the socialist movement. In their circular letters, the directors of the VChK-OGPU pressured their operatives to deepen the splits within the movement and counteract any tendencies toward conciliation. Thus, noting with alarm a "shift toward the unification of isolated and scattered populist SR groups and tendencies," the head of the OGPU's office of secret operations, V. Menzhinsky, demanded "the use of every means of information to prevent the SR groups from uniting" and "to smash these efforts at unification."[3]

The same kind of reaction was touched off by the formation of an Organizational Bureau for the Unification of Revolutionary-Socialist Populism. Even though the bureau's policy declaration ruled out any attacks on the Russian Communist Party (RKP) on political or economic grounds, the Bolsheviks saw in this organization "a group with the clear objective of struggle with the Communists."[4] Scenting the same currents in leftist populism, the OGPU asked the CC of the RKP to authorize efforts to weaken the unification trends through the "various forms of repression" available to it, and the plan was approved. "To encourage tendencies toward splits and differences among the parties hostile to us," as one prominent Chekist put it, was the constant aim of the authorities.[5]

As for the socialist parties themselves, over the course of the civil war they frequently changed their policies toward the governing regime. These vacillations were particularly broad among the populist parties. Unlike the Mensheviks, who adopted a role of quiet opposition, the SRs, who took up arms for a few days in 1918, executed a sharp change of course early the following year and switched to active cooperation. This did not save them; they were soon driven back underground. The left wing of the SRs—partners with the Bolsheviks in the seizure of power and in the government coalition during the first months after October—went into open opposition in the summer of 1918.

In the end, none of the positions adopted by their onetime fellow travelers was acceptable to the Bolshevik leaders. Their campaign to eradicate all traces of socialist dissidence was applied on a rising scale. This was not a "big game of solitaire," as Solzhenitsyn would have it, but the crushing of human beings by the fiercest terror machine known to history.

Initially, sentiment in the Russian Communist Party was not unanimous. Lenin had to contend with a fairly influential group of colleagues (L. Kamenev, V. Nogin, D. Ryazanov, G. Sokolnikov, and others) who advocated coalition with the major socialist parties under the slogan of a "homogeneous" socialist government. The idea of such a bloc arose not so much out of sympathy for the socialists but out of fear that it would be very difficult for the Communists to hold on to power all by themselves. Uncertainty about their own strength made even the most orthodox look around for allies. The result was the formation in December 1917 of a coalition with the Left SRs; by the early part of 1918, representatives of that party headed six of the sixteen central people's commissariats.

Proposals for softening the general policy toward the socialists were discussed many times within the Bolshevik ruling clique. But such ideas were uniformly opposed by the secret police, inasmuch as they presaged a diminution of that department's role in the government. Any notions of bridling the Cheka, to say nothing of abolishing it—the first such project was put forward in January 1918 by a group of prominent Bolsheviks headed by Kamenev—met with little success.[6]

In fact, not only the Chekist chiefs but the Politburo consistently rejected all attempts to include the socialists in the social and political life of the country. In April 1921, a proposal by the Chekist Vardin (Mgeladze) for formulating a more conciliatory policy toward "the more respectable" socialists and anarchists—while, of course, "holding taut the reins" of government—was sharply rebuffed. "The author is wrong," Lenin commented on Vardin's memo. "He is being formalistic. . . . The author's proposal is no good. He has not grasped the subject properly."[7] The Politburo rejected Vardin's project even before it knew Lenin's reaction.[8]

The Politburo was already working on scenarios for court trials, deciding in advance on sentencings, confinement of those arrested, places and terms of exile, and many other matters. It would often tell the secret police to have this or that socialist sentenced to a specific term of imprisonment (for example, in 1925, A. Gotz and E. Timofeyev, members of the CC of the Right SR).[9] As the covert but real master of the country, the Politburo bypassed all legal norms, in accordance with the well-known principle of "revolutionary expediency." Its actions would have proved ineffective, however, if not for the enthusiastic support—and sometimes even the *diktat*—of the secret services.

As the regime gained strength, ever greater influence on the actions of its repressive apparatus came to be wielded personally by Lenin. A cult of personality around his name was deliberately developed. It was he who installed the mechanism of repression, but in the early days he was inhibited in its use by personal ties to a number of public figures, including Yu. Martov, Georgy Plekhanov, and Prince Kropotkin. Stalin, who had a particular distaste for socialists, was free of such weakness. (In the spring of 1918 he tried to have Martov tried for slander for having brought up his 1910 expulsion from the RSDRP for taking part in expropriations—that is, open theft and robbery. The revolutionary tribunal rejected Stalin's suit.)

The spring of 1918 saw the first arrests of Anarchists and Maximalists, faithful comrades-in-arms of the Bolsheviks in the October coup and in the disbandment of the Constituent Assembly. On the night of 11–12 April, units of the Moscow Cheka and the Red

Guards carried out an operation for disarming the Anarchist groups, arresting more than four hundred persons.[10] At the same time, action was taken in Izhevsk to suppress a "mutiny" that consisted of the Maximalists' offering the Bolsheviks stiff competition in the local soviet and gaining a majority there.

Yet all this was of little help: the socialist factions in the soviets continued to enjoy considerable importance. Some large enterprises traditionally regarded as bastions of Bolshevism—for example, the Karzinkinskaya "Big Manufacturing Plant" in Yaroslavl—gave the Social Democratic electoral list more votes than they gave all the Bolshevik, Left SR, and nonparty candidates put together. Hence, on 14 June 1918, two days before the start of a new election campaign and on the eve of the 5th Congress of Soviets, the Bolsheviks pushed through the All-Union Central Executive Committee (VTsIK) a decree expelling the SRs and Mensheviks from the soviets at all political levels on all Russian territory under the Kremlin's control. (Locally, the expulsion was usually justified by the vague formula "for counterrevolutionism and sabotage of Soviet power.")[11]

Despite the decree, the populace continued to elect socialist party members to local offices. (Thus, in the elections to the Petrograd soviet at the end of June the Mensheviks and the Right SRs won 75 seats against 499 for the Bolsheviks and 109 for the Left SRs, in the Arkhangelsk Council of Deputies they won 56 seats against 168 for the Bolsheviks, and so on.)[12] The number of their delegates to the all-Russian congresses of the soviets and the VTsIK, however, fell sharply. And from 1919 on, the list of socialists admitted to the congresses had to be approved by the Politburo.[13]

In the provinces things were even cruder and more cynical. In December 1918 labor unrest broke out in Motovilikha, a village in Perm province. The workers insisted on a stop to special food privileges for Soviet government and Party workers, an end to summary executions, guarantees of freedom of speech and assembly, and the transfer of power to the Soviets of Workers' and Peasants' Deputies.[14] They threatened to go on strike if their demands were rejected.

When the usual methods of applying pressure yielded no results— at the workers' mass meetings and assemblies the spokesmen for the authorities were simply denied the right to speak—the blame for the unrest was put on the Left SRs, who held the majority in the Motovilikha Council of Deputies. The council's executive committee was disbanded and replaced by a purely Communist revolutionary committee, a state of emergency was declared in the village, the factory was closed down, and all the workers were dismissed. Thus the evolution of Bolshevik democracy.

In July 1918, after the assassination of the German ambassador Mirbach by the Chekist Blumkin, the Bolsheviks began a drive against the Left Socialist Revolutionaries, who had strongly opposed the Brest peace treaty with Germany and the government's agrarian policies. The protests of 6 July and the demonstrative arrest of Feliks Dzerzhinsky, head of the Cheka, were interpreted by the authorities as an attempt by the Left SRs to seize power. The regime immediately embarked on all-out arrests of the party's members, regardless of the extent of their participation in the demonstrations. (It remains to be clarified to what degree the assassination of Mirbach involved the top leadership of the Cheka.)

The night of 6–7 July saw the arrests not only of the sizable delegation of Left SRs to the 5th Congress of Soviets but also, in Moscow, of Left SR committees in the Rogozhsko-Simonovsky, Krasnopresnensky, and other districts, in factories and plants, and in the Moscow Council of Deputies. On 8 July fourteen Left SRs regarded by the authorities as the most active participants in the "mutiny" (V. Aleksandrovich, D. Popov, and others) were shot without any investigation whatever. All told, 964 persons were indicted in the affair.

In a telegram on 10 July, the people's commissar for internal affairs, G. Petrovsky, ordered the provincial soviets "immediately to take all measures [to] apprehend and detain" participants in the "mutiny," to "arrest those attempting to mount a rebellion against Soviet power and hand them over to military-revolutionary courts," and to "shoot any who resist."[15] Even before Petrovsky's telegram, the local authorities had begun to replace all Left SRs in positions of responsibility, to exclude their delegations from the soviets, and to arrest rank-and-file party members. Thus, in Tambov province, appropriate measures were taken by the provincial executive committee on 9 July.[16] In Kursk province, A. Baryshnikov, a Left SR member accused of attempting to "incite the masses against Soviet power," was arrested and beaten up right at the regional soviet congress and thrown in prison. Even though the local Cheka lacked any basis for detaining him and, as a member of the VTsIK, he possessed immunity from arrest, he was released only in mid-August.[17] In Kaluga province, the entire Left SR delegation was removed from a local soviet congress, even though it was the largest there. In July, Left SR committees in Tula, Vladimir, Nizhy Novgorod, and elsewhere were arrested or dissolved, and the Left SR—in effect, the peasant—component of the VTsIK was disbanded.

The period of partnership between the Left SRs and the Bolsheviks in the legislative and executive branches had come to an end. Receiving—after the arrest of the Left SR delegation—an overwhelming majority at the 5th Congress of Soviets, the authorities pushed through a resolution in which collaboration with the Left SRs in the soviets was made contingent on their unconditional and public condemnation of the actions of their Central Committee. As Zinaida Gippius wrote prophetically in her journal as early as November 1917, what the Bolsheviks demanded first and foremost was "confession." And they were ready to grant all kinds of favors, she observed, "if you fall on your knees before them."[18]

In the summer of 1918, under an avalanche of repressions and having briefly survived the death in May 1918 of its founder and leader, Georgy Valentinovich Plekhanov, the Social Democratic bloc Yedinstvo (Unity) terminated its existence. That fall the Petrograd Cheka carried out mass arrests of "alien class elements," using the electoral lists of various parties, including the socialist, drawn up during the voting for regional and city dumas. According to data compiled by a Constitutional Democratic (Cadet) Party member, A. Izgoyev, more than two hundred people were placed behind bars in this operation alone.[19] Subsequently, the authorities made extensive use of old electoral lists for arrests on the grounds of membership in this or that party. "The lust for power of this band of adventurers turned out to be so strong," the Menshevik M. Liber wrote of the Bolsheviks in 1918, "that in the struggle to hold on to it they did not shrink from any kind of crime."[20]

In the fall of 1918, at the height of the Red Terror, the authorities engaged the socialists in a tactical game that took many by surprise. The first sign of the "thaw" was an article by Lenin, "On the Character of Our Newspapers," published in *Pravda* on 20 September. The article criticized the Bolshevik press for its excessive predilection for "political babble" and for material on the "vile betrayal of the Mensheviks, lackeys of the bourgeoisie." As a result, the press campaign against the socialists was discontinued.

The expanding nature of the "new course" was augured in a speech by Lenin at a meeting of Party workers in Moscow in November 1918. Proceeding from the premise that socialism could be built only through "an entire range of agreements," including agreements with "the gentlemen of the cooperatives and the intelligentsia," who were the country's "sole cultured element," Lenin called on Party workers to learn how to "reach agreement with petty-bourgeois democracy" and "attract" it to themselves.[21]

It seemed that the ruler of Russia was ready for compromise. Actually, nothing of the kind took place. The conditions put forward by Lenin were so harsh that they were more like ultimatums, and they made it crystal clear that the Bolsheviks did not have the slightest wish to share power with anybody. "You will have good-neighborly relations with us," Lenin told the socialists, "and we will have the state power. We'll be happy to legalize you, Messrs. Mensheviks. But . . . we will keep state power in our hands, and in our hands alone. Not the smallest portion of it will we yield."[22]

In November 1918 the RSDRP regained the right to take part in the work of the soviets—and, hence, to a legal existence. Concurrently, the trial of the Left SRs implicated in the 6 July affair concluded with the handing down of comparatively mild sentences by the revolutionary tribunal; 13 of the 950 accused were sentenced to terms of one to three years in concentration camps, while the rest were released, and a few days later some of those convicted were granted amnesty. In February 1919 the Socialist Revolutionary Party was legalized.

The real attitude of the authorities toward the socialists was reflected more accurately in the VChK's Order No. 113 of 19 December 1918. While acknowledging the need to let the "petty-bourgeois elements and all socialists" go on with their work, the order provided for the "strictest covert surveillance" in order to deny them "the opportunity to hoodwink Soviet power." Thus there gradually came into being a dictatorship of two-headed power—the party of the Communists and the party of the Chekists.

The government "thaw" proved a brief episode. As early as February 1919, the repression of the socialists resumed with redoubled force. The Left SR was once again banned. The regime made a daily practice of house searches "to establish identities" and of detentions for months on end without bringing charges. Arrests not only for belonging to a socialist party but "on suspicion" of such membership became routine.

Dzerzhinsky ordered the Cheka's provincial branches to exercise the "strictest control" over the Left SRs and the Mensheviks and to take hostages from among them with the warning that they would "answer with their heads" for any anti-Bolshevik propaganda activity on the part of their confederates. All these measures had been envisaged by the Politburo in a special decision of March 1919 outlining the following aims: "To advise the press to intensify the harassment of Left SRs . . . To maintain surveillance of all former Left SRs . . . To shut down the newspapers *Golos Pechatnika* (The Printer's Voice) and *Rabochy Internatsional* (The Worker's International)."[23]

But even the countrywide implementation of the policy of repression did not satisfy Dzerzhinsky. On 14 March 1919 he wrote: "Lately we have noticed a distinct falling-off in the activity of the extraordinary commissions. . . . The Mensheviks and SRs, observing our weakness, are using it for their own counterrevolutionary ends. The denunciations submitted to the VChK make it clear that the enemies of the proletariat have stepped up their propaganda, both spoken and written, with the aim of overthrowing Soviet power."[24] The signal was heeded. In April 1919, in the course of just one "liquidation" in Moscow and its environs, fifty-five SRs and thirty-eight Mensheviks were caught in the dragnet.[25] The VChK pressed the local Chekists to maintain "close surveillance" of each and every socialist party. As one of the secret police bosses, M. Latsis, wrote in 1919, "Their every step and their every intention must be known to us."[26]

The Bolsheviks' former allies in the seizure of power had not altered their political convictions in the slightest, yet Bolshevik propaganda began to paint them as "counterrevolutionaries, no different from the Kolchakists and Denikinists." In a circular letter of 1 July 1919, the deputy chairman of the VChK, I. Ksenofontov, declared: "For the Soviet Republic at this moment, the party of the Left

SRs . . . is one of the most dangerous enemies," to be fought "merci-lessly."[27]

The archives of the FSB contain eyewitness reports on the speeches of Maria Spiridonova and I. Shteinberg at workers' mass meetings in Moscow in February 1919. The reports attest to these leaders' popularity.[28] In February–March 1919, almost all the Left SR leaders and nearly two hundred party activists were arrested on charges of participating in an antigovernment plot in Moscow, and some forty-five local party organizations in Pskov, Tula, Kazan, Bryansk, Orel, Gomel, Astrakhan, and elsewhere were closed down.

In February, Spiridonova was tried before a Moscow revolution-ary tribunal. Characteristically, not a word was uttered in court about any kind of plot, but plenty was said about her speaking for as long as three hours at workers' meetings in Moscow while represen-tatives of the government party were allotted only ten to fifteen min-utes.[29] The trial turned up no real incriminating evidence, but the court sentenced Spiridonova to a year in isolation.

The Left SR began to lose influence. Membership in both its local organizations and the party declined sharply. Even earlier, in Au-gust–September 1918, an SR wing loyal to the Bolsheviks had split off from the party as a result of the authorities' wily tactics and had formed two separate parties, the Populist Communists and the Revolutionary Communists, each numbering up to three thousand members. Both merged with the Russian Communist Party (of the Bolsheviks)—the RKP(b)—in November 1918 and September 1920, respectively.

Yet in spite of a VChK circular's judgment that "under present conditions of underground work the party of the Left SR has lost all significance and authority with the masses," the provincial Chekas were given the task of "rooting out" of Left SR ranks "the remnants of more-or-less-active workers."[30] In May 1920 Dzerzhinsky con-firmed with satisfaction that this party had been "definitively smashed by the ChK [Cheka]" and "presents no danger to us."[31]

Actually, the chief of the secret police was a little premature in his conclusions: the Left SR ended its life as a party only at the end of 1922. Its ranks depleted by arrests and torn by internal dissension, the party was by then a pale ghost of the 150,000-strong dynamic force it had been in 1918.

The hunting down of the socialists remained an important part of the Bolsheviks' policy, especially for the secret police. Information on the actions of socialist parties was unfailingly included in all reports from the provinces through Party, soviet, military, and Chekist channels. Questions connected in any way with the actions of the socialists and anarchists were routinely discussed at meetings of the Politburo of the CC of the RKP(b); in the period from April to December 1919 alone, the Politburo addressed these questions twenty-five times.

Beginning in 1919, a system of secret VChK instructions and circulars served as the legal basis for the repressive policy toward socialists and other "counterrevolutionaries." A typical sentence was confinement to a concentration camp "until the end of the civil war." Official propaganda did all it could to promote the idea that the "isolation" of socialists was merely temporary ("until the victory of labor over capital"). The end of the civil war did not, however, bring about any kind of relaxation. On the contrary, in its circulars to the local offices of the VChK, Moscow emphasized that the folding up of the external front by no means signified the termination of the struggle against internal enemies, inasmuch as "the final liquidation of counterrevolutionary manifestations is conceivable only after the victory of the socialist revolution on a global scale."

"On the external front the Soviet republic has achieved a relatively stable situation," the head of the VChK's secret department, Samsonov, wrote to local Chekist officials in June 1921, "but the liquidation of the illegal political parties by the organs of the VChK has not been concluded, because of the ChK's lack of vigilance."[32] The CC's advisories to local Party organizations emphasized the urgent need for buttressing the local branches of the VChK and other policing institutions of the republic against the "intensified operations of hostile political groups."[33]

In addition to preserving for the Cheka the broadest authority to send its victims to concentration camps by administrative fiat, Dzerzhinsky demanded that anything deserving severe punishment be placed before the revolutionary tribunals. Here he was counting on the propaganda effect, but he misjudged. The open trials of the socialists encountered an exceedingly unfavorable reception abroad. And the Chekists themselves, aware no doubt of the juridical flimsiness of their accusations, tended to avoid going to court (except in cases dealing with possession or dissemination of socialist literature), preferring to engage in reprisals on their own, beyond the bounds of the legal system.

Dzerzhinsky explained the situation as follows in a circular of 1 May 1920: "We are living in an epoch when the class struggle being waged against us by the bourgeoisie and the criminal world has not yet entered the stage where all crime is punishable by us only through the courts or where every crime is so clear-cut that we can turn it over unhesitatingly to public scrutiny with every confidence that the criminal will be punished. . . . That is why the law gives the ChK the option of isolating by administrative measures those violators of labor laws, those parasites and persons suspected of counterrevolution, against whom we do not have enough evidence for punishment by trial and whom any court, even the strictest, will always or usually find not guilty." The same thought was expressed no less candidly in January 1922 by Dzerzhinsky's deputy, Unshlikht, corresponding with Lenin on plans for reorganizing the VChK: "There is a whole range of cases where the tribunals, for lack of factual evidence, will hand down decisions of not guilty even though we have quite enough information from our agents to justify the severest sentences, up to and including capital punishment. In certain conditions in the republic as a whole or in certain localities, it is necessary to take repressive measures of various kinds against those active in the anti-Soviet parties, even when we have no concrete evidence against them. All this is feasible only through administrative measures."[34]

Only a government criminal in nature would "take repressive measures" without having "concrete evidence." Essentially, it was on such principles that the entire "legal system" of Bolshevism was built.

The policy of uprooting socialist dissidence demanded continual changes in the structure of the secret police. From 1919 on, the provincial Chekas acquired special sections with responsibility for flushing out socialists and infiltrating agents into their ranks. Starting in 1920, whole groups of Chekists took part in this endeavor.

Reporting to Moscow in January 1920, a Chekist in Tiumen wrote that the SRs and Mensheviks, "like wounded animals, cannot reconcile themselves to Soviet power and attempt in every way to regroup into one anti-Soviet camp. Admitting their defeat and their laggardness in achieving victory and the full realization of socialism, they employ various deceptions to win over the sympathies of the working masses. To attain and accomplish their criminal goals they resort to different kinds of tricks, which are everywhere visible to the all-seeing eye of the Cheka and are nipped in the bud."[35] For the struggle against "anti-Soviet" parties, Ksenofontov reported to the local branches in October 1919, "we must create a supple and sturdy information apparat, *with the aim of having every Communist as your informer*" (italics mine).[36] The experience of struggle against the counterrevolutionary socialist camp, said another VChK circular, had shown that only "when our people penetrate this or that organization are we able . . . to make arrests at the opportune moment."[37]

The repression and hounding of the socialists did not end with the civil war. In Feburary 1921 the Politburo passed an edict calling for still another "step-up in the arrests of Mensheviks and SRs," which soon found a "convenient" excuse in the Kronstadt rebellion of March 1921.[38] On the pretext that the socialists were involved, the VChK embarked on a nationwide extirpation of their organizations that went on without interruption until August of that year. In the spring of 1921 the VChK routed the SR Central Committee in Moscow. At the same time, the entire membership of the Moscow Committee and the Central Committees of the RSDRP was rounded up and Menshevik groups in Samara, Saratov, Yekaterinburg, Pskov, Rostov-on-the-Don, Odessa, and other cities were abolished.[39]

In June 1921, at the height of the arrests, the VTsIK made its mark with a decree authorizing the ChK to hold socialists in pretrial detention for up to two years on suspicion of belonging to one or another socialist party. According to the figures of the military prosecutors, more than 550 Mensheviks were imprisoned under this decree. A similar decree was passed on 10 August 1922. A special NKVD commission with the nominal participation of the OGPU was authorized to exile active members of anti-Soviet parties and confine them to labor camps for up to three years.[40] As the Presidium of the VTsIK elucidated on 22 November of that year, this measure could also be applied to those suspected of "counterrevolutionary actions."

Step by step, Lenin was closing in on his own party. A campaign to "purge" the Russian Communist Party was launched on 1 August 1921; the decision had been reached earlier at the 10th Party Congress. Among those included in the four categories of Party membership subject to "special verification," first place went to former members of other parties who had joined the RKP(b) after 1917. Special attention was to be paid to former Mensheviks and members of other "petty-bourgeois" parties.[41] On that basis, more than six thousand persons were expelled from the RKP(b) in the purge of 1921. The final cleansing of Communist ranks of the "contagious disease of Menshevism" took place later.

By the end of 1921 membership in the RSDRP was down precipitously. Whereas the Social Democratic Party could claim 200,000 members in the fall of 1917, it had only 4,000 in the fall of 1921. According to an appeal issued by the Moscow Committee of the RSDRP, "It will soon be a year that our party has been under siege, and hundreds of our comrades are filling Russia's prisons—Butyrka and Taganka in Moscow, the former convict prisons in Orel and Yaroslavl, the prisons of Riazan and Vladimir, Rostov-on-the-Don and Kharkov, and specially built prisons in every corner of Soviet Russia are packed with arrested socialists detained for months without charges, and many without even being interrogated."[42]

The illegal and foreign socialist press occasionally carried reports of the violence against the prisoners (a beating in the Butyrka prison on the night of 26 April 1921, the execution of the sit-down protesters in the Solovetsky concentration camp in December 1923, and so on). The facts were brazenly denied by the authorities. To a May 1921 inquiry by the Gomel provincial Cheka into the incident in Butyrka, Menzhinsky and Samsonov replied that no beating had taken place, and they urged that "the strongest measures be taken against those spreading these false rumors." The doctor who had revealed the beating of imprisoned Mensheviks and SRs in Butyrka paid for his action by being sent in May 1921 to the Arkhangelsk concentration camp. The camp was in the grip of a raging typhus epidemic, but the doctor was put to cleaning out the toilets.[43]

The signal for mass repressions against the Anarchists was provided by a secret circular letter of the CC of the RKP(b) to its provincial committees, approved by the Politburo on 16 April 1921. The Anarchists were accused of supporting the slogans of the Kronstadt rebellion, "provoking dissatisfaction" among workers and peasants, and seeking to bring about the ideological "decay" of the army. "The RKP, in exercising the dictatorship of the proletariat," the letter declared, "can under no circumstances make exceptions for those groups that, beneath the banner of anarchism, conceal their movement's most counterrevolutionary trends. Consequently, the CC of the RKP approves of the policy of those centers of Soviet power that, in opposing the counterrevolutionary actions of anarchist groups, are forced to impose firm limits on these groups' freedom of action."[44]

The secret police responded enthusiastically to the party's call. The spring and summer of 1921 saw mass arrests of Anarchists of various tendencies, including the Free Association of Anarchists and the Anarchists-Communists (Karelintsy). A full-scale raid carried out in March 1921 put an end to the Russian Confederation of Anarchists-Syndicalists and the Moscow Workers Union of Anarchists. Starting in August 1921, the authorities imposed a series of bans on the Anarchist-Universalist magazine *Pochin* (Initiative). On the night of 1–2 November, a sweep of Anarchists-Universalists and the breakup of their communes brought the work of that organization to a stop.

In January 1922 the Politburo of the CC decided to abolish the VChK and create the OGPU as the political administration of the NKVD, with all its work, according to the edict, to be concentrated on "setting up a system of informers of internal information and rooting out all counterrevolutionary and anti-Soviet acrtivities in all areas." The spearhead of the new department's agenda was directed toward struggle with anti-Bolshevik—above all, socialist—parties. In fact, the Politburo's decree was drawn up by a special commission "on SRs and Mensheviks" formed toward the end of 1921.[45]

Repressing the socialists and Anarchists provided grist for six of the ten subdivisions of the OGPU. The biggest and most important, the Secret-Operational, included a secret department with numbered sections—Section 1 for the Anarchists, Section 2 for the Social Democrats and related factions, Section 3 for the Socialist Revolutionaries, and so on.[46] Inherited from the VChK was the use of "special advisers," specialists in the history and current practices of socialist parties.

The experience of the 1921 struggle with the Anarchists led the OGPU to issue another circular in July 1922. As an "ideology of the lumpen proletariat" that had "nothing in common with the workers' struggle for socialism," Russian anarchism was accused of seeking to establish a "merciless dictatorship of the kulak class over the proletariat and the poorest peasantry" and of organizing "conspiratorial gangs." While calling on the OGPU's local branches to continue to wage a merciless struggle against the Anarchists, the circular added that it wasn't enough just to make arrests—that only the use of "inside informers can really paralyze the Anarchists' work."

Writing to the CC of the RKP(b) in February 1923, the patriarch of Russian anarchism, A. Karelin, stated that "on orders of the former ChK and OGPU dozens of Anarchists-Communists and Anarchists are confined" in prisons in the northern provinces—the prisons known as concentration camps—as well as in prisons in other provinces and in Moscow. He added, "Some of the Anarchists have been exiled to remote cities. Since the imprisoned Anarchists and those exiled by administrative measures are no different in ideas or methods from the Anarchists of Western Europe, who are not harassed even by their bourgeois governments, and since none of them had or have any thought of seizing government power, having been exiled or imprisoned by administrative procedures, may I, . . . knowing for certain that consumption is rife in their midst, knowing of their suffering and deprivations, appeal to the CC of the RKP(b) to release all the above-named prisoners."[47] Karelin's request received "no response."

The arrests of Anarchists continued for several years (for example, in Moscow in October 1924 and in May 1925).[48] The main Anarchist organizations in Russia fell apart once and for all. The last major arrests of individuals took place in 1929–30, when A. Andreyev, B. Barmash, N. Rogdayev, and other ideologically disparate Anarchists still at liberty were put behind bars.

There was also the practice of exiling socialists abroad without the right of return. Early on, around 1920–21, the authorities were glad to see the last of those socialists and Anarchists who went abroad for one reason or another; Martov and Abramovich were permitted to leave on party business in the summer of 1920, while the Menshevik Dalin and the Anarchists Arshinov (Marin), Volin, Shapiro, and others left in 1921. To the Left SR's appeal for permission for Shteinberg to make a foreign trip, the Politburo of the CC of the RKP(b) replied: "Permission to go, not to be readmitted." But soon after, in 1924, the Politburo rejected the proposal of a commission headed by the director of the Profintern, S. Lozovsky, for simultaneous forced expulsion from the country of all prominent Russian socialists and Anarchists of any prominence being held in prisons and concentration camps—some 1,500, all told.[49]

Of particular concern to the Bolsheviks were their erstwhile brothers in faith in the Party, the Mensheviks, who continued to operate within the Social Democratic Party framework. The archives contain quite a few Politburo decrees of 1920–23 devoted to the Mensheviks. In June 1920 all people's commissariats were instructed that "Mensheviks within the commissariats who are capable of playing the slightest political role are not to be kept in Moscow but are to be sent off to the provinces." In July the Politburo ordered the VChK to "draw up a plan for resettling Menshevik political leaders so as to neutralize them politically." An edict of December 1921 entitled "On the Mensheviks" declared, "They are to be excluded from political activity, while vigorous attention is to be paid to rooting out their influence in industrial centers. . . . The most active are to be exiled by administrative means to nonproletarian centers and denied the right of election to public office or to any position entailing contact with the broad masses."[50]

In January 1922 the foreign-policy agency and its missions abroad were forbidden to employ exiled Mensheviks or anyone "connected with them in any way."[51] In the second half of 1923, a secret investigative control commission within the CC of the RKP(b) carried out a "mop-up purge" of the entire staff of the People's Commissariat of Foreign Affairs (NKID), the People's Commissariat of Foreign Trade (NKVT), and their foreign offices, cleansing them of former members of the socialist parties, whatever their professional abilities or political beliefs.[52] From then on, all missions abroad were seeded with OGPU agents for "internal observation" of the Soviet employees' attitudes. This practice still exists.

In March 1922 the Politburo of the CC set up a system of "bureaus of support" for the OGPU within all Soviet organizations, cooperatives, and trade unions—a "public" (i.e., not part of the government) network for gathering information about former socialists and their sympathizers. A "questionnaire on members of anti-Soviet parties," with instructions on how to proceed in dealing with such cases, was sent to all local centers; the task of "catching" socialists was divided among the people's commissariats, plants and factories, the transportation system, institutes of higher education (including military ones), the army, and professional organizations.

In September 1922 the OGPU's secret section ordered the administration's provincial branches to carry out yet another mass ouster of the members of the RSDRP: "Searches to be made at the homes of active and inactive members, as well as of sympathizers. . . . Those arrested to be charged with belonging to the party of the Mensheviks and with counterrevolutionary acts, as indicated by the evidence uncovered by the search."[53] The guidelines employed by the secret police in arresting socialists are clearly reflected in the notes left by the Chekists on their "liquidation lists" of those active Mensheviks and members of the Bund who were registered by the OGPU'S provincial offices: "Elderly person. Pick him up to make him quit the party. . . . must send him to a Russian area. This will neutralize him for a while and maybe do him in financially. . . . He is the sole support of his family, to which he is greatly attached. Must be arrested, isolated, broken, and recruited."[54]

The repressions of 1922 left the Party of Socialist Revolutionaries (PSR) virtually demolished. Apart from the Moscow trial of the CC of the PSR in July–August 1922, a number of SRs in the provinces were tried in Baku in December on charges of setting fire to oil fields and laying the groundwork for an "armed attack by supporters" of Pyotr N. Wrangel, the general who led the White (anti-Bolshevik) forces in the final phase of the civil war. In the course of the trial it became clear that the case was trumped up from start to finish. Nonetheless, the Politburo of the CC of the RKB(b), briefed by the prominent Sergei M. Kirov two days before the conclusion of the trial, "did not object" to the handing down of five death sentences.[55]

In conjunction with the Moscow trial of the CC of the PSR, the authorities subjected the party to another campaign of persecution. Preparations for this trial had begun as early as the end of 1921— from the moment when the plenum of the CC of the RKP(b), at its December 28 session, decreed it would "resolve in advance the question of arraigning the party of the SR before the Supreme Court."[56] Concurrently, a Politburo commission "on the Mensheviks and SRs" was set up, and plans were made to have brief histories of the Russian socialist movement published to coincide with the trial.[57] The authors were to be certain members of the Politburo—Kamenev, Zinoviev, Trotsky, and Bukharin. When they all bowed out, pleading pressure of work, the writing of the histories was left to the second-string team of Lunacharsky, Meshcheriakov, Vardin, and others.

Everything went forward like clockwork. There was only one thing bothering the bosses. Russia was due to participate in an international economic and financial conference called for January 1922 in Genoa, and the reaction to the trial of the SRs was apt to be strong. "You yourself agree," Unshlikht wrote to Lenin on 26 January 1922, "that the terror should be intensified. If we don't do the shootings, the revolutionary tribunals will. The sentences of the revolutionary tribunals will be made public. Their number will be so large that [they] will touch off a new burst of indignation on the part of our enemies. And it is for their sake that we are making concessions."[58] Unshlikht's arguments were parried by Lenin: "The revolutionary tribunals don't always go in for glasnost. Their membership should be beefed up with 'your own' people, . . . put in to improve the speed and strength of the repressions."[59]

All these byzantine plans came to nothing. The OGPU's official announcement, on 28 February 1922, of the scheduled trial of SRs set off protest in Western Europe. Responding, the Politburo on 18 March adopted Lenin's proposal that "all comrades going abroad" be obliged to wage "the most merciless struggle" against Mensheviks and SRs.[60] In the attempt to stem the mounting outrage in the West, S. Sosnovsky and K. Radek were sent to Berlin in April to wage "counterpropaganda against the Mensheviks and SRs." The same assignment was given to Yu. Larin, who was in Berlin for medical treatment.[61]

It should be noted that Lenin was highly consistent in his decisions on many issues, especially on the use of terror. Learning of the agreement reached by representatives of the three Internationals, whereby the Soviet side renounced the use of the death sentence in the trial of forty-seven SRs and consented to having foreign observers in the courtroom, he flew into a rage. On 9 April, he handed down through the Politburo a directive to the Soviet and Party press instructing it to react emphatically to the Berlin agreement, "exposing in special detail the irrefutable fact of the real ties between the SRs and Mensheviks . . . and the international bourgeoisie."[62]

Two days later, expanding on the decree of the Executive Committee of the Comintern on "intensifying the campaign against the Mensheviks and the SRs in the entire international Communist press," Lenin again insisted on the need for a "detailed explanation" of the ties between those parties and the "broad front of the landlords and the bourgeoisie against Soviet power."[63] Lenin himself, of course, was well aware of the meretriciousness of such accusations. Having read Maxim Gorky's open letter in *Sotsialistichesky Vestnik* (Socialist Herald) to the French writer Anatole France, in which the SR trial was described as preparation for "the murder of people who are sincerely serving the cause of the liberation of the Russian people," Lenin observed that at first he had thought of berating Gorky in the press "but decided that would probably be too much" and kept silent.[64]

From 1922 on, the damning of the socialists and demands for reprisals against them became essential features of all government holidays and anniversaries. "The fifth anniversary of the October Revolution is the funeral bell tolling for the SRs, Mensheviks, and all lackeys of capital" was one suggested slogan for the festive demonstrations marking that occasion.[65]

In December 1922, on the fifth anniversary of the formation of the VChK-OGPU, the summary declaration put out by the Agency of Agitation and Propaganda for discussion within all Party organizations paid special tribute to the secret police for its merciless struggle against the pseudosocialists, who "dared to thwart the work of shoring up the achievements of the Great October Revolution." In July 1924, in line with the Comintern's proclamation of an "international week of struggle against the danger of new wars and against the Second International," the CC of the RKP(b) ordered mass demonstrations keyed to the slogan "Down with the warmonger capitalists and their lackey collaborators, the Mensheviks and SRs."[66]

The results of the struggle against the socialists and Anarchists were summed up at the 12th Party Conference, which took place during the decisive days of the big SR trial in Moscow and proved to be the culminating point of the campaign against the socialists whipped up in the spring and summer of 1922. The conference demanded that "the parties of the SRs and Mensheviks be eliminated as political factors within a short period of time." In an addendum to the resolution, Stalin noted by hand that "precisely this constitutes the most important task of the RKP."[67]

No sooner had the thunderous maledictions against the socialists died away than the Bolsheviks again went after the Mensheviks, who worried them most of all. The fact is, the Bolsheviks' policy toward the Mensheviks was neither consistent nor thought out. But some of its features, albeit minor ones, held fast. Despite their general policy of hustling the Mensheviks from power, in order to undermine the influence of their "brothers" with the masses and finish them off, the Bolsheviks, for outwardly inexplicable reasons, pretended at times to be ready to "tolerate" the Menshevik faction of socialist dissidence. Only for that reason did the Russian Social Democratic Workers Party (Unified) (RSDRP), as the Menshevik organization was officially renamed toward the end of 1917, stay alive a little longer than the other socialist parties.

The authorities would mount a campaign of persecution while turning a blind eye to the RSDRP's semilegal activities—only to fly, in quick order, into a new "paroxysm of madness" (Yu. Martov) over the very fact of the party's existence. The Bolsheviks never regarded the Mensheviks as serious contenders for power. But even the Mensheviks' timorous attempts to step out of the bounds of "quiet" opposition irritated Lenin no end. Lenin feared the Mensheviks (they were far more literate than he), but he wasn't ashamed of what he did.

A little history. In the spring and summer of 1918 the government, as I have noted, launched a mass attack against the socialist and Anarchist delegates to the soviets. Describing the course of the electoral campaign for the Moscow soviet in March–April 1918, the Press Bureau of the RSDRP wrote: "The authorities arrested speakers from among the Mensheviks and the SRs. They scheduled balloting unexpectedly, with only a tiny bunch of their own supporters present. When Mensheviks were voted in, they tried by hook and by crook to hold another round of elections with fewer voters taking part. . . . It is hard to imagine anything more despicable, more shameful and disgusting than the picture presented by the Bolshevik electoral campaign."[68] In official statements tailored for Western opinion, however, the Mensheviks, up to the end of 1920, were designated as "comrades," even if "misguided" ones. As for the Bolshevik rank and file, in the opinion of F. Dan, a sizable portion, "especially among the Bolshevik workers, felt in their hearts that those being persecuted for what our party represents are the most politically conscious and revolutionary workers and that these persecutions are an indelible disgrace for the Communist Party."[69]

Of course, the patronizing attitude toward the Mensheviks was far from consistently applied. When it came down to specific cases, there was no wavering. For example, in an election to the local soviet held in the spring of 1919 in the workers' settlement of Bogorodskoye in the Pavlovsk district of Nizhny Novgorod province, the Mensheviks gained the majority. Ignoring the results of the vote, the delegates to the former—Bolshevik—soviet continued to exercise power. On May 24 a hunger strike began in the settlement and several Communists were torn to pieces by the mob. To prevent further bloodshed, the authorities took charge of the newly elected Menshevik soviet, which succeeded in pacifying the workers and thus saving the lives of the other Communists. In spite of that, a punitive detachment sent to the settlement arrested all the Mensheviks. They were tried before a revolutionary tribunal on charges of "counterrevolutionary actions." The tribunal sentenced eleven members of the RSDRP to death, commuted to fifteen to twenty years' imprisonment and forced labor.[70]

One is hard put to find a single RSDRP member of any prominence in those years who was not subjected to searches and arrests—as a rule on fabricated charges and often without any charges at all. In 1919 A. Potresov spent several months behind bars, under conditions that were unusually severe even for that time. F. Dan and the brothers Tselerbaum were repeatedly arrested in 1920–21; one of the brothers, Vladimir, was tried in 1920 in the case of the National Center, to which he was not connected in the slightest way, and was sentenced to death, commuted to confinement in a concentration camp until the end of the civil war. Among the many others arrested were N. Rozhkov, M. Liber, B. Nikolayevsky, B. Ber, V. Krokhmal, and B. Gorev.

For all practical purposes, the war against the Mensheviks was openly declared right after the counterrevolutionary coup of 1917. As early as May 1918, Yakov Sverdlov complained of the "difficulties" being created by the Mensheviks, who were "marching in step with the saboteurs." From then on, the Mensheviks were uniformly typed as ritual scapegoats on whom the government could dump responsibility for its own failures. An edict of the VTsIK of 14 June 1918 barred representatives of the RSDRP from participating in the soviets at any level, and that autumn, in Martov's words, the party's situation became "intolerable," its press and its local organizations decimated and "the bulk of the Mensheviks arrested once again."[71]

On 21 July 1918, the authorities arrested not only delegates to a Moscow congress of workers' representatives but Mensheviks invited to the congress as guests and observers—R. Abramovich, Yu. Denike, M. Kefali, G. Kuchin-Oransky, and others. Those in power were outraged by the decision of this purely proletarian body to seek an end to "experiments in socialization and nationalization of plants and factories" and to struggle for the toppling of Soviet power and the "restoration of a democratic system." All those arrested faced the threat of execution, from which the Mensheviks were saved only by the intervention of Western European socialists.

In November 1918, at the height of the Red Terror, the RSDRP, as recounted earlier, was again unexpectedly granted the right to take part in the soviets—and thus the possibility of a semilegal existence. In an official clarification, the CC justified this softening of its stand as resulting from the position "adopted by the Mensheviks in regard to the invasion of the Entente." But the legalization extended only to those Mensheviks who "unambiguously expressed their opposition to the intervention and their support of Soviet power."[72] And, in fact, many Social Democrats were mobilized for induction into the Red Army during the civil war. One member of the Moscow

Committee of the RSDRP, Stoilov, served throughout the civil war as a divisional chief of staff, and a member of the party CC, Kuchin-Oransky, fought on the Polish front in 1921.

The legalization, however, proved very brief. In the spring of 1919, the Central and Moscow Committees of the RSDRP were dispersed, and the party's main newspaper, *Vsegda Vperyod,* was closed down, as were its papers and magazines in Kiev and Kharkov. The VChK stated officially that those Mensheviks who were under arrest were hostages whose fate depended on their party's "behavior." Pressure on Mensheviks to quit the RSDRP intensified. A number of party members—Khinchuk, Dubrovinskaya, Vilensky, Gorev, and a little later Rozhkov, who was under arrest—announced their resignations in 1919–20. At the end of 1919, a group of Mensheviks-Internationalists who had left the RSDRP in January 1918 and formed their own party merged with the RKP(b). In 1922 the CC members Yermansky, Semkovsky, Pleskov, and Groman quietly left the Social Democratic Party.

In D. Dalin's opinion, most of these party switches were motivated by "selfish or career considerations." As Martov noted, however, some of the defectors "moved to the left" out of sincere conviction. They believed that despite all the shortcomings of the new regime, the Bolsheviks had laid the foundation for building socialism and that democratization was therefore inevitable. According to eyewitnesses, these illusions were shared by S. Yezhov almost up to his tragic death. Finally, there were those among the defectors who, in opting for cooperation with the Bolsheviks, did not undergo any ideological rebirth but, on the contrary, were motivated by a preference for preserving the "oil" of authentic Marxism in the "lamp" of Bolshevism—in other words, for vulgarized Marxism.

In 1920 repressions against the "Russian Kautskyists" again intensified. In Odessa, Gomel, and Nikolayev, Menshevik factions were excluded from the soviets right from the start—in Nikolayev because of the Mensheviks' refusal to vote for Lenin in the election of an "honorary presidium." In Kiev, the authorities prosecuted ten Mensheviks on trumped-up charges of "cooperating with Denikin"; the main thrust of the indictment had to do with a memorandum containing criticism of the Bolshevik regime that was sent by local trade unions to trade unions in Europe. In Moscow, the printers union, in which the Mensheviks were influential, was disbanded and its two party clubs closed down. Shattered, too, were RSDRP organizations in Samara (in connection with a general strike), in Omsk (for the issuance of an illegal appeal), and in Tula (in connection with a strike). Mass arrests took place in Moscow in August. An amnesty announced by the VTsIK on the third anniversary of the October Revolution did not apply to members of the RSDRP.

All in all, to quote Martov, it was a "frenzied" and "shamelessly bloodthirsty" campaign that included mass searches and arrests of the more active Mensheviks, a campaign "provoked" by a number of partial successes by the RSDRP in elections to local soviets in 1919–20. In the elections of 1920, for instance, the Mensheviks won 46 seats in the Moscow soviet, 205 in the one in Kharkov, 120 in Yekaterinoslav, 78 in Kremenchug (against 62 for the Bolsheviks), and so on.[73]

The results at a chemical factory in Petrograd provide a gauge of the workers' mood. According to his own account, Martov found himself opposed as a candidate by Lenin. In an open voice vote, Lenin received eight votes to Martov's seventy-six. Greatly offended by this closest friend of his youth and learning of the Mensheviks' 46 seats (out of 1,532) in the Moscow soviet, Lenin immediately ordered that their leaders be "crushed" with onerous tasks—"For Dan, hygiene centers; for Martov, cafeteria supervision."[74] In May 1920 the Politburo of the RKP urged the Moscow soviet to "exclude members of the Menshevik faction who do not declare their disagreement with those Mensheviks arrested for provoking the strike."[75]

The year 1921 found the RSDRP in a greatly weakened state. Its numbers kept falling. Whereas under Alexander Kerensky, who headed the short-lived Provisional Government in 1917, the Menshevik candidates to the Constituent Assembly garnered 21,000 votes in Moscow, not counting those cast for the Plekhanovite group Yedinstvo (Unity), the 1921 reregistration of the party's members in the capital produced a mere 300 or so. In the RSDRP as a whole, the membership tally—as high as 200,000 members in the fall of 1917—stood at only several thousand. The departure for abroad of the party's leaders—Yu. Martov in 1920, D. Dalin in 1921, F. Dan and others in 1922—contributed significantly to the gathering crisis.

It would seem that the Bolsheviks had achieved their objectives.

Repressions against the defeated opponent should have come to an end. But that hope, too, proved illusory. From 1922 on, the Mensheviks' every activity, and hence their party's very existence, was placed outside the law. Under these conditions there was nothing left for the party to do but go underground, which it did in the autumn of 1922 in accordance with the decision of a council representing the RSDRP's local organizations. Since the party's principal organs, previously elected at a party congress, had by now ceased to exist, a CC bureau was put together by cooptation under the chairmanship of G. Kuchin-Oransky, who had escaped from exile in Central Asia.

Nonetheless, Lenin was afraid the Mensheviks might get a second wind. That, apparently, was why he stepped forward in 1922 to launch another antisocialist offensive. In an outwardly unimportant episode—a polemic between an eighteen-year-old Menshevik student named Gurvich and Leon Trotsky at a youth conference on the problems of the New Economic Policy—the leader detected a dangerous sign that what appeared to be Menshevism in its death throes concealed an enduring vitality and growing influence among the young. To Trotsky he wrote, "I have no doubt that the Mensheviks are intensifying and will continue to intensify their most malicious propaganda. For that reason I think we must increase both surveillance and repressions against them. I spoke about this to Unshlikht. . . . It would perhaps be most useful if you were to enter into open battle in the press, name this Menshevik, explain the malicious White Guard nature of his statement, and address a stern admonition to the party to improve itself."[76] Note the spite in these lines. Lenin, who passes in some quarters for a wise man, never found a way to stand up for his beliefs other than through violence, "surveillance," "repressions."

Lenin's suggestion was quickly taken up by the Chekists. In March 1922 Unshlikht reported to the "leader of the world proletariat" that "given the intensified work of the Mensheviks' Youth League, the secret department of the OGPU believes it necessary to take a number of preventive repressive measures against its harmful activities."[77] These measures yielded such a bountiful harvest that the Politburo at its session of 20 March decided to lay the groundwork for an "open trial of Social Democratic youth." But a review of the accumulated evidence by a specially created commission concluded that "to base a political trial on this would be inexpedient," and the Politburo on 20 April 1922 rescinded its decree, agreeing with the commission to "restrict itself, in this case, to administrative exile."[78]

The courts, too, received Lenin's instructions. "For public evidence of Menshevism our revolutionary courts must order executions, or else they are not our courts," Lenin declared in March 1922 in a speech at the 11th Congress of the RKP(b). Two months later, supplementing the draft of the Criminal Code of the Russian Soviet Federated Socialist Republic (RSFSR), he wrote to D. Kursky: "In my opinion, we must extend the use of executions (commutable to deportation abroad) . . . to all forms of activity on the part of the Mensheviks, SRs, and so forth; we must find a formulation linking these actions to the international bourgeoisie and its struggle against us."[79]

As a result, the first Soviet Criminal Code, of 1922, contained the "famous" article 58, prescribing the death penalty for "activities" defined in deliberately muddled form—not only for "organizing, for counterrevolutionary purposes, armed uprisings or incursions into Soviet territory by armed detachments or bands" but for "participating in any attempt, with the same aims, to seize power in the center or in the provinces."[80] By 1927, article 58 contained eighteen clauses, thirteen of them of the "shooting" variety.

In December 1922 the Politburo ordered the "removal of Mensheviks from all state, professional, and cooperative institutions, commencing the 'purge' with those institutions where the Mensheviks are able to come in contact with the laboring masses." The OGPU was given the right to substitute imprisonment in camps for administrative exile for those "active" Mensheviks against whom there were "no grounds for trial." To put a stop to intercessions on behalf of Mensheviks by prominent members of the RKP, it was decided in 1923 to subject the intercessors to Party discipline. The same penalty was envisaged for the heads of those Soviet institutions that still employed "even a handful of Mensheviks."[81]

Socialists who fell into the claws of the OGPU were rarely able to regain their freedom, even after their sentences had expired. A finding by the investigating officer of the "inadvisability" of permitting a "free existence" was enough for a prisoner to be sentenced in absentia by the Special Council of the OGPU Collegium to another term in a concentration camp or in exile. For many, to all intents and purposes, exile became forever.

From 1923 to 1925, arrested socialists were sent mostly to the special concentration camps of the Solovetsky Islands, although fairly large groups of SRs, Mensheviks, and Anarchists were imprisoned in Moscow, Vladimir, Yaroslavl, Yekaterinburg, and Suzdal. At first the socialists were favored with a privileged "political regime" excusing them from forced labor and a number of humiliating prison procedures and granting them the right to choose their own "captain." But on Yezhov's orders in February 1937, all NKVD special prisons for particularly dangerous state criminals adopted uniform regulations for keeping all prisoners strictly isolated.[82] All thought of easing conditions was given up. Categorized with socialists as "particularly dangerous political criminals" were spies, saboteurs, and members of terrorist, Fascist, and insurgent groups.

In the 1930s, an end was put to all scientific, cultural, and social organizations with the slightest connection to the socialists and Anarchists, including the P. A. Kropotkin All-Russian Social Committee (closed down in 1934), the Society of Former Political Prisoners and Exiles, with its fifty affiliates and its publishing house (1935), the Society of Old Bolsheviks (1935), and the politicized Red Cross (1937). Done away with even earlier, in the 1920s, were private and cooperative publishing houses putting out literature on the history of the socialist and Anarchist movements—*Zadruga* (Commune), *Kolos* (Sheaf), *Golos Truda* (Voice of Labor), and others.

Also in the 1930s, the secret police launched a campaign to "expose" and eliminate the so-called highly secret centers of the SR and Menshevik "underground"—in 1933 in Moscow, Leningrad, and Sevastopol, as well as in Kharkov, the Donbass, Kiev, Dnepropetrovsk, and other places in the Ukraine; in 1934 in Ivanovo and Yaroslavl; in 1935 in Kazan, Ulianovsk, Saratov, and Kalinin, and in 1936–37 in the Sverdlovsk, Voronezh, Kuibyshev, Moscow, and other oblasts.[83]

The number of those arrested in these fabricated cases totaled several thousand, most of them former members of socialist parties. They faced the usual charges of sabotage, anti-Soviet propaganda, and preparations for counterrevolutionary and terrorist actions on a mass scale. In 1937, their accusers suddenly remembered the SRs, in exile lo these many years, and Yezhov proposed that they be rearrested. Obtaining the approval of the CC of the VKP(b), he initiated another campaign, with the result that up to six hundred more persons found themselves behind bars.[84]

The second half of 1937 and the beginning of 1938 were marked by a new NKVD crackdown to "neutralize" a pack of organizations, such as the "All-Union SR Center" and the "PSR Bureau of Eastern Siberia," that in fact had never existed. The secret police trumped up numerous "conspiracies" by SRs, in league with Mensheviks, "rightists" (Bukharinists), Trotskyists, and White Guards, to overthrow Soviet power and commit terrorist acts against the "chiefs."

Increasingly, it was not just socialist party members who were arrested but their close relatives, starting with their wives, most of whom had no connection whatsoever with politics. The usual sentence passed by the "troikas" on wives and relatives was ten years in prison and five years' deprivation of civil rights.

Buckling under years of persecution, repeated arrests, and torture under interrogation, even the staunchest began to incriminate themselves or to write letters of repentance. In 1937 "honest" testimony was obtained under torture from Gots, a member of the CC of the PSR who had been with the party since 1901. He was sentenced to twenty-five years and died in August 1940 in the Krasnoyarsk concentration camp. In 1935 a letter of confession came from Kuchin-Oransky, an RSDRP member since 1907 who was on the party's CC and who by then had spent eleven years in prison or exile.

M. Nazariev (Petrov), one of the heads of the RSDRP's Petrograd Committee, died in exile in 1935; around 1938 one of the delegates to the party's 5th Congress, E. Ashpiz, died in a concentration camp; in 1938 the venerable Social Democrat P. Kolokolnikov, a prominent economist and historian and a deputy minister of labor in the Provisional Government coalition, perished in prison; on 4 October 1937 the old Social Democrat Liber (Goldman) was shot. Shot, too, were the Menshevik F. Cherevanin in 1938 and the Menshevik S. Yezhov in February 1939; B. N. Ber died in the course of an interrogation.

The list of victims is endless. Of all those indicted in the "big" trial of the SR Party CC, only one survived Stalin—A. Altovsky, who died in 1975. With the rarest exceptions (Andrei Vyshinsky, Ivan Maisky, V. Kopp), even those socialists who had broken with their parties as early as the civil war and had been serving the regime faithfully ever since were repressed in those years—for example, the former Left SR division commander Yu. Sablin, the former SR-Maximalist army commander P. Eideman, and the former Menshevik L. Khinchuk, a member of the Presidium of the VTsIK. In the autumn of 1941, the Left SRs Spiridonov, Izmailovich, and Mayorov, the Maximalist Nestroyev, and the SR Timofeyev were among the 157 prisoners shot in the Medvedevsky woods.

Monstrous as it may seem, even in the postwar period the leaders lived in fear of their former brothers in the 1917 seizure of power. Under Decree No. 416–159cc of the Council of Ministers of the USSR of 21 February 1948, the concentration-camp regime for particularly dangerous political criminals was tightened to the utmost. They were put exclusively to hard labor in trying climatic conditions; they were subjected to a ten-hour workday, confinement to cells in the camp barracks, and a special prison uniform with numbers on the back and headgear. After serving their sentences, the special-camp inmates were sent into lifetime exile in remote regions under the surveillance of branches of the MVD.[85]

In August 1953—after Stalin's death—the decree of 1948 underwent "partial changes." But these did not alter the status of Mensheviks and SRs as "particularly dangerous political criminals." By the end of 1953, there were fewer than two thousand Trotskyists, rightists, Mensheviks, and SRs left in the special camps and special prisons (Vladimirsky, Verkhne-Uralsky and Aleksandrovsky).[86] But even they, disabled and aged and infirm, continued to excite the pathological hatred of the regime.

PEASANTS

THE DESPOTISM of the authorities during the postwar period of devastation and hunger fell heaviest on the peasants. In the first place, they had grain, which had to be confiscated, and in the second place, they were automatically regarded as opponents of the new regime since, according to Marxist dogma, they were constantly re-creating the world of the petty bourgeoisie and its private-property outlook.

Immediately after the counterrevolution of October 1917, the Bolsheviks adopted a policy of economic strangulation of the peasants through the requisitioning of farm produce, the prohibition of free trade, compulsory labor duty in carting and timber processing, and so on. But soon, in mid-1918, they launched a direct military offensive against the villages with armed forces equipped with artillery, armored cars, and even airplanes. These units engaged in the consolidation of "socialist" structures within the villages—in reality, in governmental looting and the ruthless quashing of any and all peasant grievances.

As early as May 1918—even before the official inception of the Red Terror—the revolutionary tribunals, along with the VChK, were authorized to sentence to death those who refused to deliver their grain to the food-requisitioning brigades. Composed in great part of disreputable types—aside from units of the VChK, troops of the internal security services (VOKhR) and the regular units of the Workers'-Peasants' Red Army (RKKA)—this scavenging force was augmented in August 1918 by subdivisions of the Military Food-Products Office (harvesting and harvest-requisitioning detachments) numbering more than twenty thousand men, and in the spring of 1919 by Special Units (ChON), a "Party guard" created at the provincial and district Party level by a decision of the CC "to provide assistance to organs of Soviet power in the struggle against the counterrevolution"; by 1921 it included some forty thousand personnel.

The Red Army itself, in Lenin's words, was created nine-tenths "for systematic military operations for taking and retaking, collecting and delivering grain and fuel."[1] Note well: for systematic military operations. Developing their "plan for going after grain with machine guns," the Bolsheviks pursued basically political objectives.[2] Their protestations that the present measures were necessitated by famine were nothing more than a smokescreen.

Assisting the food-requisitioning agencies in seizing grain and—most importantly—in fomenting civil war in the villages were the Committees on Poverty set up by a VTsIK decree of 11 June 1918. Designating these committees as the bulwark of their peasant policy, the Bolsheviks aimed at drawing closer to the dregs of peasant society, who were eager to parcel up other people's goods and spend the proceeds on drink but not to do any work themselves.

In my village of Korolevo, in the Yaroslavl region and oblast, there was an activist, one Fyodor Sudakov, a familiar type in other villages as well. During the civil war he headed the Committee on Poverty. I remember him from the days of the kolkhoz. No one ever saw Sudakov working. His wretched wife worked herself to the bone for him. Her only solace was to clobber her husband with whatever she could lay her hands on when he was dragged home blind drunk. He liked to drink, of course, at other people's expense. And he liked to declaim, even when he was alone. He'd swagger down the village street bawling, "We"—that is, the poor—"will finish you off, you bloodsuckers," although everyone else in the village was poor, too. At first he dealt in abstractions, laying down the "Party line" in words alone, and we took him for a clown, good for a laugh. But the laughter stopped when Sudakov began to name names. Then some muzhik would step out into the street to rearrange the "ideological champion's" physiognomy. We boys would watch these spectacles with enormous curiosity. Here, after all, was the class struggle in its naked form.

Lowlifes like Sudakov called the tune in the villages. They were recruited as informers, and they boasted when drunk about their "special position" and their ability to have any villager "bundled off" when necessary. Fortunately, the peasants knew about these scoundrels and kept away from them, except to beat them ruthlessly on religious and Soviet holidays.

In the fall of 1918 the Committees on Poverty, having been designated "masters of the whole political, administrative, and economic life of the village or *volost*," were reorganized into soviets, thereby becoming even stauncher supporters of official policy.[3]

Later the Bolshevik leaders would often wax hypocritical about "local excesses" in the requisitioning of farm products and other forms of lawlessness in the villages. But facts are facts. The driving force of the campaign against the villages was the Party's ruling clique, and most of all Lenin, who had sworn publicly that he would "sooner lie down and die" than allow free trade in grain.[4] To all and sundry, the chief of state meted out his cannibalistic orders: "Merciless war against the kulaks! Death to them!" These were his instructions to the requisitioners. "Merciless mass terror against the kulaks, priests, and White Guards; all questionable persons to be locked up in concentration camps. . . . It is essential to crush the uprising of the kulaks with the greatest energy, speed, and mercilessness, taking some of the troops from Penza, confiscating all the property of the insurgent kulaks and all their grain"—his orders to the authorities in Penza. In August 1918 Lenin initiated the practice of taking hostages from among "kulaks, bloodsuckers, and moneybags," who would answer with their lives for "accurate delivery of the assessed contribution as rapidly as possible."[5]

The result was to push the peasantry to the edge of an early grave. According to reports from Tambov province, the populace in a number of volosts in the Usmansk, Lipetsk, Kozlovsk, and Borisoglebsk districts "fed not only on husks and wild grass but on bark and nettles."[6] In other provinces, too, the condition of the peasants was catastrophic. A report submitted by Chief Commissar

Sergei Kamenev in October 1920 speaks of crowds of hungry peasants in Voronezh and Saratov provinces pleading with the local authorities to give them at least some of the grain taken at the collection centers. Often, Kamenev writes, "these crowds were mowed down by machine guns."[7]

The war against the peasants produced the additional effects of a sharp decrease in planting and a slump in the harvest—which, however, did not lead to any reduction in the food requisitioning inaugurated in January 1919. On the contrary, having removed 107,900,000 poods of grain from the villages in 1918–19, the state took twice as much—212,000,000 poods—in 1921–22, in the midst of famine. Beginning at the end of 1920, moreover, the requisitioning was not limited to grain but included practically all farm products and, in some oblasts, such as the Kuban, even items of daily use (pots, pillows, forks, etc.).

The devastation of the villages and the collapse of peasant households were brought about not only by the actions of the food-requisitioning brigades but by detachments created to combat desertions, inasmuch as peasants were being forcibly recruited into the Red Army. Those caught were shot or sent to concentration camps and prisons. Their property and the property of families suspected of harboring deserters were confiscated.

The peasants' patience appeared to be coming to an end. Driven to despair, they began to sack the premises of the food agencies and to beat up Communists and food workers. Toward the end of 1921, these attacks became increasingly large-scale and the clashes with military forces increasingly fierce. In 1918, according to incomplete data, there were 245 such uprisings in the country as a whole, and close to 100 during the first seven months of 1919. At the beginning of 1921, when the peasant war reached its apogee, 118 of Russia's districts were caught up in these rebellions.

In the areas most "infected by banditism," as the authorities put it, special control agencies were set up—district political commissions, village and volost revolutionary committees. The CC of the RKP(b) received proposals that these regions be regarded as territory "occupied by the enemy" and as "comparable in importance and significance to the front lines . . . of the period of the civil war."[8]

The usual procedure followed by the food-requisitioning detachments involved beatings, floggings, torture, and shooting of peasants without trial or investigation. Even among their own kind, some provincial food commissars became known as executioners. And the Chekists did not lag behind them. "The extraordinary commissions," testified M. Latsis, "dealt mercilessly with these ravenous animals (peasants), in order to cure them once and for all of any appetite for rebellion."[9]

In the country's borderlands, the agents of the VChK engaged in bloody atrocities with impunity. In October 1920, the special representative for the northern Caucasus, K. Lander, having received his instructions from Lenin before leaving for that region, promised to crush "all attacks of the White-Green bands" with "implacable harshness." On his orders, Cossack villages and settlements sheltering Whites and Greens were subject to destruction and their adult populations to wholesale execution. Relatives of insurgents were declared hostages, and they, too, were subject to being shot when the "bands" went on the offensive; children were exiled to the central provinces. In case of mass demonstrations in the villages or cities, wrote this emissary of Lenin's, "we will subject such places to mass terror: for every murdered Soviet activist, hundreds of inhabitants will pay with their lives."[10]

Commented an eyewitness in 1921: "The Terek and Kuban oblasts have been subdued. The insurgent Cossack villages have been wiped off the face of the earth, the population has been removed—the men to forced labor in mines, the women and children scattered everywhere. All living and dead stock has been seized or has rotted or been pilfered."[11]

In February 1921, an important threshold was reached. The insurgency in Tambov province, named the Antonovshchina after its leader, Antonov, had grown enormously and begun to find support in neighboring districts of Voronezh, Saratov, and Penza provinces. With the folding up of the fronts against Poland and Wrangel, the authorities were able to move fresh troops to the affected areas. At the end of February and the beginning of March, a Plenary Commission of the VTsIK headed by V. Antonov-Ovsenko was set up as the supreme directorate in the struggle against the Antonovshchina. At the end of April, on Lenin's initiative and in response to his demand for the "quickest and most exemplary suppression" of the insurgency, Mikhail Tukhachevsky, the victor of Kronstadt, was made sole commander of the troops in the Tambov district and given the responsibility of crushing the rebellious bands. Joining him in the Tambovshchina were military commanders and secret police chiefs I. Uborevich, G. Kotovsky, G. Yagoda, and V. Ulrikh.

The "occupation regime," as it was officially called, provided for the "saturation" of insurgent areas by troops, destruction of rebel households and razing of their houses (some villages were burned to the ground), and repressions up to and including death for disobedience, harboring "bandits," and hiding weapons. Subject to execution, on orders from revolutionary tribunal member V. Ulrikh, were all "leaders, initiators, and instigators" of the peasant movement, commanders of the peasant army, those directly responsible for the death of Communists and Soviet activists, "malicious deserters," and "Communists, Soviet activists, and Red Army commanders who join Antonov's band."[12]

An order of the VTsIK Plenary Commission of 11 June 1921 provided for the execution of hostages in districts caught up in the insurgency. Under the same order, persons refusing to give their names were to be shot without trial. The next day, Tukhachevsky ordered that "forests where the bandits are hiding be cleared by poison gas." Elaborating, the army commander demanded that "the cloud of toxic gases be made to spread throughout the forest, killing anyone hiding there."[13]

As late as June 1921, when the rebellion was already subsiding, the authorities "removed" 16,000 "bandit-deserters," confiscated the property of 500 peasant households, and burned down 250 peasant homes. The province acquired a network of mobile concentration camps containing not only insurgents but hostages, including women and infants. A report on a "big influx" of children is found in the minutes of a meeting of the Commission on Child Hostages in Concentration Field Camps in Tambov Province. Even after an operation in July 1921 to "unload" the concentration camps, they still contained more than 450 child hostages between ages one and ten.[14]

In western Siberia as well, the secret police left a bloody trail. In their struggle with the peasant insurgency, the local authorities exercised no restraint in taking hostages and imposing collective responsibility. Hostages were to be shot not only when district and volost centers were approached by insurgent forces or when Communists and Soviet workers were murdered but when telegraph and railway lines were disrupted or "provocative rumors" circulated (this in the Tobolsk district), or even when there was "the slightest intent to trample on the rights of government representatives" (Kurgan district).[15] Collective responsibility was extended to whole settlements and villages if anyone there took part in the insurgency or gave the insurgents support. Thus, in February 1921, the authorities in the Ishimsk district issued an order making support for the insurgents punishable by "confiscation of all property, including, if necessary, the total destruction of villages."

At the 10th Congress of the RKP(b) in March 1921, the food-requisitioning brigades were replaced by taxation in kind and a shift to the New Economic Policy. Dropping their wild "socialist" experiments in the village, the Bolshevik leadership succeeded in calming the wave of peasant grievances. The whole business was capped by the terrible famine of 1921–22, which took more than five million lives and tragically highlighted the disgraceful results of three years of Bolshevik mismanagement in the villages. The experiment in "war Communism" was an utter failure.

Repressions against participants in armed peasant attacks and against their families continued, however, well after the suppression of the rebellion. In the 1930s, those of their number who were still alive were registered by the OGPU-NKVD and in most cases arrested. Thus, every third person out of the seventeen thousand inhabitants of the Omsk oblast subjected to repressions in 1937 was accused by the NKVD of having taken part in the Siberian uprising.

For years the formula "Stalin is the Lenin of today" was hammered into the heads of the Soviet people. It was Stalin's own brainchild. This formula, unlike most others of the time, is accurate and fair. Stalin indeed turned out to be a worthy pupil of Lenin's in his hatred and in his taste for blood. He not only carried on doggedly with Lenin's criminal endeavors but completed the destruction of the peasant class in the dreadful years of collectivization and dekulakization, the most tragic in Russia's history. To the sound of executions by rifle and machine gun, the country entered a frightful phase of its development, comparable perhaps only to the years of World War II.

The Bolshevik regime did colossal damage to the national economy, destroyed the centuries-old traditions and foundations of the Russian village, and created an essentially feudal kolkhoz-sovkhoz system. The peasantry was finished off—finished off cruelly, bloodily. Except for the lords and masters of the nomenklatura, the entire country was forced for years to stand in line for bread and meat.

It is a sin to forget this, a great sin.

The tragedy began with the November 1929 plenum of the CC of the VKP(b), which resolved to "forge ahead with a decisive struggle against the kulak, with uprooting capitalism in the rural economy." In the middle of January 1930, the Politburo of the CC of the VKP(b) set up a special commission headed by its secretary, Molotov, to work out the means of proceeding with dekulakization. The commission promptly drew up a decree that included the following:

> In carrying out in the next two months (February–March) measures aimed at exiling populations to remote regions of the Union and placing them in concentration camps, the OGPU is to figure on confining approximately 60,000 persons in concentration camps and exiling 150,000 households. With respect to the most malicious counterrevolutionary elements, to include the death penalty when necessary. . . . The places of exile to be located in the districts of the Northern Territory (up to 70,000 families), Siberia (50,000 families), the Urals (20,000 to 25,000 families), and Kazakhstan (20,000 to 25,000 families), in unpopulated or sparsely populated areas, the resettled to be put to work in farming or industry (forestry, fishing, etc.). . . . Exiled kulaks to be placed in settlements directed by duly appointed commandants.[16]

On 30 January, the CC of the VKP(b) issued a decree, "On Measures to Liquidate Kulak Households in Regions of Total Collectivization," communicated the same day to local Party organizations. In regions of total collectivization, leasing land was banned, hiring labor was forbidden, and means of production, such as cattle and agricultural facilities, belonging to kulaks were ordered confiscated. For peasant households designated as kulak the following measures were prescribed:

> A. First category—Counterrevolutionary kulak activist centers to be immediately eliminated by confinement in concentration camp, including the death penalty when necessary, for organizers of terrorist actions, counterrevolutionary attacks, and insurgent groups.

B. Second category must include the other elements of the kulaks, especially from among the richer kulaks and self-styled landowners, who are to be exiled to remote regions of the USSR within the territory in question.

C. The third category shall comprise kulaks left in their own areas, who must be resettled on other land assigned to them beyond the limits of the kolkhoz households."[17]

The Molotov commission had barely drawn up these plans when the OGPU began putting them into effect. By 18 January, its agencies had been given an order instructing them

1. To set up within the OGPU an operational group for combining all the phases of the forthcoming operation. Immediately to work out and submit to the OGPU a detailed operational plan, taking into account all operational, personnel, military, and technical questions. . . .

6. To select places along the railway lines where those to be resettled will be assembled and to determine the quantity of rolling stock and other means of transportation to be made available at these places.

7. To take careful account of the situation in the affected regions and the possibility of outbursts, so that these can be headed off without the slightest delay. To provide for uninterrupted information and agent activity in areas of operation.

8. To draw up precise plans for the deployment and use of the available troops of the OGPU and the RKKA. To select places for deploying reserves.

In villages around the country, the dekulakization campaign was, as a rule, carried out by representatives of the poor. The unrestrained power of these representatives, magnified by the enthusiasm of the utterly destitute, created an atmosphere of total despotism and all-embracing fear.

The violence spread over a widening area. On 20 February 1930 the CC of the VKP(b) adopted a decree, "On Collectivization and Struggle with Kulakism in the Economically Backward Ethnic Regions." The "liquidation of kulakism" encompassed all of the country's republics, regions, and oblasts. Freight trains packed with people began winding to the north and east; endless lines of muzhiks, the elderly, and women with little children slogged along in sleds and on foot. To help with the transfer of "kulak families," those of the populace with animal-drawn vehicles were pressed into service, and trains, trucks, and automobiles were widely utilized. Many of the exiled perished from hunger and cold—and from the bullets of their guards.

The total number of repressed kulaks exceeded the original estimates many times over. The local overlords, fearing for their own skins, knocked themselves out. Thus, the dekulakized peasants in the central black-soil region accounted for 15 percent of all peasant households. In some regions of the Nizhegorodsky territory, the figure stood at 37 percent. Mass dekulakization exceeding the quotas was the rule in the Ukraine, in the Moscow oblast, and in the Tatar and Bashkir Soviet Socialist Republics and other regions.

A good many of the dekulakized and their families—almost 1.2 million peasants—were exiled to the remotest parts of the country, to do construction work in Siberia and the far north. Millions of people found themselves homeless, without means of subsistence, denied protection against the hounding of the envious and bamboozled crowds.

In a letter to Molotov early in August 1930, Stalin recommended that "the whole group of saboteurs in the meat industry be shot without fail, with a report on this to appear in the press."[18] On 20 September the Politburo of the CC of the VKP(b) adopted a decision, "On Saboteurs in the Meat Industry and Others," that resolved:

A. To recognize the need for immediate publication of the basic testimony of the saboteurs in the case concerning sabotage in the meat, fish, canning, and vegetable industries.

To accompany this evidence with a brief introduction by the OGPU specifying that, on orders from the TsIK and the SNK of the Union, the case has been forwarded for investigation by the OGPU.

B. To publish a series of articles explaining the crux of this case and pointing out that the work of this counterrevolutionary gang has been fully exposed and that all steps for undoing the damage caused by sabotage have been taken. To devote one and a half pages to this text in the 22 September issues of the main newspapers.

C. To instruct a commission composed of comrades Menzhinsky, Yaroslavsky, Rykov, and Postyshev to review this text and the OGPU introduction prior to publication.

D. Five days later, to publish the OGPU's sentence condemning all members of this saboteur organization to be shot.[19]

The testimony of the members of the so-called organization of saboteurs of workers' supplies was duly published in the newspapers. Three days later they reported that the OGPU Collegium had sentenced forty-eight saboteurs of workers' production to be shot and that the sentence had been carried out.

From the beginning of 1931, a new wave of destruction crested against the peasantry. This time it sought out those kulaks who allegedly undermined the grain-requisitioning process and other economic and political campaigns. Decisions on a new forced resettlement of kulaks began to crop up in January 1931. The second mass campaign to "liquidate the kulaks as a class" began in March. It engulfed nearly the whole country.

A special commission of the CC of the VKP(b) was set up to help with the operation. On 18 March 1931 the commission adopted a decision to resettle 40,000 kulak households in the northern part of western Siberia and 150,000 in Kazakhstan during the months of May, June, and July. In other words, in the short period of three months and in two regions alone, 190,000 peasant families—more than a million persons—were exiled. The decision, "On Measures for the Liquidation of Peasant Households in Regions of Total Collectivization," specified that "the places of resettlement must be unpopulated or sparsely populated localities."[20] People tossed into the untamed taiga or tundra were deliberately doomed to a slow death.

One reads these documents and doesn't believe that all this happened, and not that long ago—that these crimes were committed by hundreds of thousands of our fellow citizens on orders from a criminal clique at the Party's summit.

From the very outset of dekulakization, the daily life of the specially resettled was organized along the lines of the corrective-labor camps. People were placed in "separate settlements of 100,000 families each." Supervision was organized by a commandant assisted by "two to five riflemen of the Special Units."[21] When the specially resettled were handed over to the OGPU, their regime became even more severe.

The archives contain not a few documents recounting the life of the dekulakized. Says one of them, "Lacking proper nourishment and medical supervision and assistance, a good number of the specially resettled, too weak to work, could not fulfill the quotas for timber processing, with the result that the timber industry agency ordered all the specially resettled of either sex and whatever age to join in the work of timber processing, setting a quota of two to two and a half cubic meters a day for twelve-year-old children and the aged, whereas the average quota for an adult worker had been fixed at three cubic meters a day. In view of that, the specially resettled tried to fulfill their quotas by working twenty-four hours straight in the forest, where they often froze to death or succumbed to frostbite or epidemics." As one OGPU agent reported to the chief of the OGPU headquarters for the Urals: "Out of a total of 32,000 persons, children up to twelve years of age account for 15,000, and women with infants and children up to eight years (approximately) number some 4,000. Men number 8,500, of which 1,000 are not able-bodied. Able-bodied persons capable of work of any kind total 12,000 to 13,000 (approximately), including men and women. Of course, of the 1,000 non-able-bodied men and 4,000 women and 15,000 children, 50 percent can be put to other kinds of work."[22]

Some of the specially resettled tried to escape anywhere they could. To prevent escapes the camp commanders adopted a system of collective responsibility, paid thirty rubles for the capture of every escapee, intensified agent surveillance, created Chekist flying columns, and equipped all railway stations with special barricades and security squads.

Protests against lawlessness, despotism, and slave labor took all different forms, sometimes resulting in mass unrest—as they did in the Narym territory, where more than 200,000 of the specially resettled, two-thirds of them Siberian peasants exiled to the territory's unpopulated areas as "kulak elements," were concentrated in the woods and swamps. Unrest spread to the territory of the Parbitsky headquarters, the largest of the northern headquarters of the Siberian concentration-camp administration, in charge of more than 33,000 peasants exiled from southern Siberia. (A song by the folksinger Vladimir Vysotsky is aptly titled "From Siberia to Siberia.") Dumped there in summer, they had to build their own shelter before it turned cold. But there wasn't enough time for that, since all able-bodied men were working at timber processing in the taiga, dozens of kilometers from the settlement, while their wives and children huddled in dugouts and tents. Meanwhile, winter approached. The specially resettled decided on a desperate act. They quit work and returned to their families. They disarmed their guards. In reprisal the authorities called in the troops of the OGPU. The revolt of the specially resettled was ruthlessly quashed. Those left alive fled into the taiga, where platoons of the OGPU and police continued to track them down for a long time. It was a real hunt, only for human beings. Anyone captured in the taiga was shot on the spot.

A special brand of savagery was exhibited by armed groups composed of local Party activists. On the pretext of action against the insurgents, some of them began to kill not only the specially resettled but local inhabitants, with looting as their aim. An armed Party group in the village of Tungusov, for instance, shot fifteen local inhabitants. After the bullets came looting, mass drunkenness, and yet more people shot.

A new fit of Bolshevik madness broke out in 1937. On 2 July the Politburo of the CC of the VKP(b) ordered all secretaries of oblast and territorial organizations and all oblast, territorial, and republic officials of the NKVD to carry out a meticulous registration of all kulaks who were still living in their places of exile and who had returned to their homes after the expiration of their periods of exile. The more "hostile" ones were to be "immediately arrested" and shot.

At its next session the Politburo confirmed the makeup of the troikas that were to carry out repressions against kulak and anti-Soviet elements on the republic, territorial, and oblast levels. It also set the approximate number of those who, at the troikas' discretion, should receive first-category sentences—in other words, be shot—and those in the second category, who should be sent to concentration camps for eight to ten years or imprisoned for that period. This phase began on 5 August 1937 and was to go on for four months. During that time, the plan was to arrest 186,100 persons in Russia alone and to have 47,450 of them shot.

The idiocy of the planned economy showed through in everything: even arrests and executions were planned ahead. The local Party and secret police units flung themselves with great enthusiasm into this barbaric binge.

It is the moral duty of all Russian citizens never to forget, and to pass down from generation to generation, the fact that nearly all local offices of the VKP(b) lobbied for increasing the "planned" number of those to be repressed. And although, technically speaking, the NKVD's local executioners were forbidden from letting this happen, the number of those repressed exceeded the planned levels in all republics, territories, and oblasts. In February 1938, for example, the Party's oblast committee in Gorky reported personally to Stalin that instead of the 4,500 planned for, 9,600 persons had been arrested in the area under its jurisdiction. But even this was not enough. The oblast committee asked that the figure be increased by another 5,000, of which 3,000 would be shot. The officials on the spot were well aware of prevailing sentiment in the Kremlin.

In addition to administrative methods of repression for putting an end to kulakism, the authorities resorted to economic ones aimed at cutting off the peasants' livelihood. All well-off households were subjected to an individual tax calculated on a steeply rising scale. The list of compulsory payments kept growing. The tax policy was such that often, at a certain income level, the tax payments exceeded the peasant household's earnings. For instance, if a peasant household had an income of 5,000 rubles, it had to pay 7,500 rubles in taxes. No wonder that many peasants defaulted on their payments—at which point their property, cattle, and inventory were confiscated and the household ceased to exist.

Another method of economic dekulakization widely in use was to burden kulak households with fixed assignments for basic agricultural production. Here, too, arbitrariness reigned supreme. The assignments were handed out without the slightest concern for the productive capacities of the households. In the end, the property of the peasant to whom some excruciatingly difficult task had been given was also confiscated, and he himself, in most cases, was subjected to dekulakization. It should be noted that as early as November 1930 the VTsIK and the SNK of the USSR adopted a decree, "On Excluding Kulaks and Those Deprived of Civil Rights from Cooperatives," that said: "Kulaks and those deprived of the right to vote in elections of soviets may not be members of kolkhozes and other agricultural cooperatives or of industrial cooperative associations (artels) and cooperative societies."

As a result, better-off peasants could not buy harrows or seed drills, get credit, or sell their crops; they could not buy kerosene, clothing, or other necessities in the cooperative store—and private trade was wiped out. This segment of the peasant class was not only deprived in toto of the economic basis for independent households but was, in effect, doomed to extinction.

In its war against the people, the criminal Stalinist clique had everything prearranged. In August 1932 it passed a law drawn up by Stalin himself. This monstrous statute authorized imprisonment or even death for the taking of a few sheaves of grain from a harvested field. Punishment was meted out even for the granules scraped from the burrows of field mice by starving peasants.

A direct result of the policy of dekulakization was the mass famine that gripped the country in 1932–33. Cases of cannibalism were not unknown. The authorities had their way: more than five million people died in the famine.

As a rule, dekulakization is associated with the 1930s. But on 10 February 1948 the Politburo listened to Khrushchev read a proposal to exile "harmful village elements" from the Ukraine. The same day the Council of Ministers of the USSR set up a commission composed of L. Beria, N. Khrushchev, M. Suslov, and others to work out the details. Exile was prescribed for anyone suspected of being able to "undermine labor discipline in the village economy" or "threaten the welfare of the kolkhoz by his presence in the village." Truly, these people knew no bounds—threaten the welfare of the kolkhoz by his presence in the village, indeed!

Khrushchev's initiative was emulated in other parts of prewar USSR. The "purges" swept up not only villagers but anyone regarded as a suspicious element, a potential enemy of the authorities. The scope of this campaign is demonstrated by the stark figures of official statistics, kept secret for many decades.

On 1 January 1949 the roster of the specially resettled stood close to 2.5 million. Between 1949 and 1952, up to 200,000 of them were released. In spite of that, the total number of the specially resettled did not fall but rose. After the war, hundreds of thousands of persons, primarily villagers, were deported from the Baltic states, western Ukraine, western Belorussia, Moldavia, and Siberia.

How short memory is if the agrarian barons of today—the various chairmen and other potentates—are allowed to preserve the feudal system in the village. So deeply is a slave mentality ingrained in our consciousness that many peasants still living in our villages, former "spokesmen" for the poor (only the poor are left), refuse to do any work on the land. Deranged by drink, they are unable to run a self-supporting household or live off the fruits of their labor. And the barons couldn't care less. Grain, meat, and butter we can get from abroad, and here at home we parcel out trillions of rubles in subsidies to the agrarian bureaucratic parasites.

The criminal policy of dekulakization watered the Russian land with tears and blood. The sanguinary campaign began during the earliest years of Soviet power, its goal the uprooting of the centuries-old institutions of Cossackdom, the physical annihilation of its most industrious and freedom-loving part.

The very first moves in the "socialist" transformation of the village placed the Cossacks, in the summer of 1918, in direct opposition to the new government. In all the major Cossack oblasts—Don, Kuban, Orenburg, the Urals—armed groups were formed for resistance to the Bolshevik dictatorship. From that time on, the Cossacks were regarded by the government as members of the "strike force" of the White Armies and, furthermore, as having been "bought off" by German, English, and French imperialism.[23] On 24 January 1919 the Party CC addressed a telegram to its local branches ordering them to "carry out mass terror against wealthy Cossacks, exterminating all of them; carry out merciless mass terror against any and all Cossacks taking part in any way, directly or indirectly, in the struggle against Soviet power."[24]

Apart from the prescribed executions, requisitioning, and exile, the local revolutionary committees, gleefully giving it their all in a bout of toadying and revolutionary barbarity, heaped contempt on Cossack customs, jeering at the very word *Cossack*. A particularly refined affront was the appointment of Austrian war prisoners as commissars in Cossack villages.

The Cossacks did not put up with this for very long. In March 1919 a mass uprising broke out in the upper Don. It forced the authorities to adjust their course somewhat—without changing their basic policy, to split the Cossacks, courting those who were poorer than the rest and were ready to profit at others' expense. On 16 March the CC adopted a decision to "suspend" the force of its January circular in the hope that a part of Cossack society "might assist us."[25] Needless to say, the changes had no effect whatever on the methods used in the suppression of the Don uprising, which was drowned in blood in May 1919.

In a bid to turn Cossack hostility around, the Bolsheviks declared their readiness to forgo their favorite class criteria in determining their course of action. They thought up the following formula, underscored in a document, "Theses of the CC of the RKP(b) on Work in the Don," published in September 1919: "The criterion in our relations with the different strata and groups of the Don Cossacks in the period ahead will be not so much a straightforward class evaluation of the various strata (kulaks, middle peasants, the poor) as an evaluation of the relations of the different Cossack groups to our Red Army. We shall provide steadfast patronage and armed protection to those Cossack elements that show, by their deeds, that they will go along with us."[26] The primary purpose of the new policy was to splinter and fragment the Cossack host from within.

In February–March 1920 the 1st All-Russian Congress of Cossack Workers was held in Moscow. Conforming procedurally with all Bolshevik rules—election of delegates in the presence of observers from the CC of the RKP(b), resolutions approved in advance by the CC Politburo—the congress was staged as a mass demonstration of Cossack readiness to cooperate with Soviet power. On the basis of its decisions, the Council of People's Commissars established local organs of power in Cossack oblasts, to which the VTsIK extended "all current general laws of the RSFSR on land division and land use." As a special military stratum, Cossackdom was abolished.

In spite of the various demagogic subterfuges of the authorities, the Cossacks' grievances kept growing. Their surging social and political protest took on new dimensions and new forms of struggle, including armed resistance. In 1920 Cossack territories underwent a top-to-bottom confiscation of property, leaving the peasants stripped to the clothes on their backs, without food or seeds. There was nothing to plant. Moreover, landowners saw no sense in planting, since they had learned from experience that, however much they sowed, they'd be robbed of the harvest, cleaned out, and beaten up for good measure.

By the spring of 1921 the Cossack villages had consumed the last of their food stocks. There was an outbreak of mass famine, which by summer had spread to nearly half the rural population. By the end of 1921, there were 250,000 people starving in the Don territory, and by June of the following year the number exceeded 500,000—this out of a rural population of 1.3 million people. In effect, every second person was starving. But the Kremlin did not regard the Don region as famine-stricken and, consequently, did not exempt it from taxation. Insane from hunger, people resorted to cannibalism.

The famine was man-made, the handiwork of the Bolshevik rulers.

Famine recurred in the early 1930s. The 1932 harvest was removed wholesale from the Don. As was true in other grain-producing areas—the Ukraine, the Volga region, Kuban, the southern Urals—the grain was taken for export. The authorities announced that the country had to have foreign currency to purchase industrial equipment. The Cossack villages were buffeted by one plan after another for delivery of grain. If the grain was not produced on time, the inhabitants of the village in question were declared to be saboteurs and the village was denied the right to buy supplies of salt, sugar, and matches.

Those who didn't die of hunger were finished off by the secret police. As Mikhail Sholokhov was to write, arrests were initiated by anyone who felt like it—chairmen and members of kolkhoz administrations, chairmen of rural soviets, and secretaries of Party cells. Already drained of resources, the villages fell under a reign of violence. Hundreds of thousands of Cossacks were killed, many emigrated, the villages were emptied out, and millions of hectares of land were overgrown with wild grass.

That's how the Russian peasantry was destroyed, that's how peasant Russia was ravaged.

THE INTELLIGENTSIA

TEN YEARS before the October Revolution, Lenin wrote to Gorky: "The role of the intelligentsia in our party is diminishing. The news from all sides is that the intelligentsia are bolting the party. Good riddance to the bastards."[1]

At the time, Lenin being a nobody, his sentiments attracted little notice. Who cared what might addle the pate of some ignoramus somewhere? Russia was experiencing an economic boom; everyone was attending to their own affairs.

But history ordained that Russia, succumbing to the tensions of the First World War, would take a big step toward democracy in February 1917. Who could have predicted that only nine months after this lucid moment a small group of adventurers headed by Lenin would mount a violent counterrevolutionary coup and seize power for a long time to come, to a large extent with the active support of those very "bastards" whom the new ruler of Russia had once epithetized so graciously?

It turned out that the word *bastards* had not been dropped casually as an expression of reflexive intolerance. In September 1919 Lenin wrote to Gorky: "Why these incredibly angry words of yours? Because several dozen (or maybe even hundred) Cadet or quasi-Cadet gentry will spend several days in jail as a safeguard against

conspiracies? Imagine, how awful! What injustice. . . . The intellectual grasp of the workers and peasants is growing and strengthening
in the struggle to overthrow the bourgeoisie and its accomplices,
those smart little intellectuals, the lackeys of capital, who fancy themselves the nation's brains. In point of fact, they are not the brains but
shit."[2] This coarseness tells us something about the new chief's cultural predilections. But the tragedy is that these linguistic gems reflect something far more important. They turned out to be the key to
the entire policy of the Bolshevik regime toward the intelligentsia.

It is often said that the proletarian leader, in taking steps to eliminate illiteracy in Russia, strove to replace the old bourgeois intelligentsia with a new one of workers and peasants. He himself, however, had no patience with such interpretations. In 1921, sitting for a
portrait by the painter Yu. Annenkov, he spoke his mind quite
clearly: "In general, as you probably know, I'm not particularly fond
of the intelligentsia, and our slogan 'Eliminate illiteracy' should by
no means be taken as expressing a wish to give birth to a new intelligentsia. To 'eliminate illiteracy' is necessary only so that every peasant, every worker can read our decrees, orders, and appeals by himself without anyone's help. The goal is purely practical. That's all
there is to it."[3]

The Bolsheviks' first order of business was to launch a merciless
war against freedom of speech, closing down all opposition journals
(decree of the SNK, "On the Press," of 28 October 1917). They set
up censorship offices, initially as the political department of the State
Publishing House (Gosizdat) of the RSFSR, created by a decree of
the VTsIK of 20 May 1919, and later as the Main Directorate for
Literature and Publishing (Glavlit), created by a decree of the SNK of
the RFSFR of 6 June 1922, and the Main Committee for Control of
Repertoires (Glavrepertkom) within the People's Commissariat of
Education, created by a decree of the SNK of the RFSFR of 9 February 1923. These institutions worked in close contact with the secret
police—or, rather, under the joint control and direction of the CC of
the RKP(b) and the VChK-OGPU. They always had agents of the
special services on their staffs.

In just the first three years of its existence, according to incomplete data, the Glavrepertkom closed down or banned thirty-five
plays, including the Moscow Art Theater's production of *The Broth-*

ers Karamazov (the play having been found reactionary, cultivating Christian humility), the Maly Theater's production of Friedrich Schiller's *Maria Stuart* (religious-mystical), the Kamerny and former Aleksandrinsky Theaters' *Salome* (decadent-aesthetic) and *An Ideal Husband* (affirming bourgeois parliamentarianism).[4]

In subsequent years the same fate awaited everything that fell into the clumsy hands of the fear-stricken censor. Many plays were also vetted directly by the KGB, even though many of its agents were part of the censorship apparatus itself. To take the period of World War II as an example, about half the seven hundred plays submitted to the Glavrepertkom were rejected for one reason or another.[5]

Crackdowns on freedom of speech were accompanied by arrests. In the summer of 1918 the poet Aleksandr Blok was picked up on suspicion of involvement in a Left SR plot. Arrests among the so-called Cadet intelligentsia began in August 1919. That month Vladimir Nemirovich-Danchenko and Ivan Moskvin were arrested in the trumped-up case of the CC of the Cadet Party. Fabricated trials were spawned by a conspiracy of the faculty of Petrograd University that never existed, and purges were organized in many other academic institutions and universities.

The end of 1921 saw the famous case of the Petrograd combat organization, also known as the Tagantsev case. After a review in 1992 by the prosecutor's office of the Russian Federation, the "participants" in this organization were rehabilitated. But that was seven decades later, and at the dawn of Soviet power the Chekists, perfecting their methods for the future, let the case proceed full steam ahead, indicting 833 persons.

Vladimir Tagantsev had helped political refugees flee across the border, mainly to Finland. The operation was expensive. In 1919 the price for getting someone across the border with a guide was somewhere around a thousand Finnish marks, and by 1921 it had risen to fifteen thousand. Tagantsev helped people out with money, selling family valuables and personal effects. Quite a few others helped as well, and one day they came to grief. One of Tagantsev's collaborators was killed on the border. Found on him were several pamphlets telling of workers being shot, of how the commissars and Bolsheviks were crucifying Russia.

Tagantsev was arrested. The Chekists set a trap in his apartment, bing everyone who entered. Even an innocent messenger was arrested and later shot; sent by Academician S. Oldenburg, he was delivering a manuscript analyzing Blok's poem "The Twelve" by Tagantsev's father, a well-known Russian lawyer and honorary academician. Placing his trust in the promise made by Dzerzhinsky, Unshlikht, and Yagoda not to resort to executions, Tagantsev disclosed how the money was raised, naming names. The rest was filled in by the investigators.

The Tagantsev case ended up with ninety-seven persons shot, among them the great poet Nikolai Gumilyov. Others figuring in the case included the founder of the Russian school of urology, Fyodorov; the former minister of justice Manukhin; the well-known agronomist Vyrvo; the architect Benois, brother of the famous Russian painter Aleksandr Benois; and the nurse Golenishcheva-Kutuzova. The FSB archive contains letters in defense of the accused. The intercessions included an effort to have Gumilyov released on bond. Alas, the appeal was ignored, but the authors' names were noted. Sooner or later, they were all arrested. Among them was the well-known writer and economist A. Chayanov. Like those whom he had defended, he was shot.

Choking on the blood of the terror, Russia in the 1920s suffered perhaps its greatest loss of intellectual capital. Several hundred of the most prominent representatives of the intelligentsia left the country. Lenin insisted on the need for their exile. Of Stalin he inquired:

> Has it been decided to "root out" all the Populist Socialists? Peshekhonov, Myakotin, Gornfeld? Petrishchev et al.? In my opinion, they should all be exiled. They're more harmful than any SR, because they are craftier. Also A. N. Potresov, Izgoyev and everybody on the *Economist* (Ozerov and many, many others). Me[nshivi]ks Rozanov (a wily enemy) . . . N. A. Rozhkov (must be exiled; he's hopeless); S. A. Frank (author of *Methodology*). The commission overseen by Mantsev, Messing, and others must draw up lists, and several hundred such gentlemen ought to be exiled abroad without mercy. We'll clean up Russia for a long time to come. . . . All of them—throw them out of Russia. This must be done at once. By the end of the SR trial, no later. Arrest several hundred, and without going into motives—off with you, gentlemen![6]

Thus, Lenin took on the shameful function of deciding who would be allowed to stay in Russia and who would not, of driving

them from their own home—and "without going into motives."
Banished across the border were philosophers, writers, lawyers,
artists. Leading lights of Russian culture left the country—Fyodor
Chaliapin, Ivan Bunin, Ilya Repin, Leonid Andreyev, Konstantin
Balmont, Dmitri Merezhkovsky, Korovin, Marc Chagall . . . but
who can count all the names, the roll of Russia's glory?

The pygmies were expelling the giants. Packing them off by ship
by the hundreds. When and where had there been anything like it?

Scholars were accused of refusing to reconcile themselves to Soviet power and of discrediting its initiatives. In the opinion of the un-
educated but highly placed accusers, the philosophers were propagating mysticism and backing the authority of the clergy, the doctors
were promoting anti-Soviet attitudes in their circle, and the agronomists were doing the same in theirs.

On Lenin's instructions, Stalin, Dzerzhinsky, and Semashko were
to "draw up a plan of action" against anti-Sovietism within the intelligentsia.[7] The leader's brothers-in-arms discussed the problem
within the Politburo. Lenin's proposal was accepted on 24 May
1922, and measures to implement it were drawn up in June:

> Minutes (No. 10) of the meeting of the Politburo of 8 June 1922.
> Present: Politburo members, Comrades Kamenev, Stalin, Trotsky,
> Rykov, Zinoviev; candidate members, Comrade Kalinin; CC members,
> Comrades Radek, Sokolnikov; as an observer, Comrade Tsyurupa. . . .
> VIII. On anti-Soviet groupings within the intelligentsia (Unshlikht).
> To accept, with amendments, the following proposal of Comrade
> Unshlikht:
> 1. With the aim of ensuring proper order in the universities, to create
> a commission composed of representatives of the Main Professional
> Educational Administration of the People's Commissariat of Education
> of the RSFSR (Glavprofobr) and the [O]GPU (Yakovlev and Unshlikht)
> and a representative of the Organizational Bureau of the CC, for the
> purpose of drawing up measures to deal with questions on:
> (a) The screening of students for the next semester;
> (b) The imposition of strict limitations on the acceptance of students
> of nonproletarian origin;
> (c) The requirement of attestations of the political reliability of stu-
> dents who are not sent by professional or party organizations and not
> exempted from paying tuition.
> The commission headed by Comrade Unshlikht to meet for one week.

2. The same commission (see paragraph 1) to draw up rules for the meetings and associations of the student body and faculty.

[a] To instruct the Political Department of Gosizdat to carry out, together with the GPU, a thorough examination of all publications put out by private societies, the specialist sections of trade unions, and the various people's commissariats (People's Commissariat of Land Cultivation, People's Commissariat of Education, etc.). . . .

(b) To accept as a basis paragraphs 3 and 4 of the draft order (see appendix), with the following amendments: in paragraph 3, substituting "NKVD" for "GPU"; at the end of that paragraph substituting the sentence "Local congresses and conferences of specialists to be authorized by provincial executive political committees, with preliminary inquiry as to the conclusions of the local organs of the GPU (provincial offices)."

For the final formulation of paragraphs 3 and 4 and for working out means of implementation through appropriate legislation, to set up a commission composed of Comrades Kursky, Dzerzhinsky, and Yenukidze. The commission to be called into session by Comrade Yenukidze. Length of session: one week.

(c) Paragraph 5 to be submitted to the same commission, with the mandatory involvement of Tomsky or Rudzutak.

(d) To instruct the VTsIK to issue a decree on convening a special conference of representatives of the People's Commissariat of Foreign Affairs and the People's Commissariat of Justice empowered, in those cases where more severe forms of punishment can be avoided, to substitute exile abroad or to certain areas of the RSFSR.

(e) To create a commission composed of Comrades Unshlikht, Kursky, and Kamenev for a final review of the list of heads of hostile factions of the intelligentsia subject to exile.

(f) The question of closing down publications and newspapers that do not reflect the direction of Soviet policy (the journal of the Pirogov society and so on) to be placed before the same commission (see paragraph e).

(g) Paragraph 8 of the draft decree to be rejected.

IX. On the directive on the All-Russian Congress of Doctors (Unshlikht).

(A) General measures called for by the doctors' congress to be postponed until the end of the SR trial.

(B) The question of the arrest of a certain number of doctors, which must be carried out immediately, to be placed before the commission of Comrades Unshlikht, Kursky, and Kamenev (see paragraph VIIIe [VIII2e]).

(C) The GPU to be instructed to carry out the closest surveillance of the conduct of the doctors and other intelligentsia factions during the SR trial, and not to permit any demonstrations, speeches, etc.

Appendix to paragraph VIIIb [VIII2b] of the minutes of the Politburo, No. 10, of 8 June 1922.

Proposals of Comrade Unshlikht presented to the commission. . . .

3. To establish that no congress or All-Russian conference of specialists (doctors, agronomists, engineers, lawyers, and others) may be convened without the appropriate authorization of the NKVD. Local congresses or conferences of specialists shall be authorized by the NKVD. Local congresses or conferences of specialists shall be authorized by the provincial executive committees, with preliminary inquiry as to the decision of the local organs of the GPU (provincial offices).

4. To assign the GPU to carry out as of 10 June, through the apparatus of the People's Commissariat of Internal Affairs, a reregistration of all societies and associations (scientific, religious, academic, and others), and not to permit the creation of new societies or unions without appropriate registration with the GPU. All unregistered societies and unions to be declared illegal and subject to immediate disbandment.

5. To instruct the All-Union Central Council of Trade Unions (VTsSPS) not to permit the formation and functioning of unions of specialists other than as general professional associations and to have the existing sections of specialists within trade unions registered and placed under special surveillance. The statutes of the specialists' sections must be reviewed with the assistance of the GPU. Permission for creating specialist sections within professional associations may be granted by the VTsSPS only with the concurrence of the GPU.[8]

On 18 August 1922 the OGPU leadership, under whose watchful eye the draconian decision of the Politburo was being applied, sent Lenin a list of those being exiled from Moscow, St. Petersburg, and the Ukraine, noting that the Muscovites had been informed of the decree on their exile abroad and had been warned that if they returned without permission they would be shot.

The Moscow list contained sixty-seven names, grouped by different educational institutions. The subheadings read, "Professors of Moscow University," "Professors of the Moscow Higher Technical Institute," "Professors of the Institute of Transportation," and so on. The list included the names of "anti-Soviet" writers, engineers, and agronomists.

The Petrograd list contained fifty-one names.

The first departures were from Moscow. Then the expulsions shifted to Odessa and the Crimea. The ships employed were sometimes known as "philosophic," from the number of philosophers among their "passengers," like Nikolai Berdyayev, Semyon Frank, Fyodor Stepun, Nikolai Lossky, Ivan Ilyin. The first three were exiled for having published, in Moscow, a collection of essays, *Oswald Spengler and the Decline of Europe,* in which they contested the idea of the inevitability of socialism. Lenin regarded the work as a "literary smokescreen for a White Guard organization."

Among others pushed across the border was the rector of Moscow University, the biologist M. Novikov. A severe loss was suffered in the field of history: the Bolsheviks expelled A. Kizevetter, A. Florovsky, Yu. Melgunov, and others. One of the ships took with it the famous sociologist Pitirim Sorokin.

Lenin was ridding himself of those who were more intelligent, more talented, and better educated than he.

Exile as a way of dispatching those who didn't suit him appeared to go over well with its originator. So it would seem from a note that Dzerzhinsky, right after a meeting with Lenin, left for his deputy, Unshlikht, instructing him to proceed unswervingly with the exiling abroad of the active portion of the intelligentsia, starting with the Mensheviks. Reports on the expulsions were to be collected in a "section on the intelligentsia." A separate case was to be opened for every member of the intelligentsia. Those who were exiled had to guarantee that they would never return to their homeland. The philosopher Ivan Ilyin, who was accused of not having reconciled himself to the rule of the workers and peasants in power in Russia, wrote the following statement: "As submitted herewith by me, citizen Ivan Aleksandrovich Ilyin, to the State Political Administration, I commit myself not to return to the territory of the RSFSR without permission of the Soviet authorities. (I have been apprised of article 71 of the Criminal Code of the RSFSR, providing for the death penalty for returning without permission to within the borders of the RSFSR.)"9

In the second half of the 1920s, a heavy blow fell on the intellectual elite of the old engineering and technical establishment. A large group of engineers and technicians were arrested in 1928 in the course of the notorious Shakhty case. Scholars of the first rank were persecuted in the so-called academic affair, which involved 115 persons, including S. Platonov, E. Tarle, N. Likhachev, A. Presnyakov, S. Rozhdestvensky, M. Lyubavsky, and Yu. Gotiye. They faced the standard charge of suspicious ties with émigré representatives and foreign public figures. Many of them died in camps and exile.

The many priceless manuscripts by prominent Russian intellectuals that have accumulated in the archives of the KGB would be the envy of any museum or collection in the world. The task of getting them released has turned out to be far from easy. I know from experience, having received a request a few years ago from the Commission on Literary Heritage of the Writers Union of the USSR, which appealed for help in locating and making public manuscripts of arrested writers like Babel, Artem Vesyoly, Pilnyak, Koltsov, and Chayanov. I addressed myself to the Chief Prosecutor's Office. The chief prosecutor of the USSR informed me that, according to available documents, Mikhail Koltsov's correspondence with Ilya Ehrenburg and other material confiscated at the time of Koltsov's arrest were sent in January 1965 to the Gorky Institute of World Literature for permanent safekeeping. As for the personal notes, manuscripts, and letters left by Babel, Pilnyak, Vesyoly, Chayanov, and other writers and scholars, determining what happened to them did not appear feasible. As it turned out, the chief prosecutor had far from full information as to what was being preserved by the KGB. Or else he, too, was lying. Later many of the manuscripts were found.

With the end of the civil war, the country's scientific and cultural leaders began to find their freedom to correspond and travel restricted. Rules were laid down for trips abroad, with permission granted only with the approval of the VChK-OGPU and the Politburo of the CC of the RKP(b). We know, for example, of the Politburo's decision of 12 July 1921 to reject an appeal by Lunacharsky and Gorky that the poet Aleksandr Blok be permitted to leave for Finland for medical treatment. Twice, too, the Politburo rejected a request by the First Studio of the Moscow Art Theater for permission for a foreign tour. In advocating the tour, the people's commissar for education, Lunacharsky, had an answer to Dzerzhinsky's objection that he was abetting the flight of Soviet Russia's artistic talent. Lunacharsky proposed that all artists wishing to go abroad be made to wait their turn and be permitted to leave only in numbers equal to those who had returned from earlier trips. "That way we will, in effect, establish a system of collective responsibility."[10] But even this rather shameless proposal was rejected.

By the end of the 1920s, all intellectual life had come under a system of total, all-encompassing control put in place by the VChK-OGPU. The central mechanism was divided into subsections responsible for various phases of the work—the Political Control Department for censorship by officials of Glavlit and Glavrepertkom and of letters and telegrams; the Fourth and Fifth Sections of the Secret-Political Department for agent surveillance and information gathering and for a network of informers in artistic and scientific circles. Special bureaus were set up for administrative exiling of "anti-Soviet intelligentsia."

The work of these subdivisions of the political police was astonishing in its comprehensiveness. On 4 September 1922, the head of the Political Control Department, V. Zhtingof, reported to the deputy head of the Secret Operational Administration of the OGPU, G. Yagoda, that during the month of August the department's staff had opened and examined 135,000 of 300,000 letters mailed to the RSFSR. All 285,000 letters sent abroad had also been censored.[11]

The department's employees themselves wrote reviews of literary works and were empowered to reject decisions of Glavlit and Glavrepertkom. It was on their initiative, for instance, that the OGPU ordered the confiscation of a book of short stories by Pilnyak, *Fatal Attraction,* approved by Glavlit. It was standard practice for the Chekists to attend theatrical performances, variety shows, and other public spectacles and to submit special reports on what struck them as suspicious; the "guilty" were then subjected to administrative and judicial sanctions. One such gumshoe, S. Blits, attending a circus performance by V. Durov on 10 April 1924, detected in the "animal number, with guinea pigs cast as agitators," an abundance of counterrevolutionary jokes. This "cultural expert" drew up a report on the need to ban Durov's act.

The Fourth Section of the Secret-Political Department of the OGPU established a broad network of informers in the artistic world who reported on literally every even vaguely known writer, performer, musician, painter, and film director. Vsevolod Ivanov's son,

Vyacheslav, wrote about the practice: "During those years, when members of the government wanted to get closer to young writers, Dzerzhinsky, at one of their get-togethers, told my father how much he liked his work. He promised to demonstrate this to my father in the very near future. A few days later a messenger delivered a package with a note explaining that Dzerzhinsky was fulfilling his promise and sending over all the denunciations of my father received during the previous year. One day at Gorky's home, Agranov said to my father: 'If you only knew what kind of people work for us!'"

Many of the informers were close friends of their professional coworkers, themselves writing novels, staging plays, shooting films, and painting canvases, and at the same time reporting "upstairs," regularly and efficiently, on what their friends were doing and saying. Although the poets read their work only to a small circle of friends, Osip Mandelstam's verse about Stalin, "We live, deaf to the land beneath us," and N. Kliuyev's unpublished poem "The Song of Gamayun" became instantly known to the Chekists.

During the 1st All-Union Congress of Writers in August 1934, a sheet addressed to the foreign guests was distributed among those present. It read:

> Everything you will hear and see at the All-Union Congress of Writers will be the reflection of a gargantuan lie presented to you as truth. It is entirely possible that many of us who took part in writing this letter or who fully approved of it will speak quite differently at the congress or even in private conversations with you. To understand why, you must . . . realize that for seventeen years now the country has been in a state in which any possibility of free speech is completely out of the question.
>
> We Russian writers can be compared to prostitutes in a brothel, the only difference being that they sell their bodies and we our souls; just as they have no way out of the brothel except through death by starvation, so it is with us. In addition, our families and those close to us answer for our behavior.
>
> Even at home we often avoid speaking our minds, because of the system of collective denunciations in force in the USSR. We must promise to denounce one another, and we denounce our friends, our relatives, our acquaintances. . . . Of course, those in power no longer believe in the sincerity of our denunciations, just as they do not believe us when we speak in public extolling the "brilliant achievements" of the author-

ities. Yet they demand this lie of us, since they need it as a kind of "export" for your consumption in the West. Have you at least finally understood, for example, the nature of the so-called trials of saboteurs, complete with the defendants' full confessions of their crimes? Because this, too, was part of "our export industry" for your consumption.[12]

In the course of the congress, the organs of the OGPU-NKVD, with their network of agents, kept the top leadership regularly informed (every other day) of the writers' plans and attitudes. They saw to it that every delegation at the congress had its quota of "creative officials" in secret collaboration with them.

The OGPU-NKVD paid particular attention to poets. Prior to the congress the poets Ya. Ovcharenko (I. Pribludny), Tsvelev, and Asanov were banished from the capital for "counterrevolutionary attitudes." At the beginning of the year N. Kliuyev and L. Pulin were arrested on a charge of having written anti-Soviet verses. (The OGPU Collegium sent both to Siberia, from which they never returned; N. Kliuyev was sentenced to death on 13 October 1938 by a troika of the Tomsk office of the NKVD in the case of the mythical Union for the Salvation of Russia.)

Osip Mandelstam was imprisoned for his mercilessly accurate verse on Stalin. The poet's subsequent fate was infinitely tragic. According to a letter of the general secretary of the Soviet Writers Union, V. Stavsky, he was arrested a second time and was sent on 2 August 1938 to a concentration camp, where he died. Here is the verse:

> We live, deaf to the land beneath us,
> Ten steps away no one hears our speeches.
> But where there's so much as half a conversation
> The Kremlin's mountaineer will get his mention.
>
> .   .   .   .
>
> Around him a rabble of thin-necked leaders,
> Fawning half-men for him to play with.
> They whinny, purr or whine,
> As he prates and points a finger.[13]

Just as they did during the writers congress, the secret police kept abreast of all undertakings on the part of the artistic and scientific elite. More than that, the OGPU-NKVD would at times fill in as the initiator of anti-Soviet works. Through its agents provocateurs it would induce "politically unreliable" writers to write "something lively" and then would have them arrested. For example, in the notorious 1923 case of the "anti-Semitic remarks" by a group of poets about Trotsky and Kamenev, a secret agent of the OGPU practically ordered an anti-Bolshevik composition from the poet A. Ganin, a friend of S. Esenin and his partner in the affair. Upon receipt of the poem, the OGPU fabricated the charge that the author had banded together some representatives of the intelligentsia in a counterrevolutionary terrorist organization, the "Order of Russian Fascists." Arrested and shot in March 1925 were A. Ganin, G. Nikitin, the brothers P. and N. Chekrygin, and V. Galanov.

Sad to say, the unions that were set up within the creative intelligentsia after the well-known decree of the CC of the VKP(b) of 23 April 1932, "On the Restructuring of Literary-Artistic Organizations," became, to all intents and purposes, branches of the secret police. This was particularly true of the Writers Union, many of whose leading functionaries were paid to collaborate with the OGPU-NKVD and not a few of whom were staff members of the special services.

At the apex of the power pyramid, where the information from the secret police and union heads all flowed, were the Politburo and the Party Secretariat. These closed organizations, with their tightly restricted membership, were even then outside the law; "the laws of the Constitution are not applicable to the CC," as Lunacharsky would later write in an unpublished letter to Lenin in regard to a Politburo decree closing down the Bolshoi Theater in January 1932.[14]

Basing itself on the special services, the top Party leadership gradually began to present itself not simply as the arbiter between the creative intelligentsia and the punitive agencies. It proclaimed itself the foremost expert in artistic creativity, the foremost mentor of writers, theater people, composers, and painters, trying in effect to reduce them to abject servitude to the authorities.

In coordination with the special services, the Politburo, Orgburo, and CC Secretariat put out up to one hundred "prohibitive-directive" decrees on literature and art. The disgraceful roster included decrees on the production of plays by Mikhail Bulgakov (*The Days of the Turbins, Zoika's Flat, Crimson Island, Flight*), M. Levidov (*Conspiracy of Equals*), L. Slavin (*Intervention*), Demian Bedny

(*Bogatyr*), I. Selvinsky (*Umka: The White Bear*), Leonid Leonov (*The Snowstorm*), A. Glebov (*Frankly Speaking*), M. Kozakov (*When I'm Alone*), and Valentin Katayev (*Little House*); on the elimination of the Second Studio of the Moscow Art Theater and of the Meyerhold Theater; on the banning and confiscation of works by Boris Pilnyak, I. Selvinsky, Anna Akhmatova, Mikhail Zoshchenko, and Vera Kozhevnikova; on the motion pictures *Bezhin Meadow* (director, Sergei Eisenstein), *Admiral Nakhimov* (director, V. Pudovkin), and *The Great Life* (director, L. Lukov); on the journals *Oktyabr*, *Teatr*, *Zvezda* (Star), *Leningrad*, and *Znamya* (Banner); on V. Muradeli's opera *The Great Friendship*; and on the banning of Hebrew-language anthologies.

For years on end, having taken on judicial functions, the top Party leadership and the heads of the punitive services disposed of questions of life or death for literary and artistic professionals. As archival documents reveal, the organs of the OGPU-NKVD-KGB, in their reports to Stalin on their investigations, proposed not only the scenarios of the show trials ahead but the sentences at the end. As a rule, Stalin and his underlings agreed. Sometimes, though very rarely, the boss himself would intervene in the fate of a scientific or cultural figure, on calculations known only to himself. For example, when the NKVD-KGB sent him compromising information on the poet L. Seifulina, wife of the writer and "enemy of the people" V. Pravdukhin, and on the at-large members of the pro-Trotsky literary group Pereval (Crossing)—M. Golodny, M. Svetlov, I. Utkin, D. Bedny, I. Ehrenburg, and A. Platonov—he turned down the recommendation that they be arrested. At the same time, it was he who provided the impetus for the elimination of hundreds of other prominent writers, artists, painters, filmmakers, and musicians.

In 1927 the poet Ya. Ovcharenko was exiled on a charge of promoting anti-Soviet propaganda—he had written the verse "Communist, cock your gun." In December 1928 the well-known philologist A. Boldyryov and the future eminent literary scholar M. Bakhtin were arrested in Leningrad for taking part in the study group of Professors A. Meier and K. Polovtsev, which met to discuss questions of a religious nature. (At the intercession of N. Semashko and Gorky's first wife, E. Peshkova, Bakhtin's sentence was commuted in 1930 from time in a concentration camp to exile in Kazakhstan.)

At the beginning of 1929, two other members of the Pereval literary group, M. Mirov and I. Maleyev, were sentenced by the OGPU Collegium to exile in the northern Dvinsk region and in the Urals; both would later be rearrested and would perish. The group's doyen, A. Voronsky, former editor of the journal *Krasnaya Nov* (Red Virgin Soil) and the man who had given B. Pilnyak the idea for his *Tale of the Constant Moon*, was expelled from the Party, arrested, and sentenced to five years in solitary confinement as a particularly dangerous political prisoner. At about that time the future writer V. Shalamov, then a student at Moscow University, was put in a concentration camp in the northern Urals on charges of belonging to the Trotskyist opposition; he was to spend more than seventeen years, all told, in prisons, camps, and exile.

From the beginning of the 1930s the scale of the arrests steadily expanded. In Leningrad the OGPU fabricated a case against the Oberiuty, a widely known group of writers of children's books who were followers of V. Khlebnikov, among them the poet and prose writer D. Kharms (Yuvachev), the poet A. Vvedensky, the poet and linguistic scholar A. Tufanov, the set designer E. Safonov, and the young writer I. Andronikov. Most of them were arrested on charges of anti-Soviet propaganda and were sentenced in March 1932 to prison terms.

No sooner was the OGPU done in Leningrad than a new denunciation reached its chairman's desk, this time of a group of Moscow writers, the so-called Siberians. The members of this group, N. Anov (Ivanov), E. Zabelin (L. Savkin), L. Martynov, S. Markov, L. Chernomortsev, and P. Vasiliev, were accused of criticizing Bolshevik policy on collectivization, falling for the work of White Guard poets, and dedicating their verses to Admiral Kolchak. In June 1932 these young poets and prose writers were exiled.

In the summer of 1933 the new OGPU chairman, G. Yagoda, presented to Stalin unpublished political fables by the playwrights N. Erdman and V. Mass ridiculing the censorship and cultural policies of the powers that be. At the boss's personal orders, these satirists, who had just finished the script of the motion picture *Merry Fellows*, were arrested and exiled to Yeniseisk and Tobolsk. Almost simultaneously, the OGPU Collegium visited the same punishment on the satirists M. Volpin and E. German (Emil Krotky), staff members of the magazine *Krokodil* whose only crime had been to read some of their colleagues' risky fables to acquaintances and relatives.

The Great Terror saw the elimination of many Poles living in the USSR, among them the writers B. Jasienski and G. Domski (both shot), the poet S. Stande (shot), the conductor and composer B. Przybyszewski (shot), the actress E. Szymkiewicz (shot), and the writer H. Bobinska (eight years in a hard-labor concentration camp).

At the beginning of 1935, on their own initiative, members of the Moscow Union of Artists (MOSKh) set about organizing a discussion of N. Mikhailov's "counterrevolutionary" painting of Sergei Kirov's murder. As the head of the CC's Department of Culture and Propaganda, A. Stetsky, was to report to the Politburo, the MOSKh administration demanded unanimously that appropriate measures be taken. "In view of the facts that have come to light in the Mikhailov case," Stetsky wrote in a memorandum, "I consider it necessary to have him arrested and his home thoroughly searched. I request that relevant instructions be given to the NKVD." To this memorandum Stalin, Molotov, and Voroshilov appended the words "Arrest approved."[15]

Another denunciation followed three months later. Thirteen eminent poets called on the Presidium of the Administration of the Soviet Writers Union to "take more effective steps to uproot the 'Vasilievism' present in our literary life." Their letter deserves to be quoted in full; it is a vivid example of how writers and poets devoured their own:

> For the past three years, there has hardly been a single episode of immorally bohemian or politically reactionary statements or misconduct in the literary life of Moscow that was not linked to the name of the poet Pavel Vasiliev.
>
> Unhindered and with impunity, relying on some strange support of unknown origin, this person does everything he can to discredit by his behavior the calling of a Soviet writer.
>
> Attempts by the Soviet writers' community both to reeducate and to punish him have had no effect. As his conduct reveals clearly enough, Pavel Vasiliev has ignored A. M. Gorky's stern warning in the article "Literary Follies," as well as many other warnings in the Soviet press and even his own expulsion from the union for hooliganism.
>
> These facts, and in particular the riot he caused in the House of Writ-

ers on Moscow Art Theater Street and his candidly reactionary and blatantly counterrevolutionary remarks, go to show that he has crossed the line between hooliganism and fascism. The whole pattern of his behavior attests to this eloquently enough.

To all this it should be added that through his cynically rowdy behavior and impunity Vasiliev is promoting the growth of reactionary and hooligan bohemian attitudes on the part of a certain type of young writer. More than that, Vasiliev has surrounded himself with a certain kind of "literary youth," exponents of the worst sort of bohemianism. Moreover, in talking to young people, he keeps flaunting his impunity and his disorderly conduct, trying to influence the character development of these young writers.

The incidents involving Yaroslav Smelyakov, Lavrov, Sukharev, and others make it clear that these attempts on Vasiliev's part have not been unsuccessful.

All the above confirms, first, that Vasiliev's reactionary writings are organically integrated with his public behavior and, second, that the problem of Pavel Vasiliev is not a "personal" one but a symptom of something larger and, for that reason, more harmful and dangerous.

In addition, Pavel Vasiliev's name has come to stand for the appearance and flowering in our literary life of various "salons" and "smart sets" churning out unrecognized geniuses and anointing them with artificial "reputations."

The above facts oblige us forcefully to place before the Presidium of the Administration the question of whether it is not time to take more effective steps to uproot this "Vasilievism" from our literary life. We consider that this can be done only by taking decisive and stern measures against Vasiliev himself, demonstrating thereby that for anyone and everyone within the framework of Soviet reality the display of flagrant hooliganism with a specifically anti-Soviet edge cannot go unpunished.

[Signed] Aleksei Surkov, Mikhail Golodny, Dzhek Altauzen, Mikhail Svetlov, Vera Inber, Bela Illesh, Nikolai Aseyev, Semyon Kirsanov, Boris Aganov, Aleksandr Zharov, Iosif Utkin, Vladimir Lugovskoi, Aleksandr Bezymensky[16]

This letter, we now know, was instigated by A. Shcherbakov, secretary of the Writers Union, who was to become secretary of the CC of the CPSU. What surprises me is not that someone panting with ambition beat the bushes for the necessary signatures. What is far more important is that the writers, artists, and composers themselves helped create an atmosphere of denunciation and persecution. To

our great shame, this tradition took root in our creative intelligentsia; it lived and flourished for a long time. The denunciation was
sent to the secretaries of the CC, Stalin, Andreyev, and Yezhov.
Shcherbakov sent along a cover letter with his political conclusions:

> I deem it necessary to send you a copy of a statement by thirteen po-
> ets submitted to the Presidium of the Administration of the Soviet Writ-
> ers Union of the USSR, and to comment on it as follows.
>
> In the summer of 1934, in an article entitled "Literary Follies," A. M.
> Gorky sternly condemned the hooliganlike behavior of the poet Pavel
> Vasiliev. In response to the article, P. Vasiliev published a letter of re-
> pentance, promising publicly to reform.
>
> A few months later P. Vasiliev created an uproar, with anti-Soviet and
> anti-Semitic overtones, in the House of Soviet Writers. For this offense
> P. Vasiliev was expelled from the Soviet Writers Union.
>
> Most recently, when the Writers Union offered him support, to help
> him reestablish himself as a writer, P. Vasiliev again indulged in abra-
> sive, antisocial behavior.
>
> Breaking into the poet Altauzen's apartment, he picked a fight,
> shouted anti-Soviet epithets, and so on.
>
> The main thing, however, is that he boasts before other writers, espe-
> cially the young: "You've seen that nothing's going to happen to me.
> You dumbbells, if you want to be noticed, do as I do."
>
> Staff members of the NKVD with whom I've talked declare, "It is
> time to take steps in regard to P. Vasiliev, but that can be done only on
> instructions from the CC."
>
> For my part, I believe that for his latest offense P. Vasiliev should be
> either tried or expelled from Moscow. What makes this even more nec-
> essary now is that in the last few months the poets Asanov, Tsvelev, and
> Pribludny and the writer Pestukhin have returned from exile, and they
> are part of P. Vasiliev's circle.
>
> Incidentally, may I be allowed to express the opinion that it serves no
> purpose for the NKVD to give these people Moscow residence permits.
> It would be more advisable to have them spend still more time in the
> provinces.[17]

Vasiliev's colleagues, as we have seen, asked only that he be excluded from their public and literary life. On 24 May 1935, on
Stalin's orders, their letter was published in *Pravda*. As always, the
minions of the NKVD reacted efficiently: in June, Vasiliev and his
friend the poet Yaroslav Smelyakov were arrested and sentenced to
three years in a concentration camp. (In February 1937, right after

his release, Vasiliev was to be rearrested, and in June of that year he was shot together with a group of writers of the so-called peasant school.)

In 1936 there was a sharp increase in the number of arrests among the creative intelligentsia. The KGB that year "exposed an anti-Soviet group" of writers, leading to the arrest of the poets N. Postupalsky, P. Karaban (Shleiman), and V. Narbut and the writers I. Filipchenko (shot), N. Gagen-Torn (exiled), N. Mamin (seven years in a hard-labor camp), A. Morgulis (five years in a hard-labor camp; perished in one of them in the Northeast), and M. Karpov (shot), as well as the screenwriter M. Maizel (shot), the literary scholar Yu. Osman (five years in a hard-labor camp), Bolshoi Theater orchestra members A. Gerasimov and G. Adamov (both shot), and many, many others.

The final months of A. M. Gorky's life were spent under the personal supervision of the head of the OGPU-NKVD, Yagoda. Even Gorky's newspapers were examined before being delivered. There were times when a single copy of *Pravda* was printed specially for the dean of Soviet writers, with the appropriate additions, excisions, and falsifications. The atmosphere of secrecy built up around the expiring Gorky raises serious questions about the mysterious circumstances of his death. Was illness alone the cause, or was a helping hand given by those in charge?

During 1937 and 1938, the years of the Great Terror, the scale of the arrests reached unprecedented proportions. It was then that the NKVD, on orders from above, "uncovered dozens of carefully concealed anti-Soviet organizations," composed largely of persons of "unreliable" behavior or with a "dubious" past, from the official point of view. Hundreds more writers, playwrights, moviemakers, and actors paid with their lives or with a shattered future for allegedly belonging to nonexistent organizations of one sort or another.

Thus, the former members of the Pereval literary group I. Katayev, B. Guber, N. Zarudin, Artem Vesyoly (N. Kochkurov), and A. Lezhnev-Gorelik were arrested on charges of belonging to the so-called Trotskyist terrorist literary organization headed by A. K. Voronsky. All of them were shot; Voronsky shared their fate in 1937.

A number of writers of the "peasant school," including I. Makarov, I. Vasiliev, A. Oreshin, V. Kirillov, M. Gerasimov, and S. Klychkov (Leshenkov), all friends and colleagues of the late poet Sergei Esenin, were sentenced to death for belonging to an anti-Soviet literary group in sympathy with opponents of collectivization—the "Labor Peasant Party" that had been "unmasked" at the end of the 1920s. The writers V. Zazubrin (Zubtsov), V. Pravdukhin, V. Nasedkin, and E. Permitin, all Siberians by birth, were accused of holding Trotskyist views and trying to achieve autonomy for Siberia; the first three were sentenced to death and the fourth to exile.

The former directors of the Russian Association of Proletarian Writers (RAPP) and of the literary section of the Communist Academy L. Averbakh, V. Kirshon, I. Makariev, S. Dinamov, V. Kirpotin, M. Chumandrin, A. Selivanovsky, D. Maznin, R. Pikel, and others, all formerly "faithful soldiers of the Party," were accused of organizing terrorist acts against Party and government leaders.

Yet another "Trotskyist terrorist organization" was "exposed" among writers in Leningrad. Arrested as members and sentenced to death or to prison sentences were the poets B. Kornilov, P. Kalitin, B. Livshits, S. Dagayev, N. Zabolotsky, and O. Bergolz; the writers and translators V. Stenich (Smetanich), I. Likhachev, Yu. Yurkin, G. Kuklin, Yu. Berzin, E. Tager, P. Guber, and S. Spassky; the literary critics D. Vygodsky and P. Medvedev; and many others.

In Irkutsk, in the wake of the notorious decisions reached at the February–March 1937 plenum of the CC of the VKP(b) on the struggle against Trotskyist and other doubledealers and saboteurs, the local branch of the Writers Union went on a bout of "self-criticism" in the course of which the writers A. Balin, I. Goldberg, P. Petrov, M. Basov, and others were expelled from the union and then arrested. This left only two members in the organization's oblast branch, both of whom were collaborating with the NKVD's local office.

The same tragic picture was true in other parts of the country. Thus, in Buryatia the arrests carried off the writers P. Dambinov and Ts. Don; in Tataria the writer G. Ibragimov and the playwright K. Tinchurin; in Bashkiria the writers A. Amantai, D. Yulty (Yultyev), S. Galimov, G. Davleteshin, and A. Tagirov; in Udmurtia the writers D. Korepanov-Kedra (Mitrei Kedra) and M. Konovalov; in the Mari Republic the writers I. Olyk, I. Chaivan, and M. Shketan (M. Maiorov) and the poet and actor Krylia; in Karelia the writer Ya. Virtanen; in Komi the founder of the republic's theatrical life, the poet and prose writer V. Savin; and in Yakutia the founders of Yakut literature P. A. Oiyunsky (P. Sleptsov) and A. Safronov and the writer G. Baishev (Altan Saryn).

In the fall of 1937 the artistic directors of two leading film studios, D. Sokolovskaya (Mosfilm) and A. Piotrovsky (Lenfilm), were arrested and sentenced to be shot. The editorial office of the newspaper *Kino* was sacked and its editor in chief, the film scholar G. Vovsi, perished. The secretary of the organizational bureau of the CC of the Union of Film Workers, K. Blum (Ozolin), was shot. In January 1938 the head of the Main Directorate for Cinematography within the SNK of the USSR, B. Shumyatsky, who had once shared exile with Stalin in Narym, was arrested together with his deputy, V. Usievich, and other top-level colleagues on charges of trying to organize a terrorist act against members of the Politburo in the Kremlin's screening room. All these charges were absolutely baseless.

There was probably no theatrical company in the whole country that did not suffer tragic losses. The arrests swept up the head and artistic director of the Central Children's Theater, N. Sats (sentenced to five years), and the directors and theater staff members A. Dikii, K. Eggert, I. Pravov, A. Nesterov, Z. Smirnova, M. Rafalsky, and I. Baranov. Also "exposed" was a counterrevolutionary group in the Yermolova Theater in Moscow. Its "accomplices," the actors G. Baumshtein (Bakhtarova), E. Bonfeld (Kravinsky), N. Losev, M. Unkovsky, B. Evert, N. Shernysheva, V. Radunskaya, and others, were sentenced to imprisonment. In the Moscow music-hall and circus case, fifty-seven persons were arrested and eight of them were shot.

The mass arrests virtually put an end to the Polish and Latvian state theaters established in Moscow after the revolution. The Latvian company was destroyed practically in toto: both its directors, K. Krumin and V. Forteman, and its principal actors, V. Baltgalova, Z. Boksberg, N. Zubova, A. Krumin, M. Leiko, M. Kalnina, A. Oshe, and E. Feldman, were shot in February 1938.

At the Bolshoi Theater, always the object of particular attention by the highest Party and government leaders—at one time the Politburo even had a special commission for controlling and observing its work—the opera star M. Mikhailova, the pianist L. Aptekareva, the stage manager M. Dirsky, the set designer K. Meikul, and others were arrested and sentenced to death.

With the implementation of the Politburo decision of 2 July 1937 on the arrest of "socially dangerous" elements, and of N. Yezhov's orders on the elimination of former German citizens, former employees of the Chinese Eastern Railway and repatriates from Manchukuo declared to be spies and saboteurs, as well as former kulaks, members of anti-Soviet parties, and persons who had undergone arrest in the past, the executioner's bullet took the lives of the writers P. Dorokhov and K. Shmyukle; the administrator of the Nemirovich-Danchenko Musical Theater, I. Aranovich-Arditi; the Moscow Philharmonia pianist A. Milikovskaya; the members of the Moscow Artists Union Ts. Gustav and F. Konnov; the "nonunion" painters A. Drevin, A. Berzin, and V. Lipgart; the Academy publishing house artist N. Dmitrikovsky; the painter and writer S. Broide; the film actor T. Kan; the architect O. Vutke; the director of the Moscow Soviet's architectural department, A. Pogosia; and the professor of church choral music M. Khitrovo-Kramskoy, a grandson of Field Marshal Kutuzov and a relative of Tukhachevsky.

Representatives of the cultural elite were arrested not only for participating in mythical conspiratorial groups. To be sentenced, it was enough to belong to the family of a "traitor to the motherland." Arrested as members of such families and sentenced to lengthy terms of imprisonment or exile were the writers G. Serebryakova and S. Vinogradskaya, wife of the Party worker S. Shor, who had been sentenced in the case of the "Trotskyist terrorist youth center"; the actresses O. Shcherbinovskaya and K. Andronikashvili, the first and second wives of B. Pilnyak; and the soloist of the Nemirovich-Danchenko Musical Theater S. Golemba.

After 1938, especially in the postwar period, the "disobedient" were punished more often by moral pressure and administrative whim, such as a ban on the publication of new works or the reissuing of old ones, restrictions on trips abroad, including tours, and various means of public censure—campaigns of denunciation in the press, campaigns of criticism against the miscreant by his peers in the union, and so on. Of doleful memory are the ideological campaigns of 1940 (the strictures against the writers, playwrights, and poets A. Avdeyenko, Leonid Leonov, A. Glebov, Valentin Katayev, M. Kozakova, Anna Akhmatova, and others), 1943 (A. Dovzhenko, N. Aseyeva, Mikhail Zoshchenko, I. Selvinsky), and 1946 (again Zoshchenko and Akhmatova). In 1948–49 there was the campaign against "cosmopolitanism," as well as the closing down of the Kamerny Theater.

These changes, however, did not herald a new policy. Arrests and executions continued. They acted as a reminder for those still at liberty of the ever-present possibility of their sharing the same fate. Thus, in January 1940 the writer Isaac Babel was shot on a charge of espionage and membership in a terrorist organization. Also shot was the well-known literary critic D. Mirsky (Svyatopolk-Mirsky), a former émigré who had returned to the USSR in 1932. In July 1939 the arrests netted the newly appointed director of the Moscow Art Theater, Ya. Boyarsky (Shimshelevich).

In 1940 and the first half of 1941, denunciations by informers led to a sentence of death for the writer A. Novikov, a close friend of A. Platonov, and the dragnet caught up with the Leningrad writers S. Gekhta and Ya. Larri and with I. Luppola, the director of the A. M. Gorky Institute of World Literature and a member of the Academy of Sciences of the USSR. In August 1941 Luppola was sentenced to twenty years in concentration camps; he died in custody. In 1943 the outstanding geneticist Nikolai Ivanovich Vavilov died in prison.

Control over intellectual creativity was total and incessant. In 1943, for instance, the film documentaries *Pobeda* (Victory) and *Ukraina v Ognye* (Ukraine in Flames) were found to be "harmful," inasmuch as their creator, A. Dovzhenko, had dared to criticize certain aspects of collectivization and national policy.[18] On Stalin's orders, Dovzhenko came under humiliating criticism at the plenum of the Moscow City Committee on 26 February 1944 and at the conference of the CC on 21 March. In line with a decision handed down by Khrushchev, then secretary of the CC of the VKP(b), Dovzhenko was dismissed as artistic director of the Kiev film studio.

During the war years the arrests plucked up the writer L. Ovarov, the art scholar V. Sakhnovsky, the Bolshoi opera soloist D. Golovin, and the leader of the State Jazz Orchestra of the USSR, A. Varlamov. On Stalin's instructions, the screenwriter A. Kapler was arrested in

March 1943 and sentenced to five years in a concentration camp; the boss's daughter, Svetlana, had fallen in love with him, it seems. At the Institute of Literature an investigation "uncovered" an "anti-Soviet" group of students, disciples of the "neo-Baroque." Among those sentenced to internment in a concentration camp was the future writer and literary scholar A. Belinkov, who had written an undergraduate thesis that struck the sleuths as suspicious. At the All-Union Institute of Cinematography the future screenwriters Yu. Dunsky and V. Frid were also arrested.

In the postwar period the Moscow Satirical Theater actress V. Tokarskaya drew four years in a concentration camp as a former war prisoner: early in the war she had been captured by the Germans while at the front with a concert group. Toward the end of 1946, the set designer M. Fateyev, the Bolshoi soloist N. Sinitsin, and the actor L. Bordukov were arrested on a charge of forming a group of "Anglo-American orientation." The Bolshoi actress Z. Fyodorova was arrested and sentenced to twenty-five years in prison, and a lengthy prison term was the punishment for the leader of the State Jazz Orchestra of the Belorussian SSR, Eddi Rozner. The concentration camps claimed the well-known architect M. Mershanov and the Moscow Music Hall ballet dancer E. Dobrzhanskaya.

Stalin gave the nod in the cases of the popular theater and movie actress T. Okunevskaya, the outstanding Russian singer L. Ruslanova—the real reason being her friendship with the family of the disgraced Marshal Zhukov—and his own niece, the Maly Theater actress K. Alliluyeva. All were arrested.

On 14 August 1946 the CC of the VKP(b) issued a directive on the journals *Zvezda* and *Leningrad*. The charge against them: they had published the works of Anna Akhmatova and Mikhail Zoshchenko. The directive and, even more so, the speech made by Zhdanov at a Party meeting in Leningrad were notable for their coarseness. "Literary scum . . . petty-bourgeois vulgarian and blockhead"—this about Zoshchenko. "Half nun, half harlot"—this about Akhmatova. The judgment: "persons alien to Soviet literature." Akhmatova and Zoshchenko were expelled from the Writers Union.

Three weeks later the mills of the censorship mangled the films of Pudovkhin and Eisenstein, as well as the film *The Great Life*. The same year also saw the start of the campaign against so-called decadent tendencies in the theater. In May 1948 Zhdanov would go after the composers Muradeli, Prokofiev, Shostakovich, Khachaturian, Shebalin, Myaskovsky, and others, pronouncing them exponents of an antipopulist formalist school.

Nor did Caesar's whim spare the scientists. The persecution of geneticists and biologists that had begun on the eve of the war was resumed in 1944–48 with redoubled energy. The academicians A. Zhebrak, P. Zhukovsky, L. Orbeli, A. Speransky, and I. Shmalgauzen and their students—literally hundreds of research workers— were banished from the academy and from their chairs and faculties. Genetics and other disciplines—quantum mechanics, probability theory, statistical analysis in sociology—came under a ban.

During the period of the Great Infamy—the campaign against so-called cosmopolitanism—mass arrests of Jewish intellectuals took place in Moscow, Leningrad, Kiev, and other major cities. Among those picked up were the poets and prose writers P. Markish, I. Fefer, S. Galkin, L. Kvitko, D. Bergelson, A. Kushnirov, S. Persov, D. Gofshtein, I. Platner, M. Tatalayevsky, S. Gordon, A. Gontar, M. Teif, and M. Broderzon, as well as the actor V. Zuskin and the literary critics I. Nusinov and I. Dobrushkin.

Again and again, it was demanded of workers in the cultural vineyard that they hew unfailingly to "Leninist principles of the Party" and keep magazines and theatrical repertories free of "works encouraging the cult, alien to the Soviet people, of kowtowing before the contemporary bourgeois culture of the West." The CC pointed out to the Committee on the Arts and to the publishing house Art that the committee had given its blessing to the publication of a collection of one-act plays by contemporary British and American playwrights. These plays, in the CC's opinion, were models of low-grade, banal foreign writing, openly preaching bourgeois viewpoints and morality.

Then, on 16 July 1947, came a "confidential letter from the CC" on the case of Professors Kliuyeva and Roskin. They were accused of handing over to the Americans an "important discovery" of Soviet science, a drug for the treatment of cancer—which, as we know, does not exist to this day.

As work on rehabilitation progressed, I was often asked: Did Stalin know of the systematic destruction of the intelligentsia? Did he understand that in destroying the intelligentsia he was hacking away at the roots of Russia's intellectual powers? My answer was: Of course he knew. Not only did he know, he was the instigator of these crimes. Like Lenin, he hated the intelligentsia.

Fyodor Raskolnikov's "Open Letter to Stalin" states the crux of the question with perfect accuracy. The letter begins with a quotation from Griboyedov's play *Gorye ot uma* (Woe from Wit): "I will tell you a truth about yourself that is worse than any lie." It goes on:

> While hypocritically proclaiming the intelligentsia to be "the salt of the earth," you have deprived the calling of writer, scholar, and painter of even minimal personal freedom. You have clamped art in a vise where it suffocates, wilts, and dies. . . . The writer cannot publish, the playwright cannot put his plays on the stage, the critic cannot express an independent opinion that is not sanctioned by an official stamp.
>
> You are strangling Soviet art, demanding of it a courtier's toadyism, but it prefers silence to singing hosannahs to your name.
>
> . . . You are mercilessly destroying talented Russian writers who do not suit you. Where is Boris Pilnyak? Where is Sergei Tretyakov? Where is A. Aroseyev? Where is Mikhail Koltsov? Where is Tarasov-Rodionov? Where is Galina Serebryakova, guilty of being Sokolnikov's wife?
>
> You arrested them, Stalin!
>
> Following in Hitler's footsteps, you have resurrected the medieval practice of book burning.
>
> When I was an envoy plenipotentiary in Bulgaria in 1937, I received a list of prohibited writings consigned to the flames and found therein my book of historical recollections, *Kronstadt and St. Petersburg in 1917*. Many of the authors' names carried the notation "All books, pamphlets, and pictures to be destroyed."
>
> You have deprived Soviet scholars, especially in the humanities, of even minimal freedom of scholarship, without which creative work is impossible.
>
> With their intrigues, squabbles, and harassment, stiff-necked ignoramuses are preventing scientists from carrying on with their work in universities, institutes, and laboratories.
>
> . . . You are destroying talented Russian scientists.
>
> Where is the best designer of Soviet aircraft, Tupolev? You did not spare even him. You arrested Tupolev, Stalin!
>
> There is no field, there is no corner, where one can do one's chosen work in peace and quiet. That wonderful theatrical director and outstanding artist V. Meyerhold never engaged in politics. But you arrested Meyerhold, Stalin!

Though realizing, what with your shortage of personnel, the special value of every cultured and experienced diplomat, you lured all Soviet envoys back to Moscow and destroyed them one by one. You razed to the ground the entire structure of the People's Commissariat of Foreign Affairs.

Raskolnikov's letter to Stalin, dated 17 August 1939, ends with these words: "Sooner or later the Soviet people will put you in the dock as . . . the main saboteur, a true enemy of the people, the organizer of famine and of judicial fraud."

It took a full half century for this letter to appear in our press. Raskolnikov's smoldering lines are remarkable in that this roll of political crimes is put before Stalin by a onetime fellow ideologue and confederate who had managed to look at the policies of Bolshevism with the eyes of a sobered and repentant man.

Let me quote from another letter, by the outstanding scientist and Nobel laureate Ivan Pavlov, written on 21 December 1934 and addressed to the SNK of the USSR. It was prompted by rumors that he planned to leave the country.

> What you are sowing throughout the civilized world is not revolution but fascism, and with enormous success. Prior to your revolution, fascism did not exist. Only the political innocents of the Provisional Government wanted more than just your two rehearsals before your October triumph. All other governments emphatically do not want to see in their countries what we have seen and are seeing in ours, and, of course, they have the good sense to forestall it in time by resorting to what you used and are still using—terror and violence. Is this not clear to everyone who has eyes to see?
>
> But I am sad not because world fascism will hold back for a certain period the pace of mankind's natural progress but because of what is happening among us and what, in my opinion, presents a serious threat to my country.

Poring over the documents one comes upon incredible disclosures of the torture of world-famous persons in the Lubyanka's special torture chamber. Meyerhold was naive enough to decide to complain to Molotov. The document is preserved in the Lubyanka; one cannot read it without a shudder. The investigators threw Meyerhold facedown on the floor, beat him on the back and the soles of his feet with a rubber truncheon, then sat him on a chair and beat him again on the legs. Over the next few days they beat him in the same places, which, in Meyerhold's words, were bruised red, blue, and yellow. The pain was so excruciating he felt as though the wounds were doused in boiling water. "Lying facedown on the floor, I discovered within myself a capacity to wriggle and writhe and howl like a dog being whipped by its master."

Meyerhold evidently did not know or would not believe that for the Stalinist inquisitors this performance was commonplace, mere routine.

The thaw of 1956 appeared to signal a release from spiritual tyranny. The society acquired a somewhat different face; there was hope that the authorities would renounce the practice of mass reprisals for dissidence. Not a chance. In no way did the 20th Congress retreat from the claims of the top Party nomenklatura to moral superiority over all its subjects and to the right to decide the most complicated problems of their lives and creative work.

Nikita Khrushchev was alarmed by the incipient expressions of artistic freedom. As for his immediate entourage, many were thrown into a panic. Recovering from the shock, this coterie began the methodical work of restoring the old order. The hounding of the intelligentsia resumed. The sadly remembered confrontations with writers, the public abuse of painters after Khrushchev's visit to their exhibition in the Manege, and much else all demonstrated that the country's leadership was not ready for a real turn toward democracy.

Toward the intelligentsia the state still maintained its aggressively accusatory stance. In this respect the Leninist-Stalinist legacy remained virtually untouched. Khrushchev himself once exclaimed, "We're not giving up Stalin to anyone!" The show trials resumed; dissidents were thrown out of work and harried in the mass media. Especially adept at this last was *Pravda,* ever the mouthpiece of Bolshevik reaction.

Let me recall several well-known incidents. At the beginning of 1957 the writer Vladimir Dudintsev came under criticism for his novel *Not by Bread Alone,* published in the journal *Novy Mir* (New World) the previous year. The charge was that under the banner of the struggle against the cult of personality the author was trying to expunge the achievements of the Soviet era, an offense against the people. Evident here is the fear of the ruling clique before the onset, however brief, of the thaw, all the greater as the novel provided a skillful critique of the system and its bureaucratic soul.

One of the most telling examples of political terror, and of vulgar ignorance, was the disgraceful affair of Boris Pasternak, whose novel, *Doctor Zhivago,* had been published in the West. In October 1958 he was expelled from the Writers Union. He was forced to reject the Nobel Prize. His fellow writers contributed to *Pravda* a despicable letter accusing him of every imaginable sin against the Soviet author- ities.

Many of the documents on the hounding of Pasternak have been published. Nonetheless, I think it is useful to include them here, in the context of similar facts, events, and documents, so as to demon- strate even more vividly the hatred of the regime toward the intelli- gentsia, the uncouthness and fear of the potentates before the coun- try's spiritual elite.

The whole thing began, as was often true, with a note from the KGB to the CC of the CPSU. The message was that Pasternak had written an ideologically harmful novel, which he was planning to publish in the West. As we know, publishing anything abroad, aside from articles prepared by the KGB or its affiliates, was tantamount in those days to a hostile act. Soviet publishers had refused to publish the novel. After the note from the KGB, the CC instructed all its sub- divisions to take on Pasternak and his book.

On 7 December 1957, Konstantin Simonov, editor in chief of the journal *Novy Mir,* addressed a letter to the CC.[19] *Doctor Zhivago* had just been published, in a translation by P. Tsveteremich, by the Milan publishing house of G. Feltrinelli, and Simonov had a proposal to make:

Early in September 1956, five members of the editorial staff of *Novy Mir* (Fedin, Lavrenev, Agapov, Krivitsky, Simonov), having read the manuscript of Pasternak's novel, which had been submitted to the mag- azine, wrote to the author, setting out in detail the reasons for the manu- script's unconditional rejection. This letter, thirty-five pages long, enu- merated and analyzed all of the novel's political flaws, so that in case of the novel's publication abroad, the letter, if made public, could help in implementing one of a number of possible countermeasures. The idea of writing the letter came up in a discussion with Comrades Polikarpov and Surkov at the cultural department of the CC of the CPSU.[20]

Now the novel has just been published in Italy, and almost concurrently, in December, the European Cultural Society will hold one of its regular meetings in Venice, to which our writers have been invited and which they will doubtless attend.

We presume that our opponents at this meeting will do their best to exploit the appearance of the Italian edition of Pasternak's novel to our detriment.

It seems to me that, under the circumstances, it would be useful if in the course of the meeting one of our non-Party writers of the older generation, one who in his time signed the letter to Pasternak—say, K. A. Fedin or B. A. Lavrenev—would release, on his personal initiative and for publication in the Italian Communist or Socialist press, the letter to Pasternak expressing the view of his novel taken by several well-known Soviet writers a year and a half earlier.

It seems to me that it would be particularly beneficial if this could be done by K. A. Fedin, who not only took part in the collective editing of the letter but wrote, in his own hand, several of the more sharply worded pages. This measure, along with the use of Pasternak's own letters asking the publisher to hold up the novel's printing, could help the work of our comrades at the Venice meeting and, in general, could be a positive development for our side.[21]

As it happens, I will be on a trip to France at the end of December, when Pasternak's novel is to be published there. Perhaps it would be opportune to make our letter available there, too, for publication in the French press.

The letter in question was sent in 1956 to the CC of the CPSU. It was read by the cultural department of the CC of the CPSU, it was read by the secretaries of the CC of the CPSU, Comrade Suslov and Comrade Pospelov, and its criticism of Pasternak's novel was found to be justified.

A copy of the letter to Pasternak is on file with the cultural department of the CC of the CPSU.[22]

And here is a letter from B. Polevoy to the CC of the CPSU dated 17 September 1958:

Through its friends among writers in the West, the Writers Union of the USSR was long ago informed that reactionary forces within the Nobel Prize committee allied to the United States planned to spite the Soviet Union by awarding its literary prize to Boris Leonidovich Pasternak for his creative work and also for his novel, *Doctor Zhivago*, which has not been published in the Soviet Union but has been widely and flamboyantly published in the West. Our friends are warning us that this could lead to new anti-Soviet provocations in the West, based on allegations of a lack of creative freedom in the Soviet Union, of pressure on a number of writers for political reasons, etc.

In informing the Central Committee of this, we would like to receive instructions as to what advance position we should adopt on this matter and what steps we should take.[23]

From the minutes of a meeting of Moscow writers on 31 October 1958, an excerpt from a speech by Polevoy:

The hot war that has thundered by had its traitors. There was General Vlasov, who went over to the enemy camp together with his followers, made war on us, and met a traitor's fate at the end of his loathsome life. The "cold war" also has its traitors, and in my view Pasternak is essentially a literary Vlasov—this person who, living among us, eating our Soviet bread, taking pay from our Soviet publishers, enjoying all the boons of a Soviet citizen, betrayed us, went over to the other camp and makes war on us from there. General Vlasov was shot by order of a Soviet court [he was hanged—A.Ya.] and the whole nation approved since, as it was rightly said, bad weeds have to be plucked from the field. I believe that a traitor in the "cold war" should be liable to appropriate measures, and the severest of all possible ones. We ought to say to him in the name of Soviet public opinion: "Get out of our country, Mr. Pasternak. We don't want to breathe the same air as you."

A note from Polikarpov to Suslov (dated as having been received prior to 25 October 1958):

Mikhail Andreyevich! K. A. Fedin had a talk with Pasternak. They met for an hour.

At first Pasternak took a bellicose tone, stating categorically that he would not announce he was rejecting the prize and we could do with him whatever we wanted.

Then he asked that he be given a few hours to think it over. After meeting with K. A. Fedin, Pasternak went to consult with Vsevolod Ivanov. K. A. Fedin himself recognizes the need, under the circumstances, to take strong measures against Pasternak if he does not change his behavior.

A second note from Polikarpov, sent the same day:

Mikhail Andreyevich! K. A. Fedin has just informed me by telephone that Pasternak did not show up at the appointed time for continuing their conversation. This makes it clear that Pasternak will not announce he is rejecting the prize.[24]

A letter from Boris Pasternak to the Presidium of the Writers Union of the USSR, dated 27 October 1958:

1. I sincerely wanted to come to the meeting and came into town for that purpose, but suddenly felt ill. I would not want my comrades to take my absence as denoting a lack of respect. This note is being written hurriedly, and probably not as smoothly and convincingly as I would like.

2. Even now, after all the commotion that has been raised and all the articles, I still think that one can be a Soviet individual and write books like *Doctor Zhivago*. It is just that I take a broader view of the rights and potential of a Soviet writer, and I do not thereby demean his calling.

3. I do not have the slightest hope that truth will be reinstated and justice will be done, but, at the same time, I must remind you that the account of the manuscript's delivery mixes up the sequence of events. The novel was submitted to our publishers during a period when Dudintsev's works were coming out and there was a general relaxation of literary provisions. There was reason to hope that it would be published. Only a half year later did the manuscript come into the hands of an Italian Communist publisher. Only when that became known did the editors of *Novy Mir* write the letter that was printed in *Literaturnaya Gazeta*. There is silence on the agreement with Goslitizdat, which produced a relationship lasting a year and a half. There is silence on the delays that I requested of the Italian publisher and that he granted, so that Goslitizdat could take advantage of the postponements to publish a censored version as the basis for the Italian translation. No advantage was taken of any of this.

Now newspapers of enormous circulation are running only the unacceptable parts of the novel, which stood in the way of its publication and which I had agreed to drop, though nothing came of it except the adversities threatening me personally. Why could it not have been published three years ago, with appropriate cuts?

4. I do not regard myself as a sponger off literature. With my hand on my heart, I can say there are one or two things I did for it.

5. Conceit was never one of my sins. Those who know me can confirm that. On the contrary, I asked Stalin in a personal letter for the right to do my work in silence and obscurity.

6. I had thought that my joy on being awarded the Nobel Prize would not be mine alone, that it would affect our society, of which I am a part. In my view, the honor done me, a contemporary writer living in Russia and therefore a Soviet writer, is done to Soviet literature as a whole. I am sorry I was so blind and so misled.

7. In regard to the prize itself, nothing can force me to acknowledge

that honor as a disgrace or to respond to it with rudeness instead of gratitude. As to the monetary aspect, I could ask the Swedish Academy to contribute the sum to the Peace Council, not go to Stockholm to receive it, or leave things up to the Swedish authorities. That is something I would like to discuss with one of our officials, perhaps with D. A. Polikarpov, after two weeks or so, during which time I will recover from the shocks already received and prepare for those awaiting me.

8. I am personally ready for anything, comrades, and I do not blame you. Circumstances may force you to go far in reprisals against me, only to rehabilitate me under the pressure of the same circumstances when it is too late. But that has happened so often in the past!! Don't be in too much of a hurry, I ask you. It will not bring you added glory or happiness.

The next day, 28 October 1958, Polikarpov spoke at a meeting of the CC of the CPSU, reporting on a meeting of Party members of the Administration of the Writers Union of the USSR and a joint meeting of the Presidium of the Administration of the Writers Union of the USSR, the bureau of the organizational committee of the Writers Union of the RSFSR, and the Presidium of the Administration of the Moscow branch of the Writers Union, all of which took place on 25 and 27 October:

> Discussed at these meetings was the question of "actions of the member of the Writers Union of the USSR B. L. Pasternak incompatible with the calling of a Soviet writer."
>
> Present at the meeting of the Party group on 25 October were forty-five writers—Communist Party members.
>
> Thirty of them took part in the discussion. All the comrades who spoke wrathfully and indignantly condemned the treacherous behavior of Pasternak, who had gone so far as to become a tool of international reaction in its provocations aimed at inflaming the "cold war."
>
> The unanimous opinion of the speakers was that there was no place for Pasternak in the company of Soviet writers. In the course of the discussion, however, some comrades took the position that Pasternak should not be expelled from the Writers Union immediately, as that would be exploited by international reactionary forces in their hostile campaign against us. This point of view was defended with particular force by Comrade Gribachev. He argued that Pasternak's expulsion from the Writers Union should be preceded by a wide-ranging sampling of public opinion in the press. The decision of the Writers Union to expel Pasternak should come as an expression of the people's will. Com-

rade Gribachev's position was supported by the writers L. Ashanin, M. Shaginyan, S. Mikhalkov, F. Yashin, S. Sartakov, N. Anisimov, S. Gerasimov, and several others. Gerasimov stated that "we must simply give popular opinion an outlet on the pages of the central papers." Comrades Gribachev and Mikhalkov suggested in their speeches that Pasternak be expelled from the country. This idea was supported by Shaginyan.

Many of the speakers expressed sharp criticism of the Secretariat of the Administration of the Writers Union, and of Comrade Surkov personally, for not having expelled Pasternak when they learned that he had delivered his slanderous composition to a bourgeois publisher—and, even more so, for not having arranged for the timely publication in the Soviet press of the letter to Pasternak written by the editors of *Novy Mir.*

These speakers pointed out that by not having the letter published earlier, the Secretariat of the Writers Union had now placed the union in a more difficult position. Had the letter been published a year and a half ago, said Comrade Gribachev, "Pasternak would not have been awarded the Nobel Prize, as the progressive world press would have done everything it could to prevent it." This view was shared in the statements of Comrades Kozhevnikov, Sofronov, Kochetov, Karavayeva, Anisimov, Ermilov, Lesyuchevsky, and Tursun-zade.

The writers A. Sofronov and V. Ermilov made some blunt comments on the neglected state of ideological work within the Writers Union. In recent years, said Sofronov, questions dealing with the ideological mission of the Writers Union no longer occupied center stage within the union.

Side by side with the justified and well-founded criticism of the shortcomings in the work of the Secretariat of the Administration of the Writers Union and of its first secretary, Comrade Surkov, as reflected in the speeches of Comrades Gribachev and Sofronov and, in part, of Comrade Kochetov, there was an attempt to present the question in such a manner as to portray practically the entire work of the Secretariat of the Administration as a compromise with literary doctrine and a retreat from a principled policy. Sofronov contended that the Secretariat had exhibited liberalism in relation to Pasternak, while Comrade Surkov tried this way and that to denigrate the world's foremost writer, Comrade Sholokhov. My reply that the Secretariat's literary policy cannot be called a policy of compromise did not receive any support.

As a result of a wide-ranging exchange of views, the Party group adopted a unanimous decision to submit for discussion to the Presidium of the Administration of the Writers Union a resolution providing for Pasternak's expulsion from the Writers Union of the USSR.

... On 27 October, a joint session took place of the Presidium of the Administration of the Writers Union of the USSR, the bureau of the organizational committee of the Writers Union of the RSFSR, the Presidium of the Moscow chapter of the Writers Union, nineteen members of the Administration of the Writers Union of the USSR, and the Control Committee. Twenty-six writers did not attend. Of this number, Comrades Korneichuk, Tvardovsky, Sholokhov, Lavrenev, Gladkov, Marshak, and Tychina were not present for health reasons; Comrades Bazhan, Ehrenburg, and Chakovsky because they were abroad; Comrades Surkov and Isakovsky because they were under medical treatment in a sanatorium; Comrade Latsis because of official duties; and Comrades Leonov and Pogodin without explaining why. Also absent, citing health reasons, was Pasternak's personal friend, the writer Vsevolod Ivanov. Pasternak himself did not show up, pleading illness. He sent the Presidium of the Soviet Writers Union a letter outrageous in its insolence and cynicism. In the letter Pasternak is in raptures over his award and smears our Soviet reality with filthy slander, including vile charges aimed at Soviet writers. This letter was read at the meeting and was received by all present with fury and outrage.

Comrade N. S. Tikhonov chaired the meeting, and Comrade G. M. Smarkov submitted a report.

Twenty-nine writers spoke at the meeting. Among them were the prominent non-Party writers Comrades N. S. Tikhonov, L. S. Sobolev, G. E. Nikolayev, V. F. Panova, V. N. Azhayev, N. K. Chukovsky, and S. P. Antonov. With the full support and approval of all present, the speakers exposed Pasternak's treacherous behavior and condemned it wrathfully. They characterized Pasternak as a defector to the enemy camp who had severed all ties with his people and his country. In dealing with Pasternak's moral and political decline and his slanderous composition, the non-Party writer V. Azhayev declared: "With fury and contempt we condemn this artistically shabby, vulgar work, so hostile to our socialist cause. We condemn as incompatible with the calling of a Soviet writer the actions that Pasternak took in delivering his malicious work into alien hands and that he now takes in being ready to hop, skip, and jump for his 'reward.' These actions reveal him definitively to be a man who is alien to everything that is infinitely precious to every Soviet individual."

Characterizing Pasternak's treacherous actions, the non-Party writer G. Nikolayeva declared, "In my opinion, we are dealing with a Vlasovite." Referring to the measures that should be taken against Pasternak, she said, "For me, it is not enough to expel him from the Union—this man must not be allowed to live on Soviet soil."

The non-Party writer N. Chukovsky spoke in sharp terms of Pasternak's hostile nature and his provocative actions, adding, "All the same, there is a good side to this whole despicable story—he tore off his mask and openly declared himself our enemy. Then let us deal with him as we deal with our enemies."

The writer Vera Panova gave her opinion of Pasternak in these words: "In this malevolent soul, as revealed by this whole affair, starting with the writing of the novel and concluding with the letter, there is neither a feeling for native soil nor a sense of comradeship—nothing except boundless egotism and unbearably haughty pride unacceptable in our country and alien to a collective society. To see such rejection of the motherland and such malice is in fact horrendous."

In regard to Pasternak's letter, the Armenian writer N. Zaryan spoke as follows: "This letter—it's an anti-Soviet, hostile letter. Just on the basis of this letter this man would have to be expelled from the Writers Union. With this letter Pasternak excludes himself from Soviet literature and Soviet society."

As at the gathering of the Party group, the speeches of S. Mikhalkov and Yu. Smolich at this meeting contained drastic criticism of the Secretariat of the Administration of the Writers Union for not having as yet published the letter to Pasternak by the editors of *Novy Mir* and for still having him within the Writers Union.

Significantly, only a few speeches pointed out that for a long time certain writers had gone out of their way to exaggerate Pasternak's importance to Soviet poetry. Though present at the meeting, the poet S. M. Kirsanov, who sang Pasternak's praises in his day, did not offer his opinion when this matter was raised.

All present voted unanimously for the decision to expel Pasternak from the Writers Union.

The decision states: "In view of the political and moral degradation of B. Pasternak and his betrayal of the Soviet people and of the cause of socialism, peace, and progress—a betrayal paid for by the Nobel Prize, with the aim of fomenting war—the Presidium of the Administration of the Writers Union of the USSR, the bureau of the organizational committee of the Writers Union of the RSFSR, and the Presidium of the Administration of the Moscow branch of the Writers Union of the RSFSR deprive B. Pasternak of the title of Soviet writer and expel him from the Writers Union of the USSR."[25]

The same day, 28 October, Fedin wrote a letter to Polikarpov:

> Dear Dmitri Alekseyevich, at four o'clock today, Olga Vsevolodovna (I don't remember her last name—Pasternak's friend [O. V. Ivinskaya]) paid me a visit and told me tearfully that Pasternak said to her this

morning that for him and for her "the only way out is the one taken by Lann."[26] According to her, P. asked if she would agree to "leave together," and she agreed.

The purpose of her visit to me was to find out if (in my opinion) Pasternak could still be saved or if it is too late, and if it is not too late, to ask my advice—what (in my view) would have to be done to save him.

I replied that a statement of that kind is a threat—in this case, against me and, in general, against whomever it is made to and that one cannot make such a threat and then ask for advice. I said that the only advice I deem it absolutely necessary to give her is that she must dissuade P. from his insane intention.

I also said that I do not know if, after all that has happened, it is now possible to "save" P., who flatly refused to be "saved" when it was still feasible.

O. V. said she was ready to write "any kind" of letter, to anyone necessary, and to "persuade" P. to sign it.

I replied that I cannot imagine what the letter would now say and to whom it could be addressed.

I cannot say with certainty if I should take O. V.'s visit as an approach to me by Pasternak himself (she swore that she did not tell him anything about it, although a little later she said that he did not want her to go see me).

But I think you should know about this real or feigned, serious or theatrical notion on P.'s part, about the threat—unless it is an attempt to use it as a maneuver.

In my long talk with O. V., she repeatedly asked me to whom it would be "better" to send P.'s letter or to whom to "go." I could not give her any answer to this and promised only that I would write to you that she came to see me, and you, of course, would do whatever you deemed necessary and perhaps would want to summon her or Pasternak to come to see you. For that reason I took down her telephone number to pass on to you (B-7-33-70).

Nothing came of the letter. No one was bothered by Ivinskaya's call on Fedin. The tragic sequence of persecution took its course according to the rules and methods laid down by the authorities. The shameful writers' meeting was followed a few days later by a decision of an expanded meeting of the Party bureau of the A. M. Gorky Literary Institute of the Writers Union (30 October 1958).[27] The decision deserves to be quoted in full:

Heard:
Comrade I. N. Seregin's report on a meeting of the Presidium of the

Writers Union of the USSR and the Party committee (on the question of the action by the writer B. Pasternak).

Decreed:

The Party bureau, at an expanded meeting with the Party-Komsomol active members, discussed the decision of the Presidium of the Writers Union of the USSR depriving B. Pasternak of the title of a Soviet writer and expelling him from the Writers Union of the USSR.

The Party bureau and the active members unanimously approved the decision of the Writers Union of the USSR, as well as the initiative of a group of students who addressed a letter to the Writers Union expressing outrage at Pasternak's treacherous action and demanding severe punishment for the betrayer of our motherland.

At the same time, the Party bureau and the active members are outraged by the behavior of certain students of our institute (Pankratov, Kharabarov, Akhmadulina), who have been maintaining contact with Pasternak, sharing his views on our society and literature, and trying to spread them among their fellow students. In spite of criticisms, repeated warnings, and the opportunity to reform held out to them over a period of two years, they have maintained their positions to this day, as became glaringly obvious during the general outrage over the award of the Nobel Prize to the political renegade and émigré Pasternak.

The Party bureau and the active members consider that the Administration of the Writers Union of the USSR does not provide the institute with adequate support in resolving a number of important questions and sometimes interferes with the ideological struggle waged by the institute's Party organization, directors, and members.

For example, a decision of the Secretariat of the Writers Union of the USSR has restored the rights of the students Moritz and Mil, expelled, at the demand of the institute's members, for violation of discipline and unacceptable creative work. The Secretariat of the Writers Union of the USSR ignores the views of public organizations in assigning living space (the question of living space assigned to S. E. Babenysheva).

In spite of a promise made to the students, a student delegation was denied the opportunity to address a meeting of the Presidium of the Writers Union of the USSR and make public the text of a letter denouncing Pasternak's treacherous actions.

The Party bureau resolves:

1. To approve the decision of the Presidium of the Writers Union of the USSR to expel Pasternak from the Writers Union of the USSR, as well as the initiative of the student group that sent the Writers Union a letter.

2. To enjoin the Communists and Komsomol members within the institute, as well as the faculty, to intensify their ideological-educational

work and wage a determined struggle against expressions of formalism, which is a concealed form of revisionist attitudes; to urge the art faculty and the Komsomol committee to determine the ideological-artistic position of those students who do not take a sufficiently active part in the collective (Voronel, Florov, Shaveren, Zhdanov, Androchnikov, Bzhezovsky, and others).

3. To inform the CC of the CPSU of the mistaken actions of the Administration of the Writers Union of the USSR in relation to the A. M. Gorky Institute of Literature.

Secretary of the Party bureau of the Institute of Literature, N. Zarbabov.

It would seem that nothing had been left undone to destroy Pasternak's good name. He was a "Vlasovite" and a "traitor" and an "enemy" and a "warmonger" and an "agent of imperialism." But the authorities did not rest there. On 23 April 1959 Polikarpov again addressed a note to the CC:

> As reported by TASS, the French bourgeois newspaper *France Soir* has run an interview by its correspondent with M. Sholokhov, who is in Paris. The interview says that when asked by the correspondent about the "Pasternak affair," M. Sholokhov declared: "The collective leaders of the Soviet Writers Union have lost their sang-froid. They should have published Pasternak's book *Doctor Zhivago* in the Soviet Union instead of banning it. They should have let Pasternak be given his comeuppance by his readers, instead of putting him up for discussion. If they had done that, our readers, who are very demanding, would have forgotten about him by now. As for me, I regard Pasternak's writing, taken as a whole, as lacking in any value, except for his translations, which are brilliant." (Pasternak has translated Goethe, Shakespeare, and the work of leading English poets.) "As for the book *Doctor Zhivago*, which he read in manuscript form in Moscow, it is a formless work, an amorphous mass not worthy of being called a novel."
>
> In this connection, I would think it necessary to ask the Soviet ambassador in France to check on the reliability of the *France Soir* report and, if such an interview took place, to point out to M. Sholokhov that statements of this kind, running as they do counter to our interests, are inadmissible. If the newspaper report is false, Comrade Sholokhov should be requested to disavow it publicly.
>
> A draft of a telegram to the Soviet ambassador is enclosed.[28]

And here is Boris Polevoy falling all over himself again. On 29 May 1959 he wrote to the CC:

I enclose a memorandum by a consultant of the foreign commission of the Soviet Writers Union in the field of Italian literature, in which he gives a most telling account of new unpatriotic boorishness on the part of B. Pasternak.

I also enclose three poems from among those included by Pasternak in his new book, published in Italy. Most of the poems appearing in this book have not been published in the Soviet Union.

Evidently, Pasternak uses his contacts with foreign correspondents in order to send his trash abroad with their assistance.[29]

One is ashamed and pained remembering all this. We are, after all, dealing with a Nobel laureate, a towering poet and prose writer, our best translator of Shakespeare and Goethe, a great citizen and patriot.

In 1961, acting on a denunciation by his "brothers of the pen," the KGB raided the home of Vasily Grossman. They confiscated the manuscript of the writer's new novel, *Life and Fate*, down to the very last page. All the same, after almost thirty years, the novel saw the light of day. The manuscript was rescued by the writer's friends.

In the summer of 1961 the KGB arrested V. Osipov, E. Kuznetsov, and E. Bokshtein, who had been active in the literary get-togethers at the Mayakovsky monument in Moscow. The three were sentenced under article 70 of the Criminal Code of the RSFSR ("anti-Soviet agitation and propaganda aimed at undermining or weakening Soviet power"). Osipov and Kuznetsov received seven years in a concentration camp and Bokshtein five.

In 1965 the poet Joseph (Iosif) Brodsky, a future Nobel laureate, was exiled. The film director Andrei Tarkovsky and the stage director Yuri Lyubimov, the writer Viktor Nekrasov, and the cellist Mstislav Rostropovich were deemed unsuitable by the authorities and found themselves abroad.

In September 1965 the secret police arrested the writers Andrei Sinyavsky and Yuli Daniel, whose offense, like Pasternak's, was publishing their writings in the West. Remembering their predecessor's fate, they wrote under pseudonyms—Abram Tertz and Nikolai Arzhak. The KGB classified their actions as "especially dangerous state crimes" and recommended their indictment under article 70. In February 1966 the Supreme Court of the USSR sentenced Sinyavsky to seven years in a hard-labor camp and Daniel to five years.

Their trial was overseen personally by Suslov. Just before it began he telephoned me and told me to be present from beginning to end and, while there, to coordinate all the work of information and propaganda. I tried as best I could to make excuses, pointing out that literary problems were the domain of the cultural department of the CC. I also said I was unfamiliar with the case and had never read anything by Sinyavsky or Daniel.

Prior to this conversation, I had joined the cultural department in signing a memo, routine in such cases, supporting the KGB's recommendations on how the trial was to be reported. Nothing intelligible found its way into print, though, thank God. Attached to the cultural department's memo was one by the KGB laying out the writers' "transgressions." The KGB's argument was shaky, far-fetched, and, naturally, devoid of evidence.

Of course, I didn't tell Suslov any of this but tried to squirm out of things somehow. Finally he accepted my suggestion that he send over a staff member of the cultural department, Yu. Melentiev.

Today I regret that I didn't find time to look in on the trial at least once. Igor Chernoutsan and Albert Belyayev of the cultural department told me later that the trial struck them as a revolting spectacle, stupid and vulgar. I heard that Suslov made known his dissatisfaction with the ineffective presentation of the case.

The arrests went on to net K. Babitsky, L. Bogoraz, P. Litvinov, V. Delon, V. Dremlyuga, and V. Fainberg, who had objected to the invasion of Czechoslovakia in August 1968 by troops of the Warsaw Pact. For staging a protest demonstration on Red Square, Dremlyuga was sentenced to three years' imprisonment, Delon to two years and ten months, Litvinov to five, and Bogoraz to four; Babitsky was sentenced to three years' exile and Fainberg was placed in a psychiatric ward attached to a Leningrad prison.

In the summer of 1969 the newspapers *Sovetskaya Rossiya* and *Sotsialisticheskaya Industriya* came out, one after the other, with hatchet jobs on *Novy Mir*, which by then was practically the only focal point of the country's intellectual elite. The articles launched a deliberate campaign of persecution against the journal and its editor in chief, Aleksandr Tvardovsky.

Soon after, a frankly denunciatory letter entitled "What Is *Novy Mir* Against?" appeared in the journal *Ogonyok*.[30] The letter was signed by eleven writers: M. Alekseyev, S. Vikulov, S. Voronin, V. Zakrutin, A. Ivanov, S. Malashkin, P. Proskurin, A. Prokofiev, S. Smirnov, V. Chivilikhin, and N. Shundik. In the literary and political circles of the intelligentsia it was clearly understood that the campaign to stifle the remnants of dissidence had entered a new round. Its cause was linked to the government's fear of the consequences of the events in Czechoslovakia of August 1968.

In its next issue *Novy Mir* ran an editorial deflecting the shots taken at it by the eleven "machine gunners," as they were dubbed, and, in passing, pointing out that many of the writers who signed the letter in *Ogonyok* had more than once come under "very serious criticism in the pages of *Novy Mir* for ideological and artistic laxness, poor knowledge of life, bad taste, and lack of originality." On 4 August, six members of the Administration of the Writers Union of the USSR—K. Simonov, A. Surkov, M. Isakovsky, S. Smirnov, V. Tendryakov, and S. Antonov—asked *Literaturnaya Gazeta* to publish their reply to the letter of "The Eleven" in *Ogonyok*. *Literaturnaya Gazeta* did not publish their letter.

Then, on 12 August, Simonov wrote to the Secretariat of the Writers Union of the USSR, addressing himself to Markov personally. He expressed indignation at the failure of *Literaturnaya Gazeta* to publish the letter and asked: "If the letter of the eleven writers is to be regarded as presenting their own point of view, and its publication in *Ogonyok* as reflecting the point of view of the journal's editors, then it may be asked why the organ of the Writers Union of the USSR does not want or is unable to publish in its pages the letter of the six writers presenting their point of view on this matter and contesting the point of view presented in the letter of the eleven writers in the pages of *Ogonyok*." Simonov requested that "the question of publishing our letter in *Literaturnaya Gazeta* be settled promptly, and if, for reasons beyond me, that is found to be impossible, I request that the Secretariat be convened to discuss the question of the publication of our letter in our presence."

No discussion followed, nor was the letter of "The Six" published.

The atmosphere around *Novy Mir* and its top editor, Tvardovsky, continued to darken. And just then Tvardovsky's poem, "Po pravu pamyati" (By Right of Memory), was published without his knowledge in West Germany, France, and Italy. The poem was to have been published in the June 1969 issue of *Novy Mir*, but it was pulled by the censor. Tvardovsky's appeals that the poem be discussed by the Secretariat of the Writers Union of the USSR were not answered. Instead of discussing the poem, the Secretariat of the Writers Union of the USSR (on instructions from the CC) decided to "bolster" the editorial staff of *Novy Mir*, augmenting it with new people, including some who were known to be unacceptable to Tvardovsky. Staffers close to Tvardovsky—Lakshin, Dementiev, Vinogradov, and several others—were let go. As a result, Tvardovsky was pushed out of his position as chief editor.

Tvardovsky took to drink, and *Novy Mir* ceased to be a small rallying flame flickering in the darkness of those years and holding out hope, if only a sliver, of freedom of artistic creation.

By this time the authorities were resorting more and more to psychiatry as a means of coping with dissidence. This initiative is linked primarily with the name of Yuri Andropov. In the 1960s, a new type of illness that could be used to declare anyone sick, if the authorities so ordered, was cooked up at the insistence of the KGB. It was "scientifically based" and received the name of "creeping schizophrenia." The number of inmates in the special psychiatric hospitals began to mount. According to those who were put through this course of treatment, even though they were perfectly healthy, the loony bins *(psikhushki)* were more frightful than prison or a concentration camp.

Among the "procedures" employed, according to witnesses, were the following: tying the inmate up in a straitjacket until his or her extremities were numb; injections of sulfazine, a drug whose use was banned everywhere except in the USSR—sometimes two to four injections at a time in different parts of the body, bringing on not only an intense headache and temporary loss of motor function but high fever and thirst; subcutaneous injections of gaseous oxygen, producing swelling and pain for days on end, and especially painful injections of aminazin, contributing to cirrhosis and amnesia.

In those rare cases when the doctors refused to make a false diagnosis, they were harshly persecuted. Thus, in giving expert psychiatric testimony at the trial of Major General Pavel Grigorenko, Dr.

Fedotov refused to pronounce him a mental case. The same was true of a young Kiev psychiatrist, Gluzman. Fedotov was dismissed from his position and died soon after. Gluzman was sentenced to seven years in prison and three years of exile. While in the Perm concentration camp he wrote the well-known *Manual on Psychiatry for Dissidents,* in which he revealed many of the secrets of Soviet psychiatric "help" to dissenters.

Through its agents in the journalistic profession the KGB waged a massive campaign to discredit dissidents as "psychologically deranged." Even when the dissidents were exiled abroad and stripped of their citizenship, as Valery Tarsis, Vladimir Bukovsky, and Aleksandr Yesenin-Volpin were, the campaign went on. In February 1966, for instance, right after Tarsis was exiled abroad, the deputy chairman of the KGB, N. Zakharov, and the chief prosecutor of the USSR, R. Rudenko, reported that "the KGB continues to take action to further discredit Tarsis abroad as a psychologically sick man."[31]

In other words, the authorities continued to control the representatives of the intelligentsia through the KGB, dividing them into those suspected and those temporarily free of suspicion, those cleared for trips abroad and those not cleared, those who could be published and those who could not, those to be rewarded and those to go unrewarded, those invited to Kremlin banquets and those left out.

Let me recall the most recent examples of the hounding of intellectuals. I am speaking of Andrei Dmitrievich Sakharov and Aleksandr Isayevich Solzhenitsyn.

We are still lulled by the myth of Andropov's reformist bent, of his good intentions. I will not, at this point, cite the numerous facts that indicate the opposite. I will only offer a reminder of how he took part in the harassment of great men who were the pride of Russia. In September 1973 he wrote as follows to the CC of the CPSU: "The Committee on State Security informs me that on 17 September 1973 Solzhenitsyn's wife invited Academician Sakharov and his wife to her apartment and had a two-hour conversation with them. Expressing Solzhenitsyn's opinion, his wife insisted on the need for Sakharov to make an additional appeal to world public opinion about a wider range of problems stemming from the alleged absence of freedoms in the Soviet Union.[32]

In January 1974, the Politburo held a special discussion of

Solzhenitsyn. Opening the meeting, Brezhnev said of *The Gulag Archipelago*: "This is a crude anti-Soviet lampoon. We must consult about this, what we should do now. Under our laws we have full grounds for putting Solzhenitsyn in prison, inasmuch as he has cast aspersions on what is most sacred—on Lenin, on our Soviet system, on Soviet power, on everything that is precious to us. In the past we imprisoned Yakir, Litvinov, and others, sentenced them, and that put an end to it. Kuznetsov, Alliluyeva, and others went abroad. There was some noise at first, and then everything was forgotten. But this hooligan element Solzhenitsyn has let himself go. Lashes out at everything, doesn't stop at anything. What shall we do about him?" Andropov, too, spoke: "I have been raising the question of Solzhenitsyn, comrades, since 1965. Now his hostile actions have risen to a new level. . . . He has come out against Lenin, against the October Revolution, against the socialist system. His book *The Gulag Archipelago* is not an artistic work but a political document. This is dangerous; we have tens of thousands of Vlasovites, Ukrainian nationalists, and other hostile elements in our country. . . . We must therefore take all the measures I wrote about to the CC—namely, throw him out of the country."[33] And Solzhenitsyn was soon forcibly exiled from the USSR and stripped of his citizenship.

In December 1979 Andropov gave a report on Sakharov. His denunciation included the information that Sakharov "in the years from 1972 to 1979 paid 80 visits to capitalist embassies in Moscow," had more than "600 meetings with other foreigners," and held "more than 150 so-called press conferences" and that, using his information, Western radio stations made "nearly 1,200 anti-Soviet broadcasts." As we can see from these statistics, Sakharov was under close surveillance (tailing, bugging). His every step was known. Everything was tabulated. But at the time the government did not dare to put Sakharov on trial, because of the "political costs." On 3 January 1980 the Politburo decided to deprive the academician of all his titles and "as a preventive measure to remove him from Moscow to one of the regions of the country that are closed to foreigners."[34]

Perestroika brought about a radical change in state policy on the creative arts. But the repressive machine and the spirit of intolerance were not ready to give ground.

I, for example, sincerely hoped that creative freedom would drastically reduce the denunciations, immoral squabbles, exposures of one kind or another, personal ambition, and envy that the secret police had exploited to rein in the intelligentsia. But everything remained the same. Stool pigeons in the writing profession continue to compose their compromising materials, expose "agents of influence," deal in denunciations. Today's compromising materials in the newspapers and on television are very similar to those of the secret police of an earlier day, which it fell to me to read in all their abundance.

Everything has become muddled: some former anti-Soviets have become minstrels of Soviet might, former anti-Communists have become newly christened Bolsheviks, and those who condemned the empire in the strongest language, contributing to its collapse, have turned, as though by magic, into adherents of Great Power status. And there are those "dissidents" who have soured on the Russian reformation for the simple reason that it has deprived them of an income earned exposing the Bolshevik regime.

After 1985, in spite of many promising signs of creative freedom, the KGB continued its punitive mission, even if on a reduced scale. As before, the KGB churned out memos on the hostile actions of the intelligentsia and had writers report on the literary scene—with the inevitable findings. In June 1986, for example, the KGB addressed a memo to the CC, "On the Adversary's Subversive Aims within the Soviet Creative Intelligentsia." The memo listed the many well-known writers who were allegedly being assiduously "worked over" by foreign intelligence services. It claimed that Anatoly Rybakov, Svetov, Vladimir Soloukhin, Bulat Okudzhava, Fazil Iskander, Mozhayev, Roshchin, Kornilov, and others were under the "steady gaze of the adversary's special services." Once again, the names of Aleksandr Solzhenitsyn, Lev Kopelev, Vladimir Maksimov, and Vasily Aksyonov came up as "hostile elements."[35]

The Soviet experience shows that dissidence can take a wide variety of forms. At one pole there are the creators, thinkers, artists, powerful public figures. At the other pole there are the local "truth seekers," "cranks." Both groups are to be found in every city, every village or settlement. And to those in power, they are very bothersome. In the targeted range of dissidents the KGB included people remarkable for their talent and knowledge, moral character and civic activity. So the policy of persecution was directed not only against the independent-minded sector of writers, painters, and scholars, the creative intelligentsia in general. It was aimed at everything self-reliant, enterprising, original, searching.

The persecution of dissidence, like the repressive policy as a whole, led to a grave deformation of our national character and social consciousness. Indifference, passivity, a dual standard, the collapse of social relations. Stifled was the need to take responsibility for one's life and the lives of one's children.

The Bolshevik regime is guilty not only of the deaths of millions of people and the tragic consequences for their families, not only of creating an atmosphere of total fear and lies, but of a crime against conscience, of producing its notorious "new historic community of people" distorted by malice, doublethink, suspiciousness, and pretense. Lenin and Stalin and their henchmen callously and consistently destroyed the nation's gene pool, consciously undermining the potential for the flowering of science and culture.

THE CLERGY

AS EARLY as the spring of 1918, an open campaign of terror was launched against all religions, and particularly against the Russian Orthodox Church. Its originator was, again, Lenin. His actions against religion and the Church are astonishing in their diabolical ferocity and immorality.

Arrests of the clergy began in reprisal for their appeal to the faithful not to take part in the May Day demonstrations of 1918, which, under the old calendar, fell on the Wednesday of Holy Week. In Viatka, for example, twenty participants in a pastoral-lay meeting were placed under arrest. The clergy heading the Perm diocese was destroyed in its entirety. In the Orenburg diocese more than sixty priests were arrested, and fifteen of them were shot. During the summer of 1918, forty-seven clergymen in the Yekaterinburg diocese were shot, axed to death, or drowned.

Between 1918 and 1919, some of the leading spiritual leaders of the Russian Orthodox Church perished, among them the archpriests Ioann Kochurov, Pyotr Skipetrov, Iosif Smirnov, and Pavel Dernov; Abbot Gervasy; the priest-monk Gerasim; the priests Mikhail Chafranov, Pavel Kushnikov, and Pyotr Pokryvalo; Deacon Ioann Kastorsky; Bishop Feofan of Solikamsk; and Archbishops Tikhon of

Voronezh, Mitrofan of Astrakhan, Makary of Vyazemsk, Leonty of Yenotayev, and Platon of Revelsk.

The official term *execution* was often a euphemism for murder, fiendishly refined. For example, Metropolitan Vladimir of Kiev was mutilated, castrated, and shot, and his corpse was left naked for the public to desecrate. Metropolitan Veniamin of St. Petersburg, in line to succeed the patriarch, was turned into a pillar of ice: he was doused with cold water in the freezing cold. Bishop Germogen of Tobolsk, who had voluntarily accompanied the czar into exile, was strapped alive to the paddlewheel of a steamboat and mangled by the rotating blades. Archbishop Andronnik of Perm, who had been renowned earlier as a missionary and had worked as such in Japan, was buried alive. Archbishop Vasily was crucified and burned.

The documents bear witness to the most savage atrocities against priests, monks, and nuns: they were crucified on the central doors of iconostases, thrown into cauldrons of boiling tar, scalped, strangled with priestly stoles, given Communion with melted lead, drowned in holes in the ice. According to the "Statistics on the Persecution of the Russian Orthodox Church in the Twentieth Century" assembled by the Orthodox Holy Tikhon Theological Institute, nearly three thousand members of the clergy were shot in 1918 alone.[1]

Trampling outright on the feelings of believers, the authorities ordered the disinterment of all relics of the saints of the Church throughout the country, the subject of a special decree of 14 February 1919 by the People's Commissariat of Justice. If the disinterred relics were shown to be not wholly preserved, they were passed off as a fraud on the faithful and the fact was exploited in the persecution of the Church.

On 1 November 1920 Bishop Aleksii of Khutynsk was brought up before a revolutionary tribunal in Novgorod, along with Archimandrites Nikodim and Anastasy, Abbots Gavriil and Mitrofan, the archpriest Stoyanov, and Archdeacon Ioanniky. The defendants were accused of having secretly inspected the relics enshrined in St. Sophia's Cathedral prior to their official disinterment. That same year, a number of prominent pastors and church officials were tried before a Moscow tribunal—Abbot Ion; the archpriest Nikolai Tsvetkov; the chairman of the Council of United Parishes, Samarin; and council members Rachinsky and Kuznetsov. They were accused of spreading rumors that participants in the disinterment of the relics of the venerable Savva Storozhevsky had behaved in a manner offensive to believers; Kuznetsov was also accused of making a "false complaint" to the Council of People's Commissars. The complaint read, in part: "The grossness and mockery of commission members at the disinterment of the relics went so far that one member spat several times on Savva's skull, on him whose remains are sacred to the Russian people." Samarin and Kuznetsov were sentenced to be shot, but, as the sentence read, "in view of the victorious conclusion of the struggle against the interventionists," the court commuted execution to "confinement in a concentration camp until the victory of the world proletariat over world imperialism"—in other words, for life. The other defendants received prison sentences of various lengths.

Lenin's own attitude toward religion and the clergy is made clear in many of his notes, replete with hatred of the Orthodox faith. In one of them (25 December 1919) he writes: "[T]o put up with 'Nikola' [a religious holiday commemorating the relics of St. Nikolai] would be stupid—the entire Cheka must be put on the alert to see to it that those who do not show up for work because of 'Nikola' are shot."[2]

Concurrently with the extermination of disobedient members of the clergy, the Bolsheviks began work on creating a "Red" church. At the end of 1919, local branches of the VChK around the country sought to determine whether it was possible to create a Soviet church with "Red" priests. But the creation of such a church was blocked by the position taken by some of the leaders of the RKP(b)—mainly E. Yaroslavsky and F. Dzerzhinsky. As the chairman of the VChK wrote in December 1920 to M. Latsis, "My opinion: The church is disintegrating, we must help with this, but by no means reconstitute her in a new form. For that reason, the policy of church disintegration must be carried out by the VChK and by no one else. Official or semiofficial relations between the Party and the priests are inadmissible. Our stake is on Communism and not on religion."

The rapacious Bolshevik regime cast envious eyes on the riches the Orthodox Church had accumulated over its hundreds of years of existence. Czars and emperors, aristocrats and wealthy merchants had donated enormous amounts of money and valuables and embellished icons in gold and silver settings adorned with glittering precious stones. The sacred books were bound in solid gold. The precious holy vessels, fashioned by generations of the most skilled jewelers, were the pride of temples, abbeys, and monasteries and of their parishioners.

The Church engaged in extensive social work, establishing free hospitals, orphanages, poorhouses, almshouses, schools, trade schools, and much else.

In many cases the Church submitted meekly to the villainies of the Leninist administrative thugs. But in 1921 it could not tolerate the way the government of workers and peasants gazed with the heartlessness of a Nero on a country dying of famine. Patriarch Tikhon sent Lenin a letter offering to donate some of the Church's valuables for the purchase of grain for the starving.

Lenin's perverse mind took the offer as a challenge to the new regime. In his psyche there was no room for recognition of a selfless impulse. Whatever was done was seen by him as part of a merciless political duel to the death. The Church, he reasoned, is rebuking and humiliating us; it wants to control us. Out of the question, you wily priests! That will never be! Hurriedly summoning the Politburo, Lenin read them the patriarch's letter and declared that the time had come to finish off the clerics—to accuse the Church of unwillingness to part with its riches to help the hungry, thus forcing the government to confiscate its valuables.

While the patriach was waiting for an answer, Lenin signed the decree of 23 February 1922, "On the Removal of Church Valuables for the Relief of the Starving." This step delighted all the lumpen revolutionaries, who had begun to be disillusioned with him. The work ahead was infernal. The country had almost eighty thousand Christian churches, mainly Russian Orthodox.

Detachments of the OGPU burst into the temples and monasteries. Icons were stripped of their precious settings; churches were looted of holy vessels of gold and silver, including jeweled boxes for the Eucharist and chandeliers of the fifteenth to seventeenth centuries. Solid gold crosses from the days of Ivan the Terrible and the first Romanovs were packed in boxes and sacks. Precious stones were gouged out, covers of Bibles were ripped off, all the gold and silver coins that could be found were confiscated. Ancient icons provided fuel for bonfires, books handwritten in Old Church Slavonic perished in the flames. Altars crashed to the floor.

Stunned, the patriarch appealed on 28 February 1922 to all "faithful children of the Russian Orthodox Church," saying, "In the eyes of the Church, action of this kind is an act of sacrilege. We cannot countenance the removal from churches, even as voluntary donations, of sacred articles whose use for purposes other than divine service is forbidden by the canons of the Universal Church and is punishable as sacrilege."

The appeal of His Holiness was read from church pulpits, spread by word of mouth, and posted on the walls of houses, calling on the people to resist. Throughout the country, churches were the scenes of carnage. But the unarmed believers could not offer any kind of organized resistance to the armed special brigades. In many places the crowds were simply dispersed by machine-gun fire, and those arrested were shot the same day.

Knowing, however, how deeply rooted the authority of the Church was among the common people and wary of better-organized resistance, the authorities, as usual, dissimulated, hedged, and lied. On 28 March 1922 an official announcement asserted:

> The government has no thought of persecuting believers or the Church in any way. . . . Valuable objects are created by the people's labor and belong to the people. The conduct of religious services will not lose anything from the substituting of other, plainer articles for precious ones. But the valuable items make it possible to buy enough grain, seeds, cattle, and equipment to save not only the lives but the households of the peasants of Povolzhya and all other famine-stricken areas of the Soviet Federation. . . .
>
> Only a clique of the princes of the Church, accustomed to luxury, gold, silk, and precious stones, does not want to part with these treasures to save millions doomed to die. In its greedy desire to hold on to its valuables at any cost, the Church's privileged clique does not shrink from criminal conspiracies and incitements to open rebellion. While committed as always to full understanding and tolerance of believers, the Soviet government will never, not for one minute, permit the privileged ringleaders of the Church, garbed in silks and diamonds, to create a special government of Church princes within the government of workers and peasants.

Lenin was in top form. His former energy and combative élan returned. His hypocrisy is vividly illustrated by the fact that on 19 March 1922—even before the government's appeal—he had sent the following secret directive to members of the Politburo and the heads of the OGPU, the People's Commissariat of Justice, and the Revolutionary Tribunal, which were preparing to confer on coordinating action to implement the decree on the seizure of the Church's valuables: "The conference is to reach a secret decision to the effect that the removal of valuables, and especially those in the wealthiest abbeys, monasteries, and churches, must be carried out with merciless determination, stopping at nothing whatever, and in the shortest possible time. Therefore, the more representatives of the reactionary clergy we manage to shoot, the better. We must give these people, right now, such a lesson that for decades to come they will not dare even to think of resistance."[3]

"The more . . . we manage to shoot, the better." This bequest of Lenin's was fulfilled by Stalin on the widest scale and with the greatest enthusiasm.

By the most conservative estimates, the net profit from the confiscation of the Church's valuables came to 2.5 billion gold rubles. According to Western specialists, this figure could confidently be tripled. By contrast, with a fund of $137 million for food, the American Russian Relief Administration saved more than twenty million people in Povolzhya who had been facing death by starvation. Soviet statistics show that in the years 1922–23 the government spent only one million rubles abroad on grain—and that for seeds. As for purchases of cattle or farm equipment, there weren't any. Then what did they go for, these countless treasures stolen by the Bolshevik marauders? After all, if the 2.5 billion rubles had been divided equally, as the Bolsheviks had promised they would be, even destitute Russia could quickly have flourished.

The *Manchester Guardian* reported in March 1923 that specialists attributed the recent sharp drop in the price of gold to the appearance on the world market of large consignments of it from Russia. The Bolshevik Party, the paper commented, could well be called the party of the yellow devil. Similarly, The *Times* of London observed that leftist socialists had purchased two six-story buildings in the business district of London for six million pounds each and that four million pounds had been spent for the erection of a grandiose monument at Karl Marx's grave. The Bolsheviks in Moscow evidently had money to spend, money confiscated from the Church, allegedly for relief of the starving. Only now did one realize how rich a country Russia was.

In response to the Leninist decree of 23 February authorizing the seizure of the Church's valuables, Patriarch Tikhon wrote an indignant protest.[4] It was ignored. Not only were the churches pillaged, as Lenin had ordered, "with merciless determination" and "in the shortest possible time," but tens of thousands of priests, deacons, and monks and more than a hundred thousand believers were shot. Patriarch Tikhon himself was arrested in May 1922, together with members of the Holy Synod. Thirty-two metropolitans and archbishops were executed. Earlier, at a Moscow trial on 13 April, fifty-four defendants, including twenty priests, were accused of resisting the confiscation of Church property. The tribunal handed down eleven death sentences. In five cases the sentences were carried out.[5]

The Petrograd Revolutionary Tribunal sat from 10 June to 5 July 1922. Placed in the dock were eighty-six defendants, among them Metropolitan Vaniamin; Bishop Venedikt; the senior priest of the Kazan Cathedral, Chukov; the senior priest of St. Isaac's Cathedral, Bogoyavdensky; Archimandrite Sergii; the chairman of the Administration of the Council of Petrograd Parishes, Professor Novitsky; and Administration members Koshvarov and Beneshevich. The tribunal condemned ten persons to death. Four of them were shot; the other six had their sentences commuted to imprisonment.

The archives of the FSB contain the file on Metropolitan Agafangel of Yaroslavl, its cover bearing someone's notation, "This case is of historical interest." On 5 May 1922 the "Red" archpriest Krasnitsky showed up at the Tolgsk Monastery, where the metropolitan was living, and demanded that he sign the appeal of the so-called initiative group of clergymen accusing Patriarch Tikhon and his circle of counterrevolutionary actions. The metropolitan refused. Two days later the authorities had him sign a pledge promising not to leave, and a guard was posted near his cell.

A little more than a month later the OGPU charged that between 1917 and 1922 Agafangel had "ranged the Church against the authorities; had circulated rumors that the authorities were persecuting the Church; had thereby turned believers against the Soviet authorities, interfering with the removal of valuables; had disseminated

Tikhon's appeal; and had organized protest meetings of believers against measures taken by the authorities." He was placed under guard in the city of Yaroslavl on 22 August, then transferred to the Lubyanka prison in Moscow. On 30 October the OGPU Collegium decreed that the Agafangel case be "placed before the NKVD Commission on Administrative Exile." On 25 November the seventy-year-old metropolitan, who had a heart condition, was exiled to the Narym region.

Speaking of the Tolgsk Monastery, I cannot resist telling of its rebirth. At the time of perestroika, as is well known, we in the Politburo did a complete turnaround on religious policy, putting a stop to persecution of the Church and clergy. Responsibility for this matter was assigned to me. Thousands of churches and dozens of monasteries and mosques were returned to the religious authorities of the various creeds.

I will never forget traveling with my wife to the Optina Pustyn Monastery in the Kaluzhsk oblast and to the Tolgsk Monastery. The Optina Pustyn Monastery, a holy place, rose before our eyes like a pile of stones—literally. Everywhere there were broken bricks, ruined walls, shattered windows, total desolation. And in the corners—privies. Only an utterly vile regime could have set the hands of callous wastrels and drunks to destroying Russian shrines! I proposed to the CC that the monastery be turned over to the religious authorities, which was done.

The Tolgsk Monastery housed a colony for children who had committed crimes. Only hardened villains of Stalin's type could have taken on the destruction of this most precious Russian historical monument, famous from the days of Ivan the Terrible. To be honest, I came across it by chance. I had been searching for suitable premises for establishing a school for the restoration of architectural monuments, and I was advised to look at several buildings, including the monastery. When I saw it I realized that it would be sacrilege not to restore all of the monastery's buildings and return them to the Church. The minister of internal affairs, Aleksandr Vlasov, gave the project his full attention and had the monastery vacated within half a year. Today, the Tolgsk Monastery stands over the Volga in all its beauty, astounding with its splendor all who visit the area.

To continue with the persecution of the clergy: the fate of the priest Tikhon (Sharapov), who had been a regimental chaplain in the Russian army during the First World War, was typical. His life was cut short by a sentence handed down by an NKVD troika in the Alma-Atinsk oblast on 17 October 1937:

> Heard: Case under the jurisdiction of the Fourth Department of the State Security Service (UGB) of the NKVD of the Kazakh Soviet Socialist Republic. Sharapov, Konstantin Ivanovich, born 1886, in Tula, Moscow oblast, Russian, clergyman, archbishop of Alma-Atinsk. Former émigré. Arrested by the OGPU at the beginning of 1925 for extensive counterrevolutionary activity and administratively exiled from Gomel; arrested at the end of that year and tried under article 58-10 of the Criminal Code, sentenced to three years in a concentration camp. Arrested in 1927 and tried under article 58-10, sentenced to the Solovki camp for three years. Tried in 1930 under article 58-10 of the Criminal Code, exiled to the northern region for three years. Arrested in 1931 and tried under article 58-10 of the Criminal Code, sentenced to three years in a concentration camp. Organized various anti-Soviet groups in different cities of the Soviet Union.
>
> Charged: In 1925 he was recruited by the intelligence service of one of the capitalist countries and was conveyed to the territory of the USSR for espionage missions. Until 1937 gathered information of an espionage nature on the development of the textile industry in Central Asia and on the state of the kolkhozes.
>
> Arriving in Alma Ata in 1937, organized and headed an anti-Soviet monarchist terrorist organization of clergy and churchgoers. Trained a member of the organization, one Perepechko, to carry out a terrorist act. Trained one Nishgorodov, who was due to be called up that year for military duty, to do espionage work in the ranks of the Red Army.
>
> Pleaded guilty.
>
> Arrested on 21 August 1937 and is held under guard in an NKVD prison for people under investigation.
>
> Decreed: Sharapov, Konstantin Ivanovich to be shot.

Today there is documentary proof that all these charges were trumped up. Archbishop Tikhon has been posthumously rehabilitated.

The policy of terror was felt by every religious faith.

The regularly organized anti-Moslem campaigns in the days of Uraz Bairam and Kurban Bairam, the struggle against pagan forms of religion among the Mari, Chuvash, and Udmurts—all these were harshly repressive. The far-reaching organization of the Union of Militant Atheists and the Degliryal society constituted, in effect, a Party structure for the war on religion. They took on the work of overseeing "atheist five-year plans," socialist competitions in propagating atheism and closing down churches, mosques, synagogues, and other houses of prayer. One of the first victims in Tataria was the prominent religious and social leader Mullah Gabdulla Apanayev. He was shot in 1918 on a charge of having organized the so-called Zabulachnaya Republic in Kazan.[6]

In May 1930 the mufti R. Fakhretdinov complained to the Permanent Commission on Questions concerning the Cults within the VTsIK Presidium about the shutting of mosques, the crushing taxes levied against religious bodies, the fines and arrests for their nonpayment, the despoiling of the clergy and their exiling into forced labor, the seizure of private property, and the confiscation of the Koran and other religious books from believers. After meeting with him, a member of the VTsIK Presidium, P. Smidovich, wrote to M. Kalinin: "The Moslem religious organizations are on the eve of complete disintegration and disappearance off the face of the earth. As of now, 87 percent of Moslem religious centers have closed down, as have more than 10,000 out of 12,000 mosques, and from 90 to 97 percent of the mullahs and muezzin have been left with no means of conducting religious services."[7]

In the atmosphere of official psychosis arising from the collectivization campaign, the persecutors of the clergy found a convenient weapon in the bugaboo of the "kulak." A document dated 4 April 1933, "Conclusions in Regard to Charges against Mullahs and Kulaks of the Karagushevsk Region of the Bashkir Soviet Socialist Republic," names a group of fourteen, including four mullahs, all described as kulaks. The charge states: "For a number of years, under the leadership of the mullahs, the kulaks of the villages of Teter-Arslanovo, Yashirganovo, Buzatovo, and Uchagan-Asanovo in the Karagushevsk region have engaged openly in anti-Soviet actions against measures taken by the Soviet authorities in the countryside—actions aimed at disrupting kolkhozes and undermining agricultural-political campaigns, while terrorizing the poor and farm laborers and beating up Communists."[8]

Within the Russian Orthodox clergy the largest number of victims was claimed in 1937: nearly 140,000 persons were repressed that year, and of this total 85,300 were shot. In 1938 the figures were 28,300 repressed and 21,000 shot; in 1939, 1,500 and 900; in 1940, 5,100 and 1,100. And finally, in 1941, 4,000 persons were repressed and 1,900 of them were executed.

In 1918 the Russian Orthodox Church had 48,000 parishes and in 1928 a little more than 30,000. Of Moscow's 500 churches, 224 were left by 1 January 1930 and two years later only 87. Even the Cathedral of Christ the Savior was blown up. Before the revolution there were 28 monasteries in Yaroslavl province. By 1938 they were all closed down, and more than 900 churches were destroyed.[9]

The same thing was happening to the Moslems. By 1937 there were 1,375 registered religious organizations in Tataria, as against 2,550 before the revolution. In the Dagestan Autonomous Soviet Socialist Republic (ASSR), half of all religious centers were closed down by 1936; in the Kabardino-Balkarsk ASSR, 59 percent; and in Bashkiria, 69 percent.[10]

During World War II the authorities were forced to make concessions to the clergy, but that emphatically did not mean a stop to repressions. The number of Russian Orthodox clergymen repressed in 1943 totaled more than 1,000, and half of them were shot. From 1944 to 1946, more than 100 executions took place each year.

After the war the closing down of churches continued with unabated enthusiasm. By 1963 the number of Russian Orthodox parishes had been reduced by more than half from the figure in 1953. In the summer of 1946, the Church of the Lesser Transfiguration was leveled in Moscow. In the Dnepropetrovsk and Zaporozhye dioceses, the number of parishes in 1959 stood at 285; by 1961 only 49 were left. Five seminaries were closed. And in 1963 even the Kiev-Pechersk Monastery was shut down.

The early 1960s revived the persecution of believers and clergy. Between 1961 and the first half of 1964, 806 persons were sentenced under articles 142, 143, and 227 of the Criminal Code of the RSFSR and under the relevant articles of the criminal codes of other Union republics.[11] In the wake of a decree on parasitism, 351 clergymen were exiled to remote areas.

The following figures testify to the decimation of religious organizations in the 1960s.[12]

	1960	1969
Total number of houses of worship of all faiths	20,914	16,321
Russian Orthodox	13,008	7,352
Moslem	2,308	962
Catholic	1,179	1,096
Jewish	259	226

During the Brezhnev period the rate of closings slowed a bit. On average, some fifty parishes were dissolved each year. General Secretary Yu. Andropov, however, resumed the clampdown, demanding an intensification of antireligious efforts and persecuting religious figures. The debacle in Afghanistan sent the ruling clique at the Party's summit searching for enemies to blame for its own crimes. On 5 April 1983 the CC of the CPSU issued an edict, "On Measures for Isolating the Reactionary Part of the Moslem Clergy." It was followed by a new wave of persecutions of Moslem clergymen.

Perestroika proclaimed a new policy toward religion and the Church. There were the beginnings of a revival of monasteries, churches, mosques, synagogues, and other houses of worship, and religious schools were reopened—all without the least opposition in the Politburo. Nevertheless, the momentum of many years past made itself felt, primarily in the provinces. Old rules and habits continued to prevail. All the same, in spite of everything, religious life revived fairly quickly.

I am proud of the fact that, dealing as I did with questions of culture, information, and science, I was personally involved in the recuperative process. With my direct participation and the assistance of the Russian Orthodox Church, sixteen monasteries in addition to those of Optina Pustyn and Tolgsk were returned to the Church. More than four thousand houses of worship were restored to the appropriate authorities. The patriarch of Moscow and All Russia bestowed on me the Order of Sergii Radonezhsky.

Recently, the prior of the church in Kresty (Yaroslavl) made me a present of an ancient icon for having saved the church. In the bustle of workaday life I had forgotten about it, but the father reminded me of the times when the church was in real danger of being destroyed. The Party's Oblast Committee had argued that the church spoiled the general view leading into Yaroslavl by obscuring the "beauty" of the new high-rises. I did not authorize the church's razing. It is still there in all its splendor, markedly ennobling the entrance into this ancient Russian city.

That's how it is sometimes. Not everyone's memory is short.

As for me, I do not count myself an observant believer, but I was baptized, as were my children and grandchildren, and not recently but at birth. My mother attended church to the end of her days. Even now there are icons hanging in my parents' home; they were never taken down. It so happens that throughout my life I never gave a single atheist lecture or report, never conducted a single meeting on atheist propaganda.

I was always distressed by the sight of ruined churches, which were often turned into warehouses and sheepfolds. On the road from Moscow to Yaroslavl, which I took hundreds of times, dozens of shattered monuments of the past stood like silent witnesses to the crimes of the regime. Once, in 1975, while home on vacation—I was then working in Canada—I raised the matter with Andropov, who was then chairman of the KGB. He listened attentively, agreeing that such sights created a bad impression on foreigners: that had already been reported to him. In my presence, Andropov called someone by phone and ordered the problem looked into carefully, but that's as far as it went.

I recount these facts to clarify my present thoughts. I personally regarded the return of religious property to the religious authorities as an act of elementary justice, but more than that, I hoped that the resurrection of religious activity would bring a resurrection of morality and spirituality in its wake. I can't say that all my hopes have been disappointed, but many of them, unfortunately, have faded. Quite a few clergymen in the provinces have turned out to be common thieves, engaged in the looting of Church property. Theological theory and practice seem frozen in the past, unwilling to yield even on dogma that plainly stands in contradiction to people's daily lives. For many priests, moral instruction is no longer central to their

mission. Surprisingly, some religious leaders collaborate intellectu-
ally with leaders of Bolshevik ideology, thereby helping to truncate
the already short memory of their flock.

I am particularly repelled by the statements of those activists of
the Orthodox Church who are trying to prove that Stalin wanted to
fulfill Christ's commandments on earth. No greater blasphemy could
be imagined. These activists, having wormed their way into the
Church, betray both the faith and Christ. But especially repugnant
and cynical are the present Communist Party leaders' oaths of fi-
delity to the Christian commandments. Having destroyed thousands
of churches and exterminated hundreds of thousands of clergymen,
the neo-Bolsheviks are trying to pose as upholders of morality and
defenders of spiritual values.

I cannot find words to describe the immorality of people who
vote for the heirs of the Bolsheviks. It cannot be that all those who
vote for them are atheists raised on Marxist-Leninist ideology. What
ignorance is drawing us again into the void?

For criticizing the Church, the Orthodox Synod excommuni-
cated Leo Tolstoy, a genius, the spiritual father of the Russian people. Why, then, don't the estimable and highly respected hierarchs of
our Church pronounce an anathema against the antipatriotic and
anti-Christian party that in its day destroyed the Church, declaring
the Christian religion its enemy? Let us not forget the words of Patriarch Tikhon, who denounced the "Antichrist in power."

I can well understand that many clergymen are still weighed
down by the past, when all religious activity was under the control of
the KGB. It was that organization that selected people for study in
religious schools and recruited them for work in intelligence and
counterintelligence. I know many of its double-dealers by their KGB
names, as well as many of the two-faced gentlemen in the writing
and journalistic professions. I see them sometimes at various democratic gatherings and official receptions. And I am piqued at times by
a question: What do they think about their pasts, how do they live
with their consciences? But then . . . the devil with them. As far as I
am concerned, I am not about to make public the specifics of what I
know.

TWICE BETRAYED

THE CRIMES of the regime against Soviet prisoners of war and civilians deported to Germany and German-occupied countries during World War II were boundless. To this day we have no precise information on the number of Soviet prisoners of war. The German high command gave a figure of 5,270,000; the general staff of the Armed Forces of the Russian Federation, 4,590,000. The statistical records of the Administration on Questions of Repatriation within the SNK of the USSR indicate that most of the prisoners were taken during the first two years of the war—almost 2,000,000, or 49 percent, in 1941 and 1,339,000 (33 percent) in 1942. In 1943, by contrast, 487,000 (12 percent) were taken; in 1944, 203,000 (5 percent); and in 1945, 40,600 (1 percent).[1]

The vast majority of soldiers and officers ended up as prisoners—wounded and sick—against their will. There were no weapons, there was no food. The chain of command fell apart. Yet even during the toughest year, 1941, the number of defectors on the Western front, for example, never rose above 3 or 4 percent of the servicemen who had been taken prisoner.

The fall of 1941 saw the start of mass deportations of the civilian population to Germany and the German-occupied countries. The number of men, women, and children deported during the war came to 4,829,000.[2] Their resettlement was involuntary. Exceptions totaled about 250,000, mainly Soviet citizens of German nationality and the families of those who went to work for the German armed forces and the punitive occupation units.

More than 2,000,000 war prisoners and more than 1,230,000 civilian deportees died in camps and in servitude. More than 1,866,000 former prisoners of war and more than 3,500,000 civilians were repatriated to the USSR. More than 450,000, including 160,000 former prisoners of war, refused to return.

The attitude of the Bolshevik authorities toward Red Army personnel taken prisoner was already evident during the fratricidal civil war that followed the October counterrevolutionary coup. Servicemen were often shot without trial or investigation. In 1940, at the conclusion of the Soviet-Finnish war, Finland turned over 5,500 prisoners of war to the Soviet authorities. All of them wound up in a special concentration camp in the village of Yuzha in the Ivanovsk oblast. The camp, encircled by barbed wire, was guarded by convoy troops of the NKVD. The inmates were denied the right of correspondence or visitation by relatives. The place of confinement was kept strictly secret, and the interrogation of inmates lasted almost a year. A considerable number of them were sentenced to prison terms.

In the first days of the German invasion the Soviet command lost all control over its armed forces, with the exception perhaps of the navy. The Politburo was thrown into bewilderment. Only the punitive agencies proved ready for this turn of events. As early as 28 June 1941, only a few days after the start of the war, the NKGB, the NKVD, and the Prosecutors' Offices of the USSR came out with Order No. 00246/00833/pr/59ss, "On Procedures for Bringing to Justice Traitors to the Motherland and Members of Their Families."[3] There still was no information on the course of battle, but the repressive apparat was demonstrating its readiness to imprison, exile, and shoot people it considered traitors. The punitive powers also descended on the families of those who had disappeared as prisoners of war. The country's leadership shifted its own crimes onto the shoulders of soldiers and officers.

A serviceman taken prisoner was regarded as having committed a premeditated crime. No extenuating circumstances were accepted. Even those servicemen who had returned from only a few days on the other side of the front line were placed under investigation. Soldiers and commanding officers who had broken out of encirclement were treated as potential traitors and spies.

When, at the beginning of 1942, a group of us young officers arrived at the Volkhov front to join the Sixth Special Brigade of naval infantry, we saw this practice take place under front-line conditions. It so happened that, just as we arrived, separate groups of up to forty soldiers and officers of the encircled Second Assault Army, under the command of General Vlasov, came over to our sector of the front. All this was new to us. But we were astonished to see that virtually all those who came over from the other side were immediately disarmed, placed under guard, interrogated one by one, then sorted out through some kind of test and sent to the rear.

Occasionally, however, the rules were broken. When the returnees came in twos or threes, they were assigned as privates to the constantly shrinking companies and battalions. This generally went on in agreement with officers of the special services: they placed their orders with us for captured German informants (paid for in raw spirits), and we, so to speak, ransomed their encircled servicemen. The utter confusion that reigned at the front sometimes helped in reaching sensible decisions.

On the whole, though, the situation was far more tragic than even the liveliest imagination can picture. A vivid example is the fate of division commander I. Laskin. Trying to break out of encirclement near Uman in August 1941, he was captured and interrogated by a German noncommissioned officer. A few hours later he and his comrades managed to escape and join our side. Having agreed not to tell of their brief detention by the Germans, they were returned without any difficulties to their unit. But a year and a half later, in February 1943, the story became known to the military counterintelligence organization SMERSH. Laskin had been promoted by then to lieutenant general. As commanding officer of the operational department of the general staff on the Don front, it was he who accepted the surrender of Field Marshal Paulus. Among his medals were the Order of Kutuzov, the Order of the Red Banner, and the U.S. Army's Distinguished Service Cross. Nonetheless, he was arrested and charged with treason, espionage, and deliberate surrender to the enemy. His case dragged on until 1952. General Laskin underwent the horrors of the Lubyanka, Lefortovo, and Sukhanov prisons and was sentenced to fifteen years' imprisonment. Subsequently, he was rehabilitated.

More than 994,000 Soviet servicemen were sentenced during the war by military tribunals alone, and of this number more than 157,000 were sentenced to be shot. In other words, fifteen divisions were decimated by our own side. More than half the sentences were handed down in 1941 and 1942. Most of the condemned were Red Army soldiers and officers who had escaped from prisoner of war camps or had broken out of encirclement.

The families of the supposed traitors were subjected to harsh reprisals, including exile and long prison terms. These punishments were provided for by the decree of the State Defense Committee (GKO) of 16 July 1941 and by Order No. 270 of 16 August 1941 of the people's commissar for defense, Stalin, both of which, among other things, accused the commanding officer of the Twenty-eighth Army, Lieutenant General V. Kachalov, of treason and defection to the enemy, whereas he had in fact been killed in battle on 4 August 1941. In September 1942 his wife and his wife's mother were arrested and sentenced to eight years in prison. It was only after the tyrant's death that Kachalov's good name was restored, thanks to the tireless efforts of his wife—against whom, incidentally, charges of anti-Soviet agitation were renewed in 1950.

On 27 December 1941 the GKO issued Decree No. 1069-ss regulating the checking and investigation of "former servicemen of the Red Army" who had been released from prisoner of war camps or had broken out of encirclement.[4] From that point on, all of them were sent to special NKVD camps. These camps were, in fact, high-security military stockades. The inmates were forbidden to leave the prison zone, socialize with one another, or correspond with anyone. All inquiries as to the whereabouts of these personnel were met by NKVD officials with the answer that no information was available.

Characteristically, the special camps for Soviet inmates came under the NKVD's Administration for Foreign War Prisoners and Internees. In other words, Soviet servicemen who had escaped from captivity or broken out of encirclement were equated by the Party-state leadership with war prisoners who had fought against the Soviet Union.

In April 1943 the Presidium of the Supreme Soviet handed down a decree on the creation of a system of hard labor. Convicts were put to compulsory hard labor in mines and quarries and in smelting, construction, and logging. This was the lot of "political" prisoners and of condemned soldiers and officers who had been prisoners of war.

Starting in 1944, Red Army officers who had been liberated from prison camps or had broken out of encirclement began to be assigned to "assault battalions," in which, whatever their rank, they served as privates. To atone for their "guilt" the officers had to serve in these battalions until they were wounded or were awarded a decoration or medal. Assault battalions were employed in situations where it was almost impossible to stay alive. In other words, former war prisoners of the officer class were driven to certain death.[5] Altogether, more than 25,000 officers were ground up in these assault battalions—enough men to command twenty-two infantry divisions.

As the front moved west, the wave of war prisoners and deportees returning to the USSR mounted. In response, the GKO issued a decree in August 1944 on the creation of a network of screening checkpoints in the border zone. All civilians and former war prisoners had to go through them.

The NKVD's statistical reports indicate that repatriates who did not arouse suspicion were sent on to their homes if they were below draft age while those of draft age and former Red Army servicemen were taken to recruiting offices. The fate of those who aroused suspicion was different: they were arrested or were placed under immediate and ongoing surveillance, which also meant imminent arrest and sentencing.

It is chilling to read accounts of what befell repatriates who found themselves behind barbed wire in the screening camps. Here are excerpts from a few letters:

> They put twenty thousand of us in one camp and they're holding us. Things are terrible for us here. A lot of women and children die every day. (2 August 1945; V. S. Lyashenko, repatriate)

> It seems to me that never in all the war years was life as hard as right now. We can barely stand up. The food is awful. They treat us like dogs. . . . We crawl around like flies, gorging ourselves on wormy borsht, the likes of which we never saw during three years in Germany. . . . Peo-

ple don't care if they live or die. Many have committed suicide. Every guard wants to have a girl, though he's far beneath her, to say nothing of the higher command. The girls don't submit, and as a result many of them are imprisoned in dark, cold cellars. People are dying like flies. (12 August 1945; N. M. Ostrovskaya, repatriate)

We live very badly, the food is awful, we get three hundred grams of bread a day, practically raw dough, hot food three times a day—one and a half liters of stuff half full of worms, with dried turnips and red cabbage. Frankly, we were fed much better under the Germans. A lot of girls are in the hospital, dying of hunger. All the girls go about unwashed; soon they'll be eaten up by lice. A lot of them have committed suicide. I'll go on living another week and put an end to my life, as I see no point to it. I ask you to tell Mama that her daughter died when she was liberated by Russians. Why go on when every soldier and officer insults you in the vilest possible language. They don't regard us as human beings at all. (13 August 1945; G. Gelakh, repatriate)

By the summer of 1945, there were forty-three special camps and twenty-six screening camps on the territory of the USSR. Seventy-four more screening checkpoints and twenty-two resettlement centers operated in Germany and in Eastern European countries. By the end of 1945, more than 800,000 people had gone through this network. Another 1,230,000 had been processed by six special reserve divisions. Both during and after the processing they were all put to the hardest forced labor. The best way out for a repatriate was to secure a transfer to the permanent staff of the enterprise for which the special camp was working. Such a transfer was made without any set time limit—in other words, indefinitely.

On 18 August 1945, three months after the war ended, the GKO handed down Decree No. 9871-s regulating the new policy of the authorities toward former Soviet war prisoners and civilian repatriates.[6] Now they had to go through a checking and screening process within the ranks of the labor battalions of the People's Commissariat of Defense, again with compulsory hard labor. Nearly 1,500,000 people passed through these "work battalions," 660,000 of them former war prisoners. The others were civilian repatriates of draft age.

At the same time it was decided that Vlasovites discovered during the screening process and civilians who had served in the German armed forces and police—some 145,000 persons altogether—would be exiled to special settlements for six years. The leaders of the USSR saw no difference between Vlasovites and former war prisoners innocent of any wrongdoing. Both were sent to the far north, to eastern Siberia, to Kazakhstan—to remote areas where their chances of survival were nil.

As a result of the incessant screenings, many former war prisoners and civilian repatriates were sentenced as collaborators and German agents just because, while in the Nazi camps, they had worked as doctors, paramedics, interpreters, and cooks and in other posts servicing war prisoners and *Ostarbeiters*. They were regarded a priori as having ties to the German intelligence and secret police. Those who had been liberated by the Western Allies were registered as possible agents for Western intelligence.

The screenings went on for years; the authorities were in no hurry inasmuch as the special camps and labor battalions offered a slave workforce fully comparable to the gulag's. The workers' pay went almost entirely into the coffers of the NKVD. What remained was subject to various deductions—taxes, loans. Thus, for every five hundred rubles paid out for working in a mine, less than a hundred rubles remained as cash for the worker—exactly what was allowed under the rules. But even on this pittance there was nothing to buy. As a precaution against the formation of illegal organizations, no stores were allowed in either the special camps or the labor battalions.

Children, too, had a hard time of it. Those sixteen or older were counted as adults, while those under sixteen were registered with their parents. The NKVD's directives emphasized the need for vigilance with regard to teenagers between twelve and sixteen, who could, the orders said, be recruited by the German special services for espionage and sabotage.

The files on former war prisoners and civilian repatriates came under especially wide scrutiny after 21 February 1948, when the authorities approved the creation of several camps and prisons and intensification of repressions against already sentenced Trotskyists, Mensheviks, SRs, nationalists, spies, and saboteurs. A new category of state criminals came into being: "persons presenting a danger due to their anti-Soviet ties and hostile actions."[7] This definition applied to both former war prisoners and civilian repatriates.

Special convict-labor camps of a hundred thousand persons each were created in the Kolyma, Norilsk, and Karaganda regions, as well as in Mordovia and Komi, and special prisons for five thousand persons each in Vladimir, Aleksandrovsk, and Verkhnyeuralsk. No less than half the inmates of these camps and prisons were persons "suspicious for their anti-Soviet ties"—former war prisoners and civilian repatriates.

Stalin's death brought little change. In 1955, ten years after the war, the top leadership returned to the war-prisoner problem, not, however, out of mercy. What happened was that KGB chairman Serov informed the CC of the CPSU that the "defectors" from among the former war prisoners and *Ostarbeiters* who were in the West could be used as troops in a future war against the USSR. Heeding Serov, the Presidium of the Supreme Soviet adopted a decree on 17 September 1955, "On an Amnesty for Soviet Citizens Who Collaborated with the Occupation Forces during the Great Fatherland War of 1941–1945."[8]

Fine! An amnesty for those who had served in the German police and armed forces and had collaborated with the punitive and intelligence agencies of Germany and its allies, but not for those who ended up in concentration camps through no fault of their own. Nor did the pardon apply to those who had served their sentences at hard labor and in special camps and labor battalions.

The publication of the decree touched off a flood of letters to the highest Party and government offices. Confounded by the decision, former war prisoners insisted on a speedy restoration of justice. The result was the creation of a commission under the chairmanship of Marshal Zhukov. On 4 June 1956 Zhukov submitted a report that for the first time cited compelling evidence of the arbitrary treatment of war prisoners. The marshal raised the idea of putting an end to this lawlessness.[9] It was made possible, the report said, by the "dominant personality cult of Stalin, who alone made decisions . . . on the most important political and military questions." In the decrees of the GKO and the orders of the supreme commander, the document went on, questions pertaining to war prisoners and servicemen escaping from encirclement "were considered in a biased manner, as part of a consistent unfolding of repressions against them and their families. This led to the widespread illegal practice of extrajudicial repression of former war prisoners and to violations of the law in the handling of their cases in court."[10]

The Zhukov commission proposed measures to provide former war prisoners with financial support, find them jobs in their line of work within one month, revoke all restrictions banning them from educational institutions, and so on. It also proposed government awards to former war prisoners who had been wounded or who had escaped from captivity but had not received any recognition.

The Zhukov report triggered a heated debate within the CC Presidium. Many of the proposals were rejected. However, in a decree of the CC of the CPSU and the Council of Ministers dated 29 June 1956—"On the Elimination of the Consequences of Gross Violations of the Law in Regard to Former War Prisoners and Their Families"—the Bolshevik leadership acknowledged the injustice of the Stalinist regime's policy.[11] At the same time, all it did was to grant amnesty to those who had served lengthy sentences at hard labor or in prisons, camps, and labor battalions without having committed any crimes.

To all intents and purposes, therefore, former war prisoners were equated with former members of German units and police squads, who had been granted amnesty earlier. Thus, the amnesty, while garbed in the robes of justice, was base hypocrisy. Charges of betrayal of the motherland and espionage were converted into charges of military crimes, which excluded the possibility of rehabilitation as victims of political repression.

After that, the authorities did not deem it necessary to take up the problems of former war prisoners and civilian repatriates, regarding them as having been solved. Repeated efforts on the part of the Commission on the Rehabilitation of Victims of Political Repression—and on my part personally—to return to the issue were blocked by the stubborn opposition of the Ministry of Defense (and this was equally true in the Gorbachev period). As chairman of the commission while still in the Politburo, I discussed the matter twice with the chief of the general staff, Marshal Akhromeyev, but met with strong objections. His position was the conventional one: measures of the kind proposed would harm national security, damage the army's morale, and have a negative effect on discipline within its ranks.

The regime's hatred of the former war prisoners was total and profound. Their legal rights and those of civilian repatriates were not restored. It was convenient to shift onto these unfortunates the leadership's own culpability for defeats during the war.

The Bolshevik regime never acknowledged that

- the investigating and screening of repatriated citizens who had emerged from captivity or encirclement, and their ensuing imprisonment, represented one of the forms of extrajudicial repression imposed on more than five million Soviet citizens;
- placing officers as privates in "penal battalions," thereby sending them to a certain death, was a form of extrajudicial repression— or, in plain language, premeditated murder;
- the repressions carried out against the families of Soviet war prisoners were a refined form of barbarity and an abuse of legality—in other words, a crime;
- the repressions carried out against repatriates without any proof of guilt were acts of lawlessness;
- by denying moral and social protection to Soviet servicemen captured in defense of the motherland and by stripping them of the status of war veterans, the regime provided a glaring example of its own criminal nature.

And then there were the demands of the authorities that those maimed in the Nazi camps provide written certification of their injuries and traumas. What certification could have been provided by a soldier whose leg or arm was amputated in a camp? Let us not forget, either, that the question "Were you or any of your relatives held as war prisoners or in occupied territory?" was stricken from the questionnaires only in 1992!

The full restoration of the legal rights of Russian citizens captured in battle in defense of the motherland became possible only after Decree No. 63 of the president of the Russian Federation, passed on 24 January 1995 on the recommendation of the Commission on the Rehabilitation of Victims of Political Repression. Only fifty years after the end of World War II was it possible to see justice done. In the meantime, millions of people ended their days vilified, humiliated, and betrayed by the authorities.

FOREVER SLANDERED

THE MILLS of terror seized not only on social classes and groups—the peasantry, the nobility, Cossacks, merchants, the army, the clergy—but on whole peoples, who were forcibly deported to the far north and Siberia, to Kazakhstan and Central Asia. In the tragic fate of Poles, Crimean Tatars, Volga Germans, Chechens, Ingush, Kalmyks, Balkars, Karachayevs, Turko-Meskhetins, Khemshins, Koreans, Finns, Ingermanlanders, as well as Armenians, Bulgarians, Gagauzys, Greeks, Kurds, and many others, Bolshevik fascism revealed itself in perhaps its most transparent form, exposing the chauvinist basis of its policy. Long hidden in archives, documents tracing Bolshevism's crimes against these many people now make it possible to present the full sweep of the tragedy of Soviet society's degradation.

Forced deportations began long before World War II. On 26 April 1936 the SNK of the USSR secretly decided to exile as politically "unreliable" fifteen thousand Polish and German households from the Ukrainian Soviet Socialist Republic to the Karaganda oblast of the Kazakh Autonomous Soviet Socialist Republic (ASSR).[1]

Then came the purge of border regions. The first group of deportees included 35,820 Poles. Of this number, 35,735 were sent to the Kazakh SSR, to the Alma-Atinsk, Karaganda, Kokchetav, Northern Kazakhstan, and Taldy-Kurgansk oblasts. The rest were deported in small groups of five to fifteen persons, mainly to eastern Siberia.[2] After that, the deportations enmeshed the large industrial centers of the European part of the USSR.

Among the first acts of deportation was the resettlement of "unreliable elements" in areas bordering on Iran, Afghanistan, and Turkey. On 17 July 1937 the TsIK and the SNK passed a decree creating special restricted areas. And immediately 1,325 Kurds were moved from Armenia, Azerbaijan, Turkmenia, Uzbekistan, and Tadzhikistan into the interior of the country. All told, forty regions were swept clean.

The mass exiling of Koreans living in the Buryat-Mongol ASSR, in the Khabarovsk and Primorsk regions, in the Chita oblast, and in the Jewish Autonomous Oblast was carried out in 1937. The Koreans had been classified as prime targets for Japanese espionage. Yezhov, then the people's commissar for internal affairs, reported in top secrecy to the chairman of the SNK, V. M. Molotov: "The exiling of Koreans from the Far East Region was completed on 25 October 1937. The number of Koreans exiled came to 124 trainloads, composed of 36,442 families, or 171,781 persons. The Koreans have been assigned to the Uzbek SSR (16,272 families, 76,525 persons) and the Kazakh SSR (20,170 families, 95,256 persons). Seventy-six trainloads have arrived at their destinations and been unloaded, and forty-eight trainloads are on the way."[3]

One eyewitness writes: "They brought them in trucks, leaving them amid withered clumps of wild thorns and tamarisk. Losing all self-control and dignity, people in white dresses and gray padded jackets clasped their drivers and guards by the knees, begging to be taken to some inhabited place, because in the freezing cold and wind, without shelter or a roof over their heads, the little children and the old would die, and even the young would hardly make it till morning."[4] The resettlement of the Koreans continued during World War II, but from other parts of the country.

According to official statistics, there were 1,427,222 Germans living in the country at the beginning of 1939, including 700,231 in the Russian Federation.[5] The first to be deported, at the very outset of the war, were the Volga Germans; after that it was the turn of all Germans living in the European regions.

The decision to deport the Volga Germans was made in 12 August 1941. The plan was to exile them to areas of the Novosibirsk and Omsk oblasts, the Altai region of the Kazakh and Kirgiz SSR, and other neighboring oblasts.[6]

My class's teaching assistant, Gustav Shpeter, was sent to Vorkuta together with his family. An honorable man who taught us love of country, honesty, and decency, he survived, thank God, and lives in Yaroslavl. We classmates who are still alive meet with him to this day and continue to admire his wisdom and courage.

On 27 August 1941 the NKVD put out an order, "On Measures for Carrying Out an Operation for the Resettlement of Germans from the Povolzhye [Volga] German Republic and from the Saratov and Stalingrad Oblasts." Twelve hundred staff members of the NKVD, 2,000 police, and 7,350 Red Army personnel were sent to the republic, and 250 NKVD agents and 2,300 Red Army personnel were sent to the Saratov oblast. The operation was placed under the direction of the deputy people's commissar for internal affairs, I. Serov.

The resettlement was carried out in the cruelest fashion. One of the resettled, R. Gofman, writes that within a twenty-four-hour period in September 1941 he and his entire family, father and mother and two young brothers, "were thrown out of the house without our things, placed in a convoy packed only with Germans and sent off to Siberia under guard." The new arrivals in the shattered republic found a melancholy scene: "Bewildered lambs wandered in the streets, unmilked cows flung themselves bellowing at people. In the sturdy houses everything was swept and clean, the harvest ripened in the fields and orchards—and not a soul."[7]

According to Gofman, of the 2,114 Soviet Germans who worked with him in the Gremyachinsk mine in the Molotov oblast, just over 700 were left alive by the spring of 1945. E. Airikh writes that a year later, out of the 15,000 Germans brought to the Bogoslovsk camp in February 1942, only 3,000 were alive. Compulsory resettlement applied as well to Germans living in the Crimean ASSR, the Don, the northern Caucasus, Dagestan, Kalmykia, Kabardino-Balkaria, northern Ossetia, and Checheno-Ingushetia. Resettlement of Germans from the Baltics, Belorussia, the Ukraine, and Moldavia continued to the end of the 1940s.

Scattered over the North, western Siberia, the Far East, Central Asia, and Kazakhstan, the Germans lost their autonomy. As a people, their only crime was to belong ethnically to a nation whose government was warring against the USSR.

The operation to resettle Kalmyks began with a census by *ulusy* (regions) and *khatony* (settlements), carried out by tactical teams of eight to ten persons assigned to each ulus. It was announced that enemy groups with the mission of destroying factories, bridges, and stocks of grain and fodder, poisoning cattle, and infecting the population with contagious diseases had been slipped into Kalmyk territory. The teams arrived allegedly to guard population centers, bridges, warehouses, and reservoirs of potable water. On the pretext that it was necessary to administer inoculations against contagious diseases, they registered the entire population and livestock.

After this came the expulsion, starting on 28 December 1943. It was carried out by more than 7,000 operatives and 29,000 military personnel. The Kalmyks were exiled not only from Kalmykia but from the Rostov and Stalingrad oblasts and the Stavropolsk region. The number of exiles came to 99,252.

In mid-April 1944 preparations got under way for deporting the Crimean Tatars. Utilizing some 20,000 military personnel and 8,000 operatives of the NKVD, the operation began at dawn on 18 May and was completed on 20 May. Almost 200,000 people were exiled. The expulsion of Bulgarians (12,975), Armenians (9,919), and Greeks (14,300) from the Crimea began on 26 May.

Among the autonomous entities of the northern Caucasus, the Chechen-Ingush Republic had the largest population. On the eve of the war its twenty-four regions were home to 731,400 persons, including 387,800 Chechens, 75,000 Ingush, and 205,000 Russians.

The republic was the object of incessant political experiments. Here the Gorsky [Mountainous] Soviet Republic was proclaimed in 1921, the convening of its Constituent Assembly attended by Stalin. He accepted the assembly's terms—that the Gortsy [Mountaineers] would acknowledge Soviet sovereignty if the shariat—Islamic sacred law—was recognized as the law of the land.

The Gorsky Republic was short-lived. The Chechen Autonomous

Oblast was established on 30 November 1922 and the Ingush Autonomous Oblast on 7 July 1924, and on 15 January 1934 the two were merged to create the Chechen-Ingush Autonomous Oblast, which was supplanted on 5 December 1936 by the Chechen-Ingush Autonomous Republic.

The first wave of mass arrests in the northern Caucasus sprang from the collectivization campaign and the dekulakization of the peasantry. Acting on orders from Moscow, the local Party authorities planned to make the northern Caucasus into "the first region of total collectivization based on the liquidation of the kulaks as a class."

At first the Chechens did not attach much importance to this slogan, but when the authorities seized property and made arrests, they defended themselves. The NKVD interpreted this as terrorist kulak action. Official documents reported that "at the beginning of the 1930s the oblast was confronted with a real danger of seeing the broad masses dragged into a reckless uprising; the kulaks were calling openly for rebellion and winning over a large segment of the middle-level peasants. . . . An armed insurgency of 3,000 men was organized in 1932 and spread to every aul of the Nozhai-Yurtov region and to a number of other auls."[8]

To settle things peacefully is not part of the Bolshevik canon. In response to the protests, nearly 2,000 "kulaks and their collaborators" were arrested in 1933. In 1936 the SNK enacted a decision to resettle 1,000 peasant households from Dagestan and the Chechen-Ingush Oblast to the Kirgiz SSR. The Chechen peasants thus shared in the tragedy that was befalling peasants throughout the country. (According to the OGPU, 381,026 kulak families, or 1,803,393 persons, were exiled from various areas around the country by September 1931.)[9]

The antikulak campaign was followed by the Great Terror of the second half of the 1930s. On the night of 31 July–1 August 1937, a so-called general operation for the removal of anti-Soviet elements was carried out in every aul and region. Some 14,000 persons were arrested. Arrest warrants were issued for all of them; all were tried in absentia by a single court, a special troika of the NKVD of the Chechen-Ingush Republic. They were tried not individually but by lists, with predetermined sentences: some to be shot, others to be placed in concentration camps.

For three years on end the NKVD was occupied with inventing a case against a "bourgeois-nationalist, counterrevolutionary-insurgent, Bukharinist-Trotskyist, anti-Soviet sabotage organization"—thus read the multilayered formula in the charges brought against an arrested group. This group was composed of 137 of the republic's leaders. At the end of 1938 they were sentenced to be shot, imprisoned, or exiled.

The mass deportations that took place during the war years had catastrophic consequences for the Chechen and Ingush peoples. This operation, code-named *Chechevitsa* (Lentils), is recounted in detail in various documents of the 1943–44 period, as well as in a memorandum of 5 February 1960 from the minister of internal affairs, Dudorov, to Khrushchev.

In October 1943 a team of security agents headed by Deputy People's Commissar Kobulov went to the Chechen-Ingush Republic to collect evidence on "anti-Soviet actions" that had occurred in the Caucasus from the very first days of Soviet power. The result was a document dated 9 November 1943 entitled "On the Situation in the Regions of the Chechen-Ingush ASSR." According to the report, the republic had thirty-eight religious sects, whose leaders were regarded as saints and whose members—over twenty thousand persons—were engaged in sheltering and supplying bandits and German parachutists and in calling on the people to rise up in armed struggle against the Soviet authorities. Acting on orders from German intelligence, anti-Soviet leaders had organized armed uprisings in October 1942. The Chechens and Ingush had a large quantity of weapons, which they were unwilling to turn in, saving them for the next uprising against the authorities, to take place during the "second successful German offensive in the Caucasus."

On 13 November 1943 Beria drafted a resolution: "To Comrade Kobulov. Very good report." He then called a meeting of the heads of his agency. Among the top-priority tasks he enumerated was the creation of tactical Chekist groups to be sent to Chechnya. Responsibility for carrying out Operation *Chechevitsa* was given to Beria's deputies—Serov, Appolonov, Kruglov, and Kobulov. On 18 November Beria approved a plan establishing in each region Chekist groups of ten men whose mission—aside from measures against banditry—would be to carry out an exact registration of the whole population and to do it secretly, on various plausible pretexts, with names listed in accordance with a set form. They would also produce detailed studies of the roads, trails, ravines, approaches to forests and mountains, and communications with neighboring regions and republics. All this with the aim of preventing escapes on the part of "elements" slated for "removal."

On 2 December Beria received a memorandum with a progress report suggesting ways of making sure that the preparations for the operation would be kept hidden from the population and the local authorities. In particular, in order to move more than 85,000 internal troops of the NKVD and NKGB and more than 17,000 operatives of these agencies into the Chechen-Ingush Republic, the report proposed "arranging with the commander of the northern Caucasus military district, Lieutenant General Kurdyumov, for the movement of selected NKVD troops into mountainous regions in the guise of Red Army units assigned to tactical training in mountainous conditions."

On 29 January 1944 final approval was given to "Instructions on Procedures for Carrying Out the Exiling of the Chechens and Ingush." The preamble stated that "the exiling applies to all residents of Chechen and Ingush nationality in the Chechen-Ingush Republic." Members of the VKP(b) and the Komsomol, whatever their official position, as well as Party, government, and agricultural workers, would be resettled for work in other areas. Chechen and Ingush women married to men of other nationalities, the order explained, were not subject to exile, but in principle Russian women married to Chechen or Ingush men were. They were allowed, however, to dissolve their marriages; then they would be exempted from deportation.

On 31 January the scheduled operation received its legal basis in the form of a secret decree of the State Defense Committee, "On Measures for Resettling Special Deportees within the Boundaries of the Kazakh and Kirgiz SSR." Interestingly, the decree does not refer to Chechens and Ingush specifically by nationality but provides for the resettlement in February and March of up to 400,000 persons in the Kazakh SSR and some 90,000 in the Kirgiz SSR.

Beria reported to Stalin on 17 February that preparations for the operation were coming to an end. In view of its scope and the terrain, it was decided to complete the deportation, including placement in convoys, within a week. In the first three days the operation would be completed in the lowlands and foothills and partially carried out in some villages in mountainous regions—deporting, in all, a population of more than 300,000. In the remaining four days 150,000 persons would be deported from all mountainous regions.[10]

On 18 February Beria informed the chairman of the SNK of the Chechen-Ingush Republic, Mollayev, of the impending resettlement. He justified the operation, which was in readiness, on two grounds— the dangers of armed attacks against the authorities and collaboration with the Germans in their advance in the Caucasus. On 21 February, Deputy People's Commissar for Internal Affairs Serov reported to Beria on the attitudes of the leading officials of the Chechen-Ingush ASSR. Citing examples that gave rise to apprehension, he offered this conclusion: "[P]roceeding from the above, and taking account of local conditions (weather outlook, local fairs and holidays), I deem it necessary to suggest that it would be more expedient to begin the operation on 22–23 February of this year."

On 23 February, Beria reported to Stalin that "the operation for exiling the Chechens and Ingush began at dawn. The exiling is proceeding normally. No significant incidents. There were six cases of individual resistance, blocked by arrests or use of armed force." Beria updated Stalin almost daily on the progress of this barbaric operation. On 1 March he told him: "As of 29 February, 478,479 persons, including 91,250 Ingush, have been exiled and loaded onto trains. Altogether 177 echelons have been loaded, and of these 157 have been sent off to the resettlement areas."[11]

On 29 February the leaders of the republic left for Alma Ata in a separate echelon. They were allowed to take one and a half tons of household goods with them; so were three oblast-committee secretaries and three deputy chairmen of the government. (For the population as a whole, the quota was 500 kilograms per family; for people's commissars the allowance was one ton.) This echelon was sent off without a convoy, its departure overseen by Mollayev. Beria sent a telegram to Kazakhstan with orders that those who were part of the government echelon be found housing and work.

Nor did the operation end here. It spread to include Chechens and Ingush demobilized from the Red Army (after February 1944).

Orders went out to all the fronts. Thus, instructions addressed to chairmen of the screening committees stipulated that "all Karachayevs, Chechens, Ingush, and Balkars are to be transferred to the jurisdiction of the special-resettlement branches of the NKVD in the Kazakh SSR—to Alma Ata." According to the NKVD, the number of special exiles who had served in the army from the northern Caucusus came to 8,896 (710 officers, 1,698 sergeants, 6,488 privates), and of this total the Chechens numbered 4,248 (238 officers, 724 sergeants, 3,286 privates).[12]

Two weeks after the start of the operation, on 7 March 1944, a decree was handed down on the dissolution of the Chechen-Ingush ASSR. And the following day, another—on awards for "exemplary accomplishment of government assignments in wartime conditions." The supervisors of *Chechevitsa*—Appolonov, Kobulov, Kruglov, Serov, People's Commissar for State Security Merkulov, and the head of SMERSH, Abakumov—were awarded the Order of Suvorov, First Class.

The edict on the dissolution of the Chechen-Ingush ASSR justified the exiling of two whole peoples by claiming that in World War II, especially during Germany's military operations in the Caucasus, many Chechens and Ingush betrayed the motherland, joining saboteurs and spies dropped by the Germans in the rear of the Red Army and forming armed bands for action against the authorities. There is some truth to these charges, but not in the Chechen-Ingush Republic alone. The fact is that Red Army desertions and draft evasion assumed significant proportions in the entire northern Caucasus region during the war. In the first three years of the war there were 49,362 cases of desertion and 13,389 cases of draft evasion.[13] Those involved made up the principal source of manpower for the outlaw groups that were helping the Germans. Let me cite a few lines from a report of the NKVD in August 1942: "With the front approaching the territory of the Chechen-Ingush Republic, the anti-Soviet operations of counterrevolutionary and bandit-insurgent elements have been signficantly activated. . . . More than 240 bandits are operating within the republic, the Dzumoyevsk village soviet has been destroyed, kolkhozes have been closed down. . . . Communication lines with Grozny have been wrecked." And in August 1943: "In the Chechen-Ingush Republic, according to our figures, there are 33 bandit groups (175 persons) and 18 individual bandits; in addition there was action by 10 other bandit groups (104 persons). Discovered in the course of an inspection tour of the region: 11 bandit groups (80 persons); thus, on 15 August 1943 there were 54 bandit groups, or 359 participants, operating within the republic."[14] Operational summaries cite instances of terrorist acts against Red Army units: soldiers and officers killed, supply lines attacked, livestock stolen, and more. The communiques cite evidence of sabotage and espionage.

All in all, many of these and other reports are true. But they are true not only of the northern Caucasus. According to the NKVD department dealing with the struggle against banditry, 7,163 insurgent groups numbering 54,130 persons were smashed during the first three years of the war.[15] The breakdown for the northern Caucasus is: Dagestan—148 groups (3,380 persons); Kabardino-Balkaria—50 groups (3,241 persons); northern Ossetia—39 groups (323 persons); Krasnodarsk region—303 groups (2,985 persons); Stavropolsk region—88 groups (3,316 persons).[16]

Terror remains terror. To try to justify it is immoral. Absolutely immoral, too, were the actions of the authorities when, as punishment, they forcibly drove whole peoples, including veterans and heroes of World War II, from their native homes. The deportations were accompanied by mass abuse on the part of NKVD agents and troop units.

The deportation of the inhabitants of the Nashkhoisk rural soviet in the mountainous Galangozhsk region began on 27 February 1944. Equipment for transporting the sick, the elderly, and children was unavailable, and the horses and oxen belonging to the population had already by confiscated. The deportees prepared for a trudge of almost forty-eight hours along snow-covered mountain paths—whereupon the NKVD announced that the sick and elderly would have to stay behind for treatment, after which they would be reunited with their families. When all the able-bodied men and women had been taken away, the NKVD agents drove the remaining inhabitants, about three hundred in number, into the kolkhoz barn, locked it, and proceeded to rake the structure with automatic-rifle and machine-gun fire. Then they banked it with hay and torched it. In Melkhasti, the biggest rural soviet of the region, all the inhabitants of thirty-two of its thirty-four hamlets were massacred. During the tramp over the mountains, those who lagged behind were beaten with rifle butts, while those whose strength gave out were shot, their corpses left along the way.

Many columns were not even supplied with drinking water. One of the deportees, Magomed Tagayev, who was then forty-four, recalls: "I was brought with my family to the railway station in Grozny. We were packed into a freight car, about sixty persons; people found room wherever they could. Except for the appointed group leader, who was taken under guard to get food at the station stops, the deportees were not allowed to leave the train. . . . There were many deaths; I saw how the Chechens in the cars next to ours would carry out corpses, under guard, lay them down on the snow, cover them with it, and go back inside."

The republic's economy and culture suffered an enormous loss. Unique historical monuments were demolished. In the mountain regions almost a thousand monuments to ancient and medieval cultures were blown up and burned. Priceless manuscripts in Arabic and community chronicles *(teptary)* were seized and fed to the flames; encrusted silver and wooden tableware, goblets, vases, trays, men's and women's ornaments, swords, sabers, daggers, carpets, and much else were pillaged. Archives were destroyed.

After the 20th Party Congress, the question naturally arose of changing the lot of these humiliated and blighted peoples. But the attitude of the punitive agencies had undergone little change. The minister of the MVD, Dudorov, presented this conclusion: "To restore the autonomous status of the Chechens and Ingush within the borders of their previous territory would be a difficult and hardly practicable task, since the return of the Chechens and Ingush to their former places of residence would inevitably lead to a whole range of undesirable consequences. Here we could look into the question of creating autonomous oblasts for the Chechens and Ingush in the territory of the Kazakh and Kirgiz SSRs."[17]

At the same time, trying somehow to adjust to the new political situation, the MVD of the USSR, on 30 June 1956, submitted a proposal to the CC that the Chechens and Ingush and their family members be taken off the special registration lists and freed from the administrative surveillance of the MVD, although with the proviso that the removal of these restrictions not entail the return of property confiscated during the exiling or the right to return to the areas from which these peoples were exiled.[18] On 16 July 1956, the Presidium of the Supreme Soviet issued an edict, "On the Lifting of Restrictions on Special Resettling for the Chechens, Ingush, and Karachayevs and Members of Their Families Exiled during the Period of the Great Fatherland War," enacting instead the restrictions proposed by the MVD of the USSR.

Then, on 9 January 1957, there followed an edict of the Presidium of the Supreme Soviet of the RSFSR, "On the Restoration of the Chechen-Ingush ASSR and the Elimination of the Groznensk Oblast," and an edict of the Presidium of the Supreme Soviet of the USSR, "On the Restoration of the Chechen-Ingush ASSR within the Framework of the RSFSR." The latter edict is important in that it abrogated the repressive edict of the Presidium of the Supreme Soviet of the USSR of 7 March 1944 abolishing the Chechen-Ingush ASSR and repealed the edict of 16 July 1956 forbidding the Chechens and Ingush to return to their earlier homes.

The documents show that the return of the Chechens and Ingush to their native lands went forward under very difficult conditions. Their resettlement began in the second half of the 1950s in chaotic circumstances, with armed clashes with the people who had settled in the region after 1944. Thus, at the end of August 1958, in response to threats and violent actions by Chechens, more than ten thousand Russians and Ukrainians demanded the protection of the local authorities. A crowd tried to take over the postal and telegraph offices and the buildings of the MVD and KGB and to storm the building of the Party's oblast committee. The area was placed under the control of regular troops.

The population of the republic at the end of 1961 stood at 892,400, including 432,000 Chechens and Ingush. Of the 418,000 Chechens and 106,000 Ingush who had been living in the Kazakh and Kirgiz republics, those who left for the Chechen-Ingush Autonomous Republic totaled 468,000 (384,000 Chechens and 84,000 Ingush). All in all, 432,000 (356,000 Chechens and 76,000 Ingush) moved into Checheno-Ingushetia and 28,000 into the Dagestan ASSR. Some 56,000 (34,000 Chechens and 22,000 Ingush) remained in the Kazakh and Kirgiz republics.

A new stage in the rehabilitation of the maltreated peoples began on 14 November 1989 with a declaration by the Supreme Soviet of the USSR, "On the Recognition as Illegal and Criminal Repressive Acts against Peoples Subjected to Forced Resettlement and on the Guarantee of These Peoples' Rights," in which, for the first time, the illegality of the deportations was acknowledged and the practice of forced resettlement condemned.

On 26 April 1991 the Supreme Soviet of the RSFSR passed a law, "On the Rehabilitation of Repressed Peoples," with an addendum on 1 July 1993 making a law of the Russian Federation, "On the Re-habilitation of Victims of Political Repression," applicable to those citizens who had been subjected to repressions on the territory of the Russian Federation on grounds of nationality or other affiliation.

The main reason I have dwelt in detail on the fate of the Chechen people is that the knot tied by the Bolshevik regime is one we have not been able to undo to this day. Moreover, this knot is becoming tighter and tighter, especially after the criminal war in Chechnya. Personally, I do not see any real sense in separatism, as it serves the interests only of a narrow ruling elite. Singling out this or that people for sovereignty as a separate state is justifiable, in my view, if no less than 75 percent of the population vote for it. At the same time, the criminal actions of the Stalin regime could not fail to engender a deep-seated hatred of the imperial power. Russia will have to go on paying for a long time for the infamous policy of Stalinism toward the country's nationalities.

ANTI-SEMITISM

AS FAR BACK as the end of the nineteenth century the populist Nechayev said: "There must always be a rumor afloat about some kind of attack on the people." Stalin and Hitler, as the real "attackers of the people," pinned the rumor on the Jews.

All governments are hypocritical, but none have surpassed the Bolshevik regime. On the surface it had its catchphrases about the equality of nations, the barbarity of chauvinism, nationalism, and anti-Semitism. But in practice it exercised a policy that had nothing whatever in common with these declarations. In one of his interviews Stalin likened anti-Semitism to cannibalism, whereas in reality, as attested by his daughter, Svetlana Alliluyeva, he saw Zionists under every bed and repeatedly insisted that the history of the Bolshevik Party was a history of struggle against the Jews.

True, in the initial years after the October coup, the authorities took steps against instigators of pogroms (for example, the decree of the SNK of the RSFSR of 20 July 1918). Articles denouncing anti-Semitism appeared in the press. But these expressions of attitudes at the top counted little around the country. During the civil war, more than 300,000 people fell victim to anti-Jewish pogroms in the Ukraine and Belorussia alone. Pogroms and the slaughter of Jews were especially prevalent in the theater of operations of Budyonny's cavalry.

Still, on the whole, the authorities disapproved of anti-Semitism, in particular of anti-Jewish pogroms, and at times rampaging anti-Semites were brought to justice. The Black Hundreds of the "Union of the Russian People," whom Berdyayev had dubbed the "refuse of the Russian people," were actively pursued. Lenin had enough political intuition to realize that any persecution on ethnic grounds would mean the collapse of his proclaimed policy of internationalism.

But with Stalin's rise to power the picture changed radically. Restrictions began to be placed on the development of Jewish national culture, language, and religion. Jews began to find themselves forced out of the Party apparatus and political and economic posts. There were arrests of Jewish writers, the closing down of Jewish educational and cultural institutions, prohibitions on publishing books in Hebrew. Lenin's wife, Nadezhda Krupskaya, wrote to Stalin in 1938: "At times it seems to me that great-power chauvinism is beginning to raise its head a little. . . . Among children you begin to hear the swear word *zhid* [kike]."[1]

In a conversation with Ribbentrop on the eve of the war, Stalin spoke candidly of his views on the Jewish question. He is purported to have promised Hitler to put an end to "Jewish domination," which he saw as particularly strong among the intellectuals.[2] Two kindred souls and kindred systems began to work in rapport with each other.

Even during the war the keepers of the Bolshevik flame repeatedly demonstrated their vigilance. In August 1942 the Administration on Propaganda and Agitation of the Party CC reported that "in the arts, non-Russians predominate (mostly Jews)" and that the administration doubted that such artistic luminaries as Samosud, Faier, Shteinberg, Gabovich, Messerer, and others could be offered work in the Bolshoi Theater. In October 1943, with the approval of the CC of the CPSU, the actress F. Ranevskaya was rejected for a role in the film *Ivan the Terrible* because her "Semitic features clearly stand out, especially in close-ups." The head of the propaganda administration, G. Aleksandrov, wrote repeatedly during the war of the need to cleanse Soviet culture of Jews.

After World War II anti-Semitism became virtual state policy. Former Deputy Minister of State Security M. Ryumin declared that within his agency "a tendency to regard people of Jewish nationality as potential enemies of the Soviet state began to be clearly apparent" after the end of 1947.[3] Before the war the demand had been only for devils and witches; they were called "enemies of the people." After the war there was a need for new enemies, although the previous ones still provided plenty of corpses. Discontent with the difficulties of daily life (hunger, the housing shortage, crime, the stifling of free thought, and so on) had to be redirected into the usual demagogic channel: It's the Jews' fault. As the grim joke went about one anti-Semitic poet: "He's a hunchback and his verses are hunchbacked. Who's to blame? The Jews are to blame."

The campaign against "rootless cosmopolitanism" hastened the descent of the Iron Curtain between the USSR and the West. Within the country, the regime could not exist without grand political trials and permanent civil war. The punitive agencies worked hand in glove with the Party. Special commissions for flushing out cosmopolitans, for example, were created on orders of the CC. One such commission, chaired by the secretary of the Party Committee of Moscow State University, N. Poltyev (himself a professor at the university), submitted a denunciation of physics faculty members "with dubious political characteristics":

A. Prof. S. D. Gvozdover, department chairman and head of the radiophysics division. His father was a Menshevik and his brother was repressed under article 58. He himself was born in Munich. . . .

B. The Party organizer in this department, M. D. Karasev, was expelled from the Komsomol for defending Trotskyism and concealed this incident on joining the Party. Karasev was expelled from the Party and was reinstated with a stern reprimand. His father-in-law (Martynov) is a former Menshevik. . . .

C. Prof. G. B. Spivak, department head, has a sister living in Palestine.

D. The docent Krasilnikov, in the acoustics department, is the son of Trotskyites. His father and mother were repressed; his father died in prison and his mother served her sentence and now lives with him.

E. Prof. N. A. Koptsov, department head, merchant's son. Two brothers were repressed; one of them was shot in the Promparty case [the case of Party workers in industry]. Wife German, with family from Konigsberg.

There were times when the authorities' freedom from restraints and their blind chauvinism led to odd conclusions. The monk Mendel was numbered among the Jews, as were Morgan, Tatlin, Meyerhold, and Academician Varga. It didn't matter to the ignorant that many among those arrested were not Jewish, so long as their last names sounded "convincing."

Under this anti-Semitic policy two cases stand out—that of the Jewish Anti-Fascist Committee (EAK) and that of the "doctors' plot."

The Jewish Anti-Fascist Committee was created during the war alongside other public organizations—the Anti-Fascist Youth Committee, the All-Slavic Anti-Fascist Committee—to mobilize energies for the struggle against Nazi aggression. The committee contributed greatly to the exposure of Fascist ideology and policy. The EAK's contacts with progressive organizations in North America and Europe helped in the obtaining of food, clothing, medicine, and hard currency from abroad in the form of outright grants.

But the secret police do not change their spots. On 12 October 1945 the MGB sent a report to the CC and to the government, "On the Nationalistic Manifestations of Some Staff Members of the Jewish Anti-Fascist Committee." "Some" would later become all. The CC's Foreign Policy Department accused EAK staff members of neglecting the class attitude toward problems and developing their international contacts "on a nationalistic basis." What this meant was that Soviet Jewish anti-Fascists were meeting, say, with American Jewish anti-Fascists, and, since the principals on both sides were Jews, it followed that the meetings had a nationalistic basis.

Then, on 26 November 1946, a report by Mikhail Suslov turned a new page in the history of repression. He accused the EAK of anti-Soviet actions and espionage. An investigation was promptly opened. Through the use of torture, the secret police were able to extract testimony from I. Goldshtein and Z. Grinberg, arrested in December 1947, that served as grounds for bringing criminal charges against the EAK.

As a matter of fact, the secret police had been working the organization over from its founding. As in other public organizations with foreign ties, during the war the posts of executive secretary and

his deputies were occupied by civilian staff members of the state security agencies or by those agencies' informers—in the EAK, by Sh.
Epshtein, I. Fefer, and G. Heifetz. They informed on the committee
members' every step and every utterance.

The gory assault on the committee began with the murder of
Solomon Mikhoels, a cultural figure of world stature. Extensive torture of one of the prisoners in the Lubyanka yielded testimony "acknowledging" Mikhoels's involvement in alleged espionage activity
and his manifest interest in Stalin's private life. On 10 January 1948
the transcript of the interrogation was presented to the dictator himself. He immediately ordered that Mikhoels, who was then in Minsk,
be liquidated.

Mass arrests of people linked in one way or other to the EAK began in the second half of 1948. The investigation was headed by a
certain V. Komarov, who even among his drinking companions was
known as an executioner. Minister of State Security Abakumov was
arrested in 1951 (after being denounced by the investigator, Ryumin,
who accused him of harboring nationalists and enemy agents.) The
same fate befell Komarov. Confident of his innocence, he sent Stalin
a letter whose language faithfully conveys prevailing attitudes within
the secret services—and not only there. Here it is:

> My fellow workers in the investigative branch know well how much
> I hated our enemies. I was merciless toward them—wringing out their
> souls, as we say, demanding that they reveal their enemy dealings and
> connections. Those who were arrested literally trembled before me;
> they feared me like fire. The minister himself did not fill them with the
> kind of fear they betrayed when I interrogated them personally. Ar-
> rested enemies well knew and felt my hatred of them; they saw in me an
> investigator prepared to punish them harshly, and consequently, as the
> other investigators told me, they did all they could to avoid meeting up
> with me, to escape being interrogated by me. . . .
>
> Most of all I hated, and was merciless toward, Jewish nationalists,
> whom I saw as our most dangerous and malicious enemies. Because of
> my hatred of them, not only those arrested but former staff members of
> the MGB of the USSR of Jewish nationality regarded me as an anti-
> Semite and tried to compromise me with Abakumov. In my days with
> the MGB of the USSR I kept Abakumov informed of my political dis-
> trust of Shvartsman, Itkin, and Broverman.
>
> Learning of the villainies perpetrated by Jewish nationalists, I was

filled with even greater anger toward them and I most earnestly ask you to give me an opportunity to use all my inborn hatred of our enemies to take revenge on them for their villanies, for the damage they have done to the state. . . . I beseech you, Comrade Stalin, do not deny me your trust. Do not put me on trial.[4]

In the voluminous investigation reports, full of denunciations, filth, and blood, a curious detail stands out—a rare photograph used as "material evidence" of the subversive actions of the accused. The picture shows the great physicist Einstein and Mikhoels side by side. The picture was taken at Einstein's home in Princeton.[5] What need of further proof?!

When P. Zhemchuzhina, a member of the EAK and V. Molotov's wife, was placed under arrest, Molotov took it silently. His wife remained in prison until 1953.

On 20 November 1948 the Politburo issued a decree "that the Jewish Anti-Fascist Committee be immediately disbanded, since it has been shown that this committee is a center of anti-Soviet propaganda and regularly transmits anti-Soviet information to foreign intelligence, and that the committee's publications therefore be shut down and its files confiscated."[6] The decree cleared the way for mass repressions against Soviet Jews. Those arrested included well-known scholars, political and public leaders, poets, and writers. The necessary evidence was torn out of them by torture.

The methods are described in a letter that B. Shimeliovich, former chief physician of the Botkin Hospital, sent on 6 June 1952 to the chairman of the Military Collegium of the Supreme Court of the USSR: "On the very night of my arrest the investigator, Lieutenant Colonel Shishkov, took me to the minister's waiting room, where his secretary, a colonel, and three other staff members in military uniform were present. . . . They told me to take off my glasses and proceeded, like a football team, to throw me from side to side, punching me all the while in the face. Each time I fell to the floor (a yellow carpet) the voice of someone standing next to the table said: 'Get up.' . . . I got to my feet, and it all continued. It was here that I first heard it said, repeatedly, 'All Jews are anti-Soviet,' and, finally, 'All Jews are spies.'" As Shimeliovich tells it, the minister, Abakumov, taught his investigators to "beat them half to death." The doctor writes: "I heard him use the word *beat* at our first meeting, at which

Ryumin was present. . . . The investigator Shishkov told me, '. . . If you are unable to walk to the interrogations, we will carry you in on a stretcher and we'll keep beating you.'" Ryumin admitted that for the initial interrogations the badly beaten Shimeliovich "was literally carried" into his office.

Another example of the investigators' methods was given by I. S. Yuzefovich, a research associate of the Institute of History of the Academy of Sciences of the USSR and a member of the Jewish Anti-Fascist Committee, who was arrested in January 1948: "Minister of State Security Abakumov summoned me and said that if I did not confess he would transfer me to the Lefortovo prison, where I would be beaten. And I had already been 'softened up' for several days. I responded to Abakumov with a refusal, and they transferred me to the Lefortovo prison, where they beat me with a rubber truncheon and stamped their feet on me when I fell." On 12 August 1952 the Military Collegium of the Supreme Court of the USSR sentenced Yuzefovich to be shot.

On 3 April 1952 Minister of State Security Ignatiev sent the text of an indictment to Stalin: "I enclose herewith a copy of the indictment in the case of the Jewish nationalists, the American spies Lozovsky, Fefer, and others. I am reporting that the case has been forwarded for consideration by the Military Collegium of the Supreme Court of the USSR with the recommendation that Lozovsky, Fefer, and their accomplices, except for Shtern, be sentenced to death. Shtern to be exiled to a remote region for 10 years." The Politburo approved the indictment and decided to have all the accused executed, except for L. Shtern, an elderly woman whose term of exile was reduced to five years. This bit of clemency was granted by the "all-merciful" Stalin.

Not one of the charges was proven during the trial. The accused rejected the charges, exposing the falsification of evidence and recounting the tortures and beatings. The case fell apart. But that wasn't of the slightest import, inasmuch as the sentences had been confirmed in advance by the Politburo. In July 1952 the Military Collegium put its stamp on this decision. On 12 August, S. Lozovsky, P. Markish, L. Kvitko, B. Shimeliovich, D. Bergelson, and the others accused were shot.[7]

Trials were also staged of members of the so-called organizations of Jewish bourgeois nationalists in industry (the Stalin Works in Moscow, the Kuznetsk metallurgical complex, and elsewhere), in the mass media, and in the field of health care. The leaders of the Jewish Autonomous Oblast were placed on trial; Jewish staff members of the Ministry of Foreign Affairs and the Ministry of State Security were arrested. All told, more than seventy such cases were trumped up. For all practical purposes, Stalin had organized an all-Union pogrom.

The widest-ranging of the anti-Semitic provocations was the "doctors' plot."

The persecution of Jewish doctors began soon after the war. There were endless screenings on the basis of anonymous letters—in the field of psychiatry, for instance, in the Institute of Nutrition, and elsewhere. The screenings were followed by arrests. In 1950 the CC issued two decrees ordering the intensification of anti-Jewish purges in medical institutions. The same year, the well-known cardiologist Etinger and his adopted son, Yakov, were arrested. Among other charges, they were accused of listening to foreign radio broadcasts. On 2 March 1951 Etinger was no more. He died in prison, allegedly of heart failure.

A few months later, M. Ryumin, the MGB investigator who had headed the Etinger case, sent Stalin a letter accusing the minister of state security, Abakumov, of having concealed the terrorist plans of the "Jewish nationalist" Etinger against the Soviet leadership. Abakumov was arrested, and the new minister, S. Ignatiev, was ordered to track down the group of doctors engaged in subversive plotting against the leaders of the Party and the government.

The first step was to concoct a letter by one Timashuk as a basis for mass persecution of the biggest names in medicine, doctors entrusted with the care of the country's top leaders in the Kremlin hospital. The secret police doggedly searched for evidence that the doctors had employed "criminal methods of medical treatment" with the aim of "causing the death of prominent leaders of the Party and the state." Those arrested included Russians, Ukrainians, and Jews. Nonetheless, all were charged with participating in a Zionist plot.

The KGB investigators failed to find any evidence of a doctors' plot or of espionage. In the fall of 1952, however, Stalin took matters in hand, setting a schedule for open trials. On his orders, persons who were well past their youth and in poor health were subjected to monstrous tortures. He himself, the chief inquisitor, decided which tortures would be used on which detainees to obtain "admissions of guilt," and he personally checked on how well his orders were being carried out.

On 13 January 1953 *Pravda* reported the arrest of a group of "doctors-saboteurs." Although the case was still under investigation, the account was couched in terms of already proven crimes:

> [S]ome time ago, the state security agencies uncovered a terrorist group of doctors whose purpose was to shorten the lives of prominent leaders of the Soviet Union by the use of subversive methods of medical care. . . .
> This band of beasts in human form claimed Comrades A. A. Zhdanov and A. S. Shcherbakov as their victims. . . . It has been established that all the members of this terrorist group of doctors were employed by foreign intelligence services, had sold out to them body and soul, and were hired and paid agents. Most of the members of the terrorist group—Vovsi, B. Kogan, Feldman, Grinshtein, Etinger, and others—were bought by American intelligence. They were recruited by an affiliate of American intelligence, the international Jewish bourgeois-nationalist organization "the Joint." . . . Other members of the terrorist group (Vinogradov, M. Kogan, Yegorov) are . . . longtime agents of British intelligence.

A new wave of arrests of Jewish doctors rolled across the country. The KGB sought to create the impression that the plot was widespread, opening the way for a campaign of unbridled anti-Semitic propaganda. The very phrase *doctors-murderers,* trumpeted in the propaganda drive, was calculated to exploit people's natural concern for their health. The organizers aimed to foment, as in the 1930s, an outbreak of mass hysteria and to use it to prompt further widescale arrests.

I remember well the stifling atmosphere of those days. I was working in the Yaroslavl oblast committee of the CPSU as head of the department for schools and higher education. The first secretary of the committee was Vladimir Vasilievich Lukyanov, a calm, even-tempered man who behaved quite decently, figuring that questions of cosmopolitanism had nothing to do with life in Yaroslavl. But on one occasion he called me in and told me, with alarm in his voice, that I had been summoned by Shkiryatov, the chairman of the Party Control Committee, the Party's main repressive agency. He didn't know why, he said, but just in case, I should take along the data on the personnel of the educational institutions.

Frankly, I was scared. I was only twenty-eight. I phoned the reception desk, got an appointment. Shkiryatov received me glumly. He began by saying that the CC had received a letter accusing me of a lack of vigilance as to the dominant influence of the cosmopolitans in the universities, especially in the medical institute. Shkiryatov taxed me with failing to understand the Party's policy and thus promoting cosmopolitanism—for which I had to be punished. The Party did not excuse such behavior . . . and more in the same vein. I didn't follow much of this monologue and mumbled something unintelligible, such as that in Yaroslavl cosmpolitanism was in no way evident.

"Go," Shkiryatov grunted. "We'll decide."

But when I reached the door he asked, "Why are you limping?"

"The war."

"Where did you serve?"

"The Volkhovsk front."

"What branch?"

"Naval infantry."

He told me to come back to the desk, and then, in a milder tone, he went on about vigilance, the perfidy of imperialism, and so on. And let me go in peace. For the role of scapegoat they apparently chose someone else.

My other interview on the subject ended in embarrassment. I was first summoned by Inspector Vasilenko, then taken to see Shkiryatov. He was sitting at his desk, bent over some papers. He didn't recognize me. Before him lay a letter. Without lifting his head, he began saying that I didn't understand the Party's policy toward the intelligentsia, that I permitted excesses in the struggle with cosmopolitanism, and he read some names from his papers, names that meant nothing to me, except for Professor Genkin's. I told him Genkin had left for Voronezh University and a promotion as department head. He had passed an exam. The other names, I said, were unfamiliar to me, but I supposed that many of the instructors had gone home to

Leningrad, since the medical institute had been evacuated from Leningrad to Yaroslavl during the war.

And then I said to Shkiryatov, "Matvei Fyodorovich, you had a talk with me a year ago, but then you accused me of exactly the opposite."

He looked up and apparently remembered me; he asked what the earlier case had been about. I told him. He got someone to bring him the papers from the year before. And suddenly he exclaimed: "Look, the same handwriting. What a bastard!"

While I was still there Shkiryatov phoned the first secretary of the oblast committee and ordered him to find out who the anonymous informer was. He turned out to be a former secretary of one of the Party's regional committees, dismissed from his post for drunkenness.

Returning to Yaroslavl, I asked the first secretary of the oblast committee why I had had the honor to be singled out by Shkiryatov himself.

"Very simple," Lukyanov replied. "They were looking for some figure for exemplary punishment before the country at large. And then this letter turned up."

That was how things were done. But I am grateful for those meetings. They challenged my naïveté at the very start of my Party career.

The campaign to root out cosmopolitanism was followed by the adoption of a blatantly open policy of destroying Jewish culture and all forms of national self-expression. The authorities closed down Jewish theaters in Moscow, Chernovtsy, Minsk, Odessa, Birobidzhan, Baku, and Kishenev; Jewish academic centers and libraries in Kiev, Lvov, and Minsk; and the Hebraic studies section of the Department of Oriental Studies at Leningrad State University. Superb collections in Jewish museums in Tbilisi, Vilnius, and Birobidzhan were partially devastated. Synagogues were shut down. Torah scrolls, religious literature, and prayer books were destroyed. Hundreds of Jewish literary and theatrical figures, community leaders, and rabbis were arrested, and most of them perished in prison or exile or were shot.

Preparations for the mass deportation of Jews from Moscow and other major industrial centers to the northern and eastern regions of the country were launched in February 1953. They began like this: On Stalin's orders, a group of Jews sent a letter to *Pravda* asking the government to separate the "good" Jews from the "bad." Khavinson, the director of TASS, the Soviet news agency, and Academician Mints then made the rounds, inviting people to come to *Pravda*'s editorial offices, read the letter, and sign it. Sad to say, they were able to collect a sizable number of signatures.

Only the dictator's death averted a new bloodbath.

The anti-Semitism whipped up by Stalin after the war did not leave the country unscathed. Its malignant consequences are still lodged in the public conscience. Stalin's strategic plans included the fomenting of grassroots anti-Semitism as well, and this he succeeded in doing, as present-day events in Russia confirm all too clearly.

With the onset of perestroika in 1985, state-sponsored anti-Semitism came to an end. However, the dawn of real political and civic freedom not only gave rein to people's best qualities but laid bare all the dark and despicable impulses encouraged and cultivated in the human soul by Bolshevism and its chieftains through decades of terror, officially inspired denunciations, and deceitful propaganda.

Today, more than 150 Fascist and anti-Semitic newspapers are published in the country. There are many functioning organizations of similar orientation, and they are free to put forward candidates for legislative and executive office. For example, the governor of the Krasnodarsk region, Kondratenko, and the Duma deputy Makashov hold frankly extremist views, and they are not alone. The Communist contingent in the Duma, having inherited Stalin's commandments, gives overt support to anti-Semitism. The Fascist organization RNE (Russian National Unity) is growing, with official tolerance. Unfortunately, many disgraceful anti-Semitic episodes, with their public displays of far-rightist views and their unabashed use of Fascist terminology and emblems, go unpunished.

Is all this an unexpected development? Of course not. After Stalin's death, the persecution of Jews on grounds of nationality came to a stop, but an unspoken understanding or conspiracy took form within the Party and government elite: Jews were to be kept out of positions of authority at all official levels. The personnel departments of the Party, the ministries, and the agencies kept careful watch, under the overall control of the KGB.

True, in line with their pharisaic policy, every ministry had two or three Jews working for it—usually staff members of the special services—as though to be able to reply, if challenged: "Why accuse us of anti-Semitism? We have a Jew working for the Ministry of Foreign Affairs, another in the Ministry of Defense, a third in the CC, a fourth in some other ministry. . . ." In academia the situation was more complicated. Here the bald pragmatism of the authorities took over, especially in the applied military sciences. So they had to tolerate even Jews.

Any violation of the unspoken understanding was severely chastised. This baseness was something I was to experience. No sooner had I written an article in 1972 on the dangers of chauvinism, nationalism, and anti-Semitism in the USSR—hung out the dirty laundry, as it were—than I was removed from all Party work. Moreover, I remain labeled to this day as a "Russophobe" and a leader of "kike-masons" and supplied with four different surnames—Epshtein, Yankelevich, Yakobson . . . and a fourth I have forgotten and am too lazy to look up in the archives.

If the intelligentsia and all decent people in Russia do not raise their voices against the rampant thugs and their political ringleaders, trouble is unavoidable. The old and tattered card of anti-Semitism, an insult to the Russian people, will be played again, and as demagogically and vilely as before.

I should like to end this chapter with the words of Patriarch Tikhon's message to his flock in the Russian Orthodox Church. In 1919 he wrote:

> All Russia is a battlefield! But that is not the end of it. What follows is even more terrible. There is word of anti-Jewish pogroms and beatings without distinction as to age, guilt, sex, or beliefs. Embittered by the conditions of daily life, the individual looks for others to blame for his misfortunes, and, in order to take out on them his own resentments, sorrows, and sufferings, he lashes out so violently that his vengeful blow fells a great number of innocent victims. In his mind, his miseries have been identified with the evil done him by the actions of one or another party, and his bitterness against some has been transformed into bitterness against all. And this mass carnage claims the lives of people without any connection to the reasons that engendered such bitterness.

Orthodox Russia, may this disgrace pass you by. May you escape this curse. May your hands not be stained in blood crying unto Heaven. Do not allow Christ's enemy, the devil, to tempt you with the passion for revenge and to make you belittle the suffering of the victims instead of acknowledging and confessing your guilt; do not allow the devil to belittle your suffering at the hands of tyrants and persecutors of Christ. Remember: pogroms mean the triumph of your enemies. Remember: pogroms bring dishonor to you, dishonor to the Holy Church![8]

FROM KRONSTADT
TO NOVOCHERKASSK

BOLSHEVISM began its bloodsoaked harvest right after the counterrevolutionary coup of 1917. Its more brazen methods of violence were worked out at the expense of the sailors and soldiers of Kronstadt. And it went on from there, from Kronstadt and Tambov, through hundreds of peasant uprisings, through camps and executions, prisons and insane asylums.

For decades, Soviet historiography portrayed the bloody events in Kronstadt in the spring of 1921 as a mutiny organized by White Guards, SRs, Mensheviks, and Anarchists, with the active support of foreign intelligence services, in particular the French. It was asserted that the Kronstadt rebellion, aimed at the overthrow of the Soviet government, was joined by the sailors of only a few ships and by a small group of soldiers in the garrison. It was emphasized that the leaders of the Party and the state did everything they could to avoid bloodshed and that only after all peaceful appeals to the sailors and soldiers were rejected was armed force employed. It was given out that, after the fortress was captured, only the more active members of the mutiny, primarily White officers, were sentenced to death and that no other repressions followed. Documents show that all this was a contemptible lie on the part of the Bolshevik authorities.

The Kronstadt events have their bloody prelude.

During the fratricidal civil war, a large part of the peasantry and working class, while still giving support to the Soviet government, protested strenuously against the Bolsheviks' monopoly on power. In the cities, as well, a highly explosive situation developed. There was a food shortage. Many plants and factories were shutting for lack of fuel and raw materials, and workers were being thrown out into the street. The situation was particularly bad in the major industrial centers, especially in Moscow and Petrograd. On 11 February 1921, it was announced that ninety-three Petrograd enterprises, including such giants as the Putilovsk, Sestroretsk, and Triangle complexes, would be closed down on 1 March.

On 28 February 1921 the CC of the RKP(b) met to discuss the problems in Moscow and Petrograd and agreed on the need to crush the political opposition. The Cheka was ordered to step up the arrests of Mensheviks and SRs, including workers, "especially when they expose themselves by their actions."[1]

Rumors of the events in Petrograd had reached Kronstadt some time earlier, and a delegation of sailors and soldiers had been sent to Petrograd to determine the causes and scope of the unrest. On their return they reported on the results of their mission. The next day, 28 February, the sailors of the warships *Petropavlovsk* and *Sevastopol* passed a resolution, which they put forward for discussion by representatives of the crews and military units of the Baltic Fleet.

The resolution stated:

1. Since the existing Soviets do not express the will of the workers and peasants, we demand the immediate holding of new elections to the soviets by secret ballot, with unrestricted preelection campaigning among all workers and peasants.

2. Freedom of speech and publication for workers and peasants, Anarchists, and left socialist parties.

3. Freedom of assembly for both trade unions and peasant organizations.

4. The holding no later than 10 March 1921 of a nonparty conference of workers, Red Army men, and sailors of Petrograd, Kronstadt, and Petrograd province.

5. Release of all members of socialist parties held as political prisoners, as well as all workers, peasants, Red Army men, and sailors held in connection with the workers' and peasants' movements.

6. Election of a commission to review the cases of those held in prisons and concentration camps.

7. Elimination of all political departments, since no party may enjoy a privileged position in propagating its ideas or receive state funds for this purpose. Instead, there should be locally elected cultural-educational commissions financed by the state.

8. Immediate removal of all barrage units.

9. Equal benefits for all workers, except for those in hazardous industries.

10. Elimination of Communist armed detachments in all military units, as well as of the various Communist duty shifts; should such units or duty shifts become necessary, they could be appointed within the units of military companies and in plants and factories at the discretion of the workers.

11. Full rights for peasants to utilize their land any way they wish and to own cattle, which they must maintain by themselves—that is, without hired labor.

12. We ask all military units, as well as our comrades in the military academies, to join us in this resolution.

13. We demand that all resolutions be widely disseminated in the press.

14. We ask for the appointment of a mobile monitoring unit.

15. We demand permission for people to have their own home industries, maintained by their own labor.[2]

It should be noted that the Kronstadt sailors who passed this resolution had given their support to the Bolsheviks in October 1917. Essentially, the resolution did not depart from the program on the basis of which the Bolsheviks had seized power. It was the Bolsheviks who had demanded the transfer of all power not to any one party but to the soviets, which represented all socialist organizations. It was they who had promised to give the land to the peasants. It was they who had spoken in support of the Constituent Assembly that was slated to establish a form of government for Russia. Less than four years later, all these demands were stigmatized by the new regime as counterrevolutionary.

On the afternoon of 1 March, sixteen thousand people met on Yakor Square to discuss the resolution. The commissar of the Baltic Fleet, N. Kuzmin, tried to defuse the fervor of the meeting, but unsuccessfully. The speakers demanded an end to the barrage detachments, the hunger, the lack of fuel—an easing of living conditions. The resolution adopted by the sailors of the *Petropavlovsk* and *Sevastopol* was approved by an overwhelming majority.

On March 2 a Provisional Revolutionary Committee, headed by a sailor from the *Petropavlovsk*, S. Petrichenko, was set up in Kronstadt. Its task was to prepare for secret-ballot elections to the soviet, with all political forces of socialist orientation entitled to present candidates and campaign without restrictions. Soviet institutions in the city continued to operate. No one was arrested.

The unrest in the fortress was accompanied by the collapse of the Communist Party cells. In January 1921 there had been 2,680 members and candidate members of the RKP(b). Many of them left Kronstadt during the first days of unrest, although no one was after them. Of the remainder, more than 900 people left the Party.

The Kronstadt leaders sought open and public negotiations with the authorities, who took, however, a sharply confrontational stance from the outset: no negotiations, no compromises, the "mutineers" had to be punished. Delegations were sent repeatedly from Kronstadt to Petrograd, and each time they were arrested.

On 3 March the government published an announcement headlined "A New White Guard Conspiracy!" It declared that everything that had happened in Kronstadt "was undoubtedly prepared by French counterintelligence" and that "spies have been apprehended." The sailors' and soldiers' resolution was described as "Black Hundreds–SR" in character. In view of this, it said, the Soviet of Labor and Defense (STO) had issued a decree placing Petrograd and Petrograd province under martial law. This wild set of lies was approved by the chairman of the STO, Lenin, and by the chairman of the Revolutionary Military Soviet, Trotsky. They clearly sought to present the events in Kronstadt in the most threatening light, confident that the ignorant masses would swallow this latest provocation. And that is what happened. The masses swallowed it.

On 5 March an order was given for operational measures to put down the rebellion. To this end, the Seventh Army was reconstituted under the command of Mikhail Tukhachevsky. Meanwhile, in Moscow, preparations for the 10th Congress of the RKP(b) were being completed. It had been decided to open the congress on 6 March. The delegates arrived, but the congress did not meet on the scheduled date. A plenum of the CC of the VKP(b) was convened on 7 March and reset the congress for 8 March. The reason was that the night of 7–8 March was the time set for the storming of Kronstadt. It was expected that the Kronstadters would be wiped out in one blow and the capture of the fortress would be announced to the delegates as a new victory over the counterrevolutionaries.

Why were the dates for the opening of the congress and for crushing Kronstadt so closely linked?

By that time, the situation in the country was dangerous enough that Lenin had to look for a radical way out. He decided that in addressing the congress he would announce a New Economic Policy (NEP) and, as part of it, the elimination of the requisitioning of farm produce and the substitution of a tax in kind of food products. This provision was one the Kronstadters had demanded.

But Lenin, naturally, did not want the changes in economic policy to be seen as concessions made in response to the Kronstadt uprising or to the worker and peasant unrest. That would serve as a dangerous precedent. So the leader preceded his economic concessions with punitive action. He realized that economic changes, especially if made under pressure from the masses, would create momentum for political reform. The suppression of the Kronstadt revolt was required primarily to demonstrate the immutability of the Bolshevik monopoly on power.

However, the plan to crush the rebels with one blow on the opening day of the congress fell through. The government troops retreated with heavy losses. A basic reason for the failure lay in the political attitudes of the Red Army soldiers thrown into the assault on the fortress, who went so far as to commit flagrant insubordination, even actions in support of the Kronstadters.

In the line of attack by the Southern Group, the 561st Regiment disobeyed orders to storm the fortress. A telegram report described events: "The 561st Regiment, after moving one and a half versts toward Kronstadt, refused to advance any further. The reason is unknown. Comrade Dybenko ordered a second formation to deploy and open fire on any troops returning to the rear. The commander of the 561st Regiment is taking repressive measures against the Red Army men under him, so as to make them advance."[3] A part of the regiment went over to the Kronstadters.[4] In the northern sector, it was only with great difficulty that the Petrograd cadets, regarded as the most combat-ready unit of the Northern Group, were made to join in the offensive.

After intensive artillery shelling, a new assault on the fortress was launched on the night of 17 March. Orders by telegram from Petrograd were to "deal harshly with the mutineers, shooting them without mercy," and not to "be too particular about taking prisoners."[5] In the course of the assault it was even decided to use chemical weapons. Tukhachevsky issued an order "to attack the battleships *Petropavlosk* and *Sevastopol* with asphyxiating gas and toxic shells no later than tomorrow."[6] There was not enough time, however, to put the order into effect. On the afternoon of 17 March, when it became clear that further defense of the fortress was useless, the Kronstadt rebels determined to retreat to Finland. About eight thousand made it there.

The fortress fell on the morning of 18 March, and the round of repressions began immediately. It was decided that the very fact of being in Kronstadt during the uprising would be regarded as a crime. Even giving medical aid to the wounded defenders of Kronstadt was made a punishable offense. Just one example: Two sisters, Zinaida and Maria Nikiforova, were arrested on the night of 29–30 March. Zinaida, the investigator's report said, "picked up wounded mutineers and worked in a hospital." The investigator recommended that "citizen Nikiforova be sent to a forced-labor camp for five years, suspended sentence." As for Maria Nikiforova, she was to have been released, but a special troika decree sent both sisters to five years of forced labor and exiled them to Arkhangelsk.[7]

Several dozen open trials were held. The harshest treatment was meted out to the sailors of the *Petropavlovsk* and *Sevastopol*. Just having served aboard these vessels was cause enough for one to be shot. The courts were particularly merciless toward the Red Army soldiers of the 560th Kronstadt Regiment and those of the 561st Regiment who had gone over to the Kronstadters during the assault on the fortress of 7 March.[8] The open trials, however, were only the tip of the iceberg. The fate of thousands of persons was decided at closed sessions of the special troikas and sometimes even *dvoikas,* or two-man tribunals.

On 20 March 1921 a special troika heard the case against 167 crew members of the *Petropavlovsk*. All were sentenced to death. The next day 32 sailors from the *Petropavlovsk* and 30 from the *Sevastopol* were shot; so were another 27 from the *Petropavlovsk* on 24 March.[9] The chairman of the mobile session of the Revolutionary Military Tribunal, S. Tsvetkov, sent a telegram to Petrograd: "Further arrests are being made and will continue to be made until I am sure that Kronstadt has been bled white and disarmed."

Most of those arraigned before the courts and troikas had taken virtually no part in the defense of the fortress. Among those who show up in the troika transcripts, for instance, is Pyotr Samsonov, twenty-nine, of peasant stock, a semiliterate, non-Party telephone operator with the First Naval Air Division; he was sentenced to death simply because he was an elected delegate to a conference aboard the *Petropavlovsk* on 2 March. And there is Arseny Petrov, forty, a junior clerk of a supply section, shot because he did guard duty on three occasions. There are many such examples.

The punitive forces were particularly prejudiced against those who quit the Party during the Kronstadt events. They were divided into four categories. The first category included commissars, secretaries of Party organizations, and "persons who made malicious announcements raising the hopes of the mutinous revolutionary committee and contributing to its authority." They were sentenced to death. The second category included those who had made "less malicious announcements and who were politically undeveloped, young, and played a passive role in the mutiny." They were sentenced to five years in a concentration camp. Finally, the third and fourth categories comprised "persons who declared that they were leaving the Party but did not give any reason, persons whose declarations that they were leaving the Party have not been found, though they themselves admitted that they submitted such declarations, and persons who declared they were leaving the Party but had been under the surveillance of the revolutionary committee members." These received a one-year suspended sentence of public service or were released.[10]

For "taking part in the Kronstadt mutiny," 2,103 persons were sentenced to death by the summer of 1921 by just four of the tribunals—the Presidium of the Petrograd Provincial Cheka, the Collegium of the Special Section of the Finnish Border Defense Forces, the special troika of the Kronstadt Special Section, and the Revolutionary Tribunal of the Petrograd Military District. Another 6,459 persons were sentenced to prison terms. Of these, 1,464 were released, but the charges against them were not dismissed.[11] They were dealt with later; all were tracked down and all were repressed.

This ever more inhuman system instituted the use of hostages and concentration camps. Here is an excerpt from one of many similar files: "Tukina, Olga Vladimirovna, wife of revolutionary committee secretary Tukin, taken hostage on 9 May 1921 and sentenced by a special troika to a concentration camp as a hostage, the sentence to be carried out when she recovers and is released from the maternity ward of the Kronstadt hospital."[12] So many people were sentenced that the need for more concentration camps was addressed by the Politburo of the CC of the RKP(b). At a session on 20 April 1921 it set up a commission chaired by Menzhinsky and charged with preparing for discussion the question of "creating a disciplinary colony of 10,000 to 20,000 people, if possible in the far north, in the Ukhta region, far removed from populated centers."[13]

By the beginning of April the principal phase of the investigation into the Kronstadt mutiny was completed. The conclusions of the chief investigator, Ya. Agranov, clearly diverged from the propaganda version. His report said, in part:

> The task facing my investigation was to clarify the roles of different parties and groups in the inception and development of the rebellion and the links between the rebellion's organizers and instigators and counterrevolutionary parties and organizations active on the territory of Soviet Russia and abroad. But to establish such links proved impossible. . . . The rebellion broke out spontaneously and drew into its vortex almost the entire population of the city and the fortress. In general, the Kronstadt rebellion constitutes the climax of a long-standing spontaneous petty-bourgeois reaction against the dictatorship of the proletariat and the Communist regime, as well as discontent on the part of the peasantry and backward elements of the working class with the food policy of the Soviet authorities and their evident wish to break the fetters placed by the authorities on small property owners' free trade.

Agranov's report reached only a narrow circle of Party and government leaders.

In 1921 and 1922 the TsIK announced amnesties for participants in the "White movement," including Kronstadters. Those who had fled to Finland were permitted to return. Some of them were naive enough to do so and found themselves at once in camps and prisons.

The winter of 1922 saw the start of mass exiling of Kronstadters. A committee was set up to carry out the evacuation. The first to be exiled were families with members who had been shot or sentenced, who were missing, or who had been expelled from the Party in a purge or had left the Party voluntarily. From 1 February 1922 to 1 April 1923 alone, 2,514 persons were exiled, 1,963 of them as "Kronstadt mutineers and their families." The overwhelming majority of the latter group were women and children. On arrival at their new places of residence, all the exiles had to register with the local offices of the VChK. For years to come, investigators would periodically scour the archives for cases that had been closed, trying to find evidence for fresh charges.

The reaction of the Bolshevik authorities to the Kronstadt events clearly revealed the Party's totalitarian essence and demonstrated the betrayal by its ruling clique of the ideals for which millions of misguided people gave their lives.

When, after the 20th Congress, the threat of personal responsibility for the villainies committed against the people hung in the air, a pitiful squabble broke out at the topmost levels of the Party and the secret police. The scourges of the special services said they had been merely executors, implementing the direct orders of the Party big shots. The Party leaders, in turn, insisted that all the crimes had been the work of the VChK, the OGPU, the NKVD, the MGB, the KGB.

Both were right. The elite of the Party and the elite of the security services were blood brothers. They committed crimes together. That from time to time the heads of Politburo members and special-service chiefs fell in the general carnage and thousands of Communist and Chekist apparatchiks died at the executioner's hands only testifies to the system of dual power that had developed in the country. In the final analysis, both Khrushchev and Gorbachev were toppled by the KGB; the Party bonzes were onstage only as extras.

Stalin had not trusted anyone. To rule freely, he had always sowed conflict among his followers. That is why the apparatchiks now feared punishment. That's how the apparatchiks lived—with fear and with a lust for power simultaneously.

Khrushchev's speech at the 20th Congress of 1956 condemned Stalin's crimes, but the system and the Stalinist henchmen remained untouchable. The latter did all they could to crush the barely budding process of de-Stalinization, realizing that at some point it would lead to the matter of their own legal responsibility. An attempt to widen the area of responsibility for the crimes of Stalinist fascism was made at the June 1957 plenum of the CC of the CPSU, but it failed.

As the first speaker, Marshal Zhukov raised the issue, revealing documents containing data on the execution of tens of thousands of people without trial, solely on the direct orders of members of the Politburo or with their approval. "Sleeves rolled up, axe in hand, they lopped off heads," he declaimed. "They packed them off by freight like cattle: so many bulls, so many cows, so many lambs."[14]

As Kaganovich spoke, Zhukov interrupted:

> Let's speak about responsibility for crimes, for executions—that's also an important question.
> Kaganovich: If the Plenum members wish me to put the other questions aside. . . .
> Zhukov: Tell us, why did you send three hundred railroad workers to kingdom come?
> Kaganovich: The question that was put, that's a political question.
> Zhukov: And a criminal one.
> Kaganovich: It should be examined not from the vantage point of 1957 but from the vantage point of the years 1937 and 1938. That's what is demanded by Marxist dialectics. I will say that we had a political struggle going on in the country. . . .
> Zhukov: You, brother, answer straight out. You had CC members shot—were they our enemies?
> Kaganovich: There were enemies, there was an intense class struggle. Together with our enemies, did we permit distortions, outrages, crimes? We did.
> I agree with and approve of Khrushchev's report at the 20th Congress, although I must say that I was very shaken by it. But I don't think that members of the CC took this dethroning of Stalin and exposed their sores and wounds with a light heart. I suffered through this report and I support it. I consider that we did right in uncovering and exposing these things. But, of course, that does not relieve me of responsibility. I am responsible politically.
> Zhukov: And criminally. . . . Abuse of power leads to criminal punishment.

Kaganovich: I am talking about political responsibility. The situation was drastic, we all acted very fast, and the fact that Comrade Zhukov pulled out the names of only two or three who signed documents and does not mention the others—that's a factional maneuver. There's factionalism for you. Drown everyone it suits you to and keep your mouth shut about the others. The whole Politburo. And how about the oblast troikas—all the oblasts had troikas headed by the obkom secretary.

Voices: On whose orders? Who created them?

Khrushchev: Who set up this criminal procedure of creating these troikas? Everyone who came before these troikas was shot.

Voices: That's right.

Kaganovich: Not all.

Khrushchev: The absolute majority were shot.

Kaganovich: And you, didn't you sign papers about executions in the Ukraine? I left Moscow in March 1935, I left the TsKK in 1934, I worked in the economy.

Voices: They shot people there, too.

Zhukov: Three hundred railroad workers.

Khrushchev: Were the judicial and Chekist organs subordinated to the obkoms? They never were. I was considered a Polish spy.

Kaganovich: Many were, and maybe me among them. I'll tell you now. The situation was tense.

Voices: You yourself created it.

Kaganovich: I'm being asked about railroad workers. There was an endless flow of papers from the NKVD. Ask the railroad workers how I was constantly accused of holding up the questioning. I defended hundreds of thousands of railroad people, and we arrested some of the people who according to the papers appeared to be enemies. And you, Comrade Zhukov, as division commander, you never signed?

Zhukov: I never sent a single person to be shot.

Kaganovich: That's hard to believe.

Zhukov: Please believe it.

Kaganovich: And you, what, you didn't approve of the policy of the CC, the policy of struggle with our enemies?

Zhukov: Of struggle with our enemies, but not of executions.[15]

Concluding his address, Zhukov said: "If the nation only knew their hands dripped with innocent blood, it would have met them not with applause but with stones."[16]

After the 20th Congress things eased up a bit. The camp system was gradually shrunk. But the war on dissidence went its own way, as I recounted earlier. Bloody repressions continued as well. Let us recall the events in Novocherkassk.

During the first six months of 1962, the administration of the Novocherkassk electric locomotive plant repeatedly readjusted its salary scales, with the result that the pay of many workers fell by 30 percent. The decline in wages and the simultaneous increase in food prices made life unbearable.

On the morning of 1 June 1962, the plant's workforce, gathering in groups, debated the government's decision to raise retail prices on meat and dairy products. The stormy discussions gradually spread from the workshops throughout the grounds of the factory. The number of those taking part swelled rapidly. At the workers' demand, the plant director came out to speak to them. The workers complained about abnormal working conditions, unsafe work rules and equipment, poor living conditions, and low wages. The atmosphere became heated. When the workers asked the director how they could go on making ends meet, he replied cynically, "If you don't have enough money for bread, eat pirozhki with liver." This proved to be the spark that set off the explosion.

A large group of workers moved on the administration office. Slogans appeared: "Meat, milk, pay raise!" More than four thousand people gathered in the factory square. During this meeting, a group of workers stopped a train on the Saratov–Rostov-on-the-Don line. The strikers told the passengers about their demands and their dire straits and asked them to pass the information on to people in other cities. A group of KGB operatives who had arrived at the plant with the head of the oblast administration attempted, with the help of the police, to force the crowd of workers off the railroad tracks and let the train go. They were unsuccessful. All movement on the line came to a halt.

That afternoon a member of the CC Presidium, A. Kirilenko, arrived in Rostov and proceeded to dress down the commander of the military district, General Pliyev, and the head of the political administration, Lieutenant General Ivashchenko, for their passivity. Kirilenko demanded that troops stationed in the district be sent immediately to Novocherkassk to put a stop to these "hooligan actions." After a telephone conversation with Kirilenko, Khrushchev agreed to his proposal. Pliyev gave orders for the deployment of subdivision units to Novocherkassk.

Kirilenko, Pliyev, and Ivashchenko proceeded that same day to Novocherkassk, establishing themselves in a military township where a temporary command post had been set up. Mikoyan, Kozlov, Shelepin, Polyansky, the heads of the KGB's central agencies, and the command of the internal troops of the MVD came from Moscow. On orders from members of the Presidium of the CC of the CPSU, units of the northern Caucasus military district and of the internal troops of the MVD in Kamensk-Shakhtinsk, Grozny, and Rostov-on-the-Don moved on Novocherkassk.

Toward the end of the day, five truckloads of soldiers and three armored personnel carriers moved toward the square in front of the plant's office. A crowd of factory workers blocked their way. The officers and soldiers were confused and uncertain what to do. Workers made speeches from the armored cars calling for a continuation of the strike and appealing to the soldiers to join them. Presidium members Kirilenko and Shelepin ordered tanks and more soldiers in armored personnel carriers to advance on the plant, which was placed under martial law. A curfew was declared in the city and arrests of workers began.

On the morning of 2 June the workers' demands gained the support of workers in the petroleum equipment plant and other enterprises in the city. Unarmed demonstrators started in a column toward the city center to express their grievances. It was a peaceful march with red flags, portraits of Lenin, and fresh flowers.

The demonstrators included many women and children. On the way to the city they were joined by a large group of young people. The troops were ordered to stop these peaceful marchers. The bridge across the Tuzlov River was blocked in three places by tanks and armored personnel carriers. But even this did not help. The crowd flowed over to the other side and continued on to the city committee of the CPSU.

When the thousands-strong crowd of demonstrators was four or five kilometers from the committee building, CC Presidium members Kozlov, Kirilenko, and Mikoyan reported the situation to Khrushchev and asked for permission to issue orders through the minister of defense and the commander of the northern Caucasus military district troops to break up the demonstration by force. All the internal troops and army units were issued weapons and ammunition. By ten that morning all the military subunits were brought to combat readiness.

The crowd of workers and their relatives—wives and children—approached to within fifty or a hundred meters of the committee building. It was encircled by troops. A mass demonstration was held, the speakers demanding lower food prices and higher wages. They wanted to convey their demands to the Party and government leaders. But the Party bosses were afraid to come out to them. They preferred to deal with them through the municipal radio network, which broadcast the texts of appeals to the city's population by Mikoyan and Kozlov. The workers insisted on meeting with representatives of the top leadership face to face.

The response was an order to open fire on unarmed people. Shots rang out. Twenty persons, including two women, were killed on the spot. The wounded and injured numbered more than forty; later, three of them died.[17]

This, however, did not bring the bloody reprisal to an end. Mass arrests of "instigators of the disturbances" began to take place in the city. Among the demonstrators there had been quite a few KGB members in civilian clothes who had noted down and photographed the more active participants. It was on their testimony that residents of Novocherkassk were rounded up.

The investigations failed to uncover any evidence of robbery or seizure of property by the accused. The investigators could dig up only two accusations of attempted seizure of weapons. And even here, one of the accused rejected the charge at his trial, and the other, having been killed, was unable to either admit or reject it.

The case files contain some curious testimony. Hearing the roar of tanks, a tractor driver named Katkov ran out of his house in his drawers (a detail duly noted in the file). Being not exactly sober, he exclaimed: "Oh Lord, they too are on their way to meet the requests of the toilers!" The tractor driver was tried and condemned; the sentence declared that "being near his house, he maliciously obstructed the movement of military vehicles on their way to the defense of the

Novocherkassk Electrical Locomotive Plant, giving vent at the same time to hostile, slanderous shouts."

All told, 116 persons were sentenced, seven of them to death and many to lengthy imprisonment—from ten to fifteen years in correctional hard-labor camps. Realizing the futility of blaming what had happened on "hooligan elements," the authorities did everything possible to keep the affair secret—including the cold-blooded murder of dozens of people. Even the bodies of the victims were buried secretly in different cemeteries of Rostov oblast.

Not a word about the events in Novocherkassk appeared in the newspapers. The only mention of the city came on 6 June in *Pravda*—that the workers there had "given a correct assessment to the increase in purchase and retail prices of meat and butter." The same newspaper commended the people of Novocherkassk for their zealous labor. That's what it said: "Good work is being done by the collectives of the Novocherkassk electric locomotive and electrode plants. . . ." Moreover, it reported, a number of meetings had been held in the city in support of the "wise policy of the Party and government."

All this took place during the Khrushchev "thaw," when the propaganda line called from time to time for de-Stalinization, democracy, and a wider role for workers in the conduct of government. But in practice, the authorities pursued something entirely different—the preservation of the Bolshevik dictatorship, which was using the same old Stalinist instruments of violence.

On 5 June 1962, three days after the executions, the servicemen of the Novocherkassk garrison and the subdivisions of the internal troops were addressed by a member of the CC Presidium, CC Secretary Kozlov. On behalf of the CC of the CPSU, the Soviet government, and Khrushchev personally, he praised them for putting an end to the "disorders" in Novocherkassk and thanked them for their discipline, staunchness, and courage.

From Kronstadt to Novocherkassk—stages in a tide of blood and shame.

HARVEST OF CROSSES

(In Lieu of an Epilogue)

FROM horizon to horizon Russia is sown with crosses and with the nameless graves of its citizens, felled in wars, killed by famine, or shot at the whim of the Leninist-Stalinist fascist regime. The crosses mark the last remains of millions, and more millions lie in unmarked graves. They lie in ditches and trenches, in swamps, in mountain clefts, and some are just skeletons scattered in the forests of the Russian land.

There are no precise documented figures on the scope of this national tragedy. A variety of figures are bandied about. Academician Vernadsky, an astute observer, wrote in his diary in January 1939 that the number of persons exiled or sent to prison or concentration camp in the last half of the 1930s was being quoted as 14 to 17 million. The authorities naturally espoused a different version. In 1954, the minister of internal affairs, S. Kruglov, an active participant in the repressions and the organizer of the deportations from the northern Caucasus, reported to Khrushchev that between 1930 and 1953 the number of those repressed in the USSR totaled about 3.7 million, including 765,000 who were shot.

These figures, of course, are false. But they pop up officially to this day. They do not take account of the number of people confined in the internal prisons of the NKVD, and those prisons were jam-

packed. They do not break down the mortality rate in camps for political prisoners, and they ignore the number of arrested peasants
and deported peoples. To these categories should be added the victims of the Leninist repressions, whom nobody counted, and the 13
million killed in the civil war—plus the 3.4 million arrested during
the collectivization campaign and the 3.3 million who were of repressed nationalities or were repatriates from prisoner of war camps
in Germany and other European countries.

My own many years of experience in the rehabilitation of victims
of political terror allow me to assert that the number of people in the
USSR who were killed for political motives or who died in prisons
and camps during the entire period of Soviet power totaled 20 to
25 million. And unquestionably one must add those who died of
famine—more than 5.5 million during the civil war and more than
5 million during the 1930s.

Documents that have already been published give some idea of
the scope of the punitive policy. In the Russian Federation alone, according to incomplete data, the number of people sentenced between
1923 and 1953 totaled more than 41 million. Of course, among
them there were people who had committed crimes—but there were
also millions imprisoned for being late to work, for falling short of
daily production quotas in kolkhozes, and for other such minor mis-
demeanors. On orders handed down between 26 June 1940 and 15
April 1942, the number of people sentenced in 1940 for such offenses totaled more than 2 million; for 1946 the figure was 1.2 million, for 1947 more than 938,000, and so on. Even as late as 1953,
more than 308,000 people were sentenced under these statutes.

During the postwar years, the number of people sentenced for
being late to work and falling short of work quotas totaled more
than 6 million. Many of them served their time in the gulag.

But who can tell it all.

The advent of Bolshevism in Russia was predicted by Fyodor
Dostoyevsky, who wrote in *The Possessed* that "one hundred million people will perish."

What did Bolshevism give to the world, to its peoples, to the individual?

To the world: revolts, destruction, violent revolutions, civil wars,
violence toward the individual.

To its peoples: poverty, destitution, lawlessness, slavery both material and spiritual.

To humankind: endless suffering. The Bolshevik state deprived the individual of freedom, honor, morality, prosperity, even faith in God.

Bolshevism is a many-faced demonic frenzy, a militant antihuman grotesquerie. Its ideological models were Marxism of German origin and its English counterpart. But Bolshevism's first real victory was won in Russia.

As we know, the land of Rus accepted Christianity from Constantinople in 988 A.D. Characteristics of Byzantine rule of that era—baseness, cowardliness, venality, treachery, overcentralization, apotheosis of the ruler's personality—dominate in Russia's social and political life to this day. In the twelfth century the various fragmented Russian principalities from the Volga to the Carpathians were conquered by the Mongols. Asian traditions and customs, with their disregard for the individual and for human rights and their cult of might, violence, despotic power, and lawlessness became part of the Russian people's way of life.

The tragedy of Russia lay first and foremost in this: that for a thousand years it was ruled by men and not by laws. The rulers were princes, czars, various chairmen, general secretaries. They ruled ineptly, bloodily. The people existed for the government, not the government for the people. Russia avoided classical slavery. But it has not yet emerged from feudalism; it is still enslaved by an official imperial ideology, the essence of which is that the state is everything and the individual nothing.

Russia found itself on the margins of civilization, inasmuch as it never knew the institution of normal private property. Property always belonged to the state, to its feudal elite—and today to the nomenklatura oligarchy of former apparatchiks. The lack of private property, especially land, is the primary reason for Russia's woes, for its cruel fate.

Russia made several desperate attempts to overcome its backwardness. There were the reforms of Peter I and Alexander II, as well as the reforms—commonly associated with the name of Pyotr Stolypin—of Nicholas II. And all of them were accompanied by upheaval and war. Serfdom was abolished in Russia in 1861. Only at the end of the nineteenth century did the country, with agonizing difficulty, take the road of democratic development.

The beginning of the twentieth century is the brightest period in Russian history. Industrial development leaped forward at a rate that was equaled only later by Japan in the 1950s; finances stabilized, agricultural productivity rose. Parliamentarism was born. Compulsory primary education was instituted; universities, centers of higher education, traditional and modern secondary schools were opened. Science, art, and literature flourished. But in 1914 the First World War broke out. Early in the spring of 1917 the czar abdicated and a republic was proclaimed.

It lasted only nine months: the Bolsheviks drowned it in blood, staging a counterrevolution. Three generations of Russians suffered through economic slavery and unimaginable terror, both physical and psychological, through World War II, Stalinism, the dictatorship of the Communist Party and its leaders.

In August 1996 I appealed to Russian and world public opinion, to the president of Russia, to the Constitutional Court, to the government, to the Chief Prosecutor's Office, and to the Federal Assembly to initiate proceedings against the fascist-Bolshevik ideology and its exponents. There was no response except from a group of Communist deputies who lodged a demand with the chief prosecutor that I be indicted for persecution of dissidence. Democrats confined their support to congratulatory phone calls.

But even though the Bolshevik forces, twisting and turning, dissembling and playing innocent, are doing all they can to promote a creeping restoration, I still believe that the Russian people will have sense enough to cure themselves for good of their lingering illness.

We managed to give the remains of Emperor Nicholas II and his family a dignified burial. The president of Russia and Patriarch Aleksii acknowledged at long last the need for a spiritual cleansing, the need for repentance.

Under these circumstances, and with full awareness of Russia's tragic history, I am convinced that:

Bolshevism cannot escape responsibility for the counterrevolution, for the violent coup d'état of 1917.

Bolshevism cannot escape responsibility for the establishment of a dictatorship instilled with hatred for the individual. As a result of its criminal actions, more than sixty million people were exterminated. Bolshevism, as a species and forerunner of fascism, made itself the principal force in the genocide of its own people.

Bolshevism cannot escape responsibility for unleashing the fratricidal civil war that devastated the country; in the course of its senseless and bloody battles and destruction more than thirteen million people were killed, died of hunger, or emigrated.

Bolshevism cannot escape responsibility for the destruction of the Russian peasantry. Peasant Russia was demolished, its morality, traditions, and customs trampled. The productive capacity of the village was undermined so badly that for many years now, in order to avert famine, the country has been buying food from abroad.

Bolshevism cannot escape responsibility for the destruction of Christian churches and monasteries, Moslem mosques, Jewish synagogues, and other houses of worship, for the mass execution of clergy, for the persecution of believers, actions that have brought the country eternal disgrace.

Bolshevism cannot escape responsibility for the destruction of entire strata of Russian society—the officer caste, the nobility, the merchant class, the true intelligentsia, the community of scholars, scientists, and artists.

Bolshevism cannot escape responsibility for violations of elementary rights, for falsifications, spurious accusations, and extrajudicial sentencings on a scale unheard of in all history; for executions without investigation or trial; for torture and torment; for organizing the system of concentration camps, including camps for children held hostage; for the use of poison gas against peaceful civilians—for the meat grinder of Leninist-Stalinist repressions in which more than twenty million people perished.

Bolshevism cannot escape its responsibility for abolishing freedom of speech, for eliminating all democratic parties and movements, including those with a socialist orientation.

Bolshevism cannot escape responsibility for its inept waging of the war against Hitler's fascism. Only the sacrifice of thirty million of our citizens and the heroism of the people saved the country from subjugation.

Bolshevism cannot escape responsibility for its crimes against former Soviet prisoners of war and repatriates, for driving them after the war into Soviet camps and exploiting their hard labor with the aim of working them to death.

Bolshevism cannot escape responsibility for waging genocide against non-Russian citizens of the USSR, for forcibly resettling in the country's most sparsely populated regions Germans, Poles, Tatars, Chechens, Ingush, Karachayevs, Koreans, Balkars, Kalmyks, Turko-Meskhetins, Armenians, Bulgarians, Greeks, and Gagauzy.

Bolshevism cannot escape responsibility for organizing the hounding of scholars and writers, of those active in film, theater, and music, of doctors and others; for the colossal damage done to the nation's culture and science. Out of criminal ideological motives, genetics and cybernetics, as well as progressive movements in economics, linguistics, and literary and artistic endeavor, were ostracized.

Bolshevism cannot escape responsibility for organizing racist trials—against the Jewish Anti-Fascist Committee, against the "doctors-murderers"—aimed at fomenting enmity among the country's national groups and playing on the masses' vilest instincts.

Bolshevism cannot escape responsibility for organizing criminal campaigns against every kind of dissidence, whose many adherents were subjected to the widest array of punishments—prison, exile, special resettlement, expulsion abroad, psychiatric institutionalization, loss of jobs, slanderous attacks in the press, and other indignities.

Bolshevism cannot escape responsibility for the total militarization of the country, which rendered the people destitute and drastically stunted the development of society.

Bolshevism cannot escape responsibility for the antigovernment mutiny of August 1991, which led to the disorderly breakup of the state and to unimaginable hardship for all the peoples of the former Soviet Union.

How short our memory is, even today. We crawl pitifully along, bogged down in the mire. The main source of our troubles has yet to dawn on us: without the de-Bolshevization of Russia there can be no question of the nation's recovery, its renascence and its resumption of its place in world civilization. Only when it has shaken free of Bolshevism can Russia hope to be healed.

Notes

FOREWORD

1. Alexander Yakovlev, *The Fate of Marxism in Russia*, trans. Catherine A. Fitzpatrick (New Haven: Yale University Press, 1993).

2. Stephane Courtois et al., *The Black Book of Communism: Crimes, Terror, Repression* (Cambridge: Harvard University Press, 1999).

3. Most notable are Djilas's *The New Class* (New York: Praeger, 1957) and *Conversations with Stalin* (New York: Harcourt, Brace & World, 1962).

4. Anatoly S. Chernyaev, *My Six Years with Gorbachev* (University Park: Pennsylvania State University Press, 2000), pp. xvii, xv–xvi.

5. Quoted in Robert V. Daniels, "Overthrowing Utopianism" [review of Yakovlev's *The Fate of Marxism in Russia*], *New Leader*, 14–18 February 1994, p. 17.

6. Jonathan Steele, *Eternal Russia: Yeltsin, Gorbachev and the Mirage of Democracy* (Cambridge: Harvard University Press, 1994), p. 175. In a conversation I had with Yakovlev in 1998 in Washington, D.C., he confirmed that his visit to Prague had made "a terrible impression" on him; he asked Soviet tank drivers why they were there, and they had no idea.

SOCIALLY DANGEROUS CHILDREN

1. *Sbornik zakonodatelnykh i normativnykh aktov o repressiakh i reabilitatsii zhertv politicheskikh repressii* (Compilation of Legal and Normative Acts on the Arrest and Rehabilitation of Victims of Political Repression) (Moscow: Respublika, 1993), pp. 86–93.

2. The letter is in the archive of the Administration of the President of the Russian Federation (AP RF) on communications from citizens.

3. L. Trotsky, *Diaries and Letters* (New York, 1986), p. 101.

4. *Yezhenedelnik ChK* (Cheka Weekly), Moscow, 1918, no. 1, p. 11.

5. Gosudarstvennyi arkhiv russkoi federatsii (State Archive of the Russian Federation) (GARF), f. 8415, op. 1, d. 114, l. 62.

6. *Krestianskoye vosstanie v Tambovskoi gubernii v 1919–1921 gg. ("Antonovshchina"). Dokumenty i materialy* (The Peasant Uprising in Tambov Province in 1919–21: "Antonovshchina." Documents and Materials) (Tambov, 1994), p. 246.

7. All three letters are in the archive of the AP RF on communications from citizens.

8. *Sobranie zakonov SSSR* (Collected Laws of the USSR) (SZ SSSR), no. 19, 1935, p. 155.

9. *Detstvo v Tiurme: Memuary Petra Yakira*, s. 84–85. The quotation is from the English-language edition, by Pyotr Yakir, *A Childhood in Prison* (London: Macmillan 1972), p. 82.

10. AP RF, op. 1, d. 795, l. 126.

11. Ibid., ll. 40–41.

12. Ibid., l. 128

13. Tsentr dlya khraneniya sovremennoi dokumentatsii, f. komissiya Shvernika (Center for the Preservation of Contemporary Documentation, File of the Shvernik Commission) (TsKhSD) d. 3, ll. 45–51.

14. Tsentralnyi arkhiv federalnoi sluzhby bezopastnosti (Central Archive of the Federal Security Service) (TsA FSB), f. 3, op. 4, d. 16, ll. 147, 310, 311.

15. AP RF, f. 3, op. 58, d. 174, l. 107.

16. GARF, f. 9401, op. 1a, d. 20, l. 199.

17. Ibid., l. 199 ob.

18. Ibid., d. 29, ll. 28–28 ob.

19. GARF, f. 9401, op. 2, d. 1, pp. 610–13.

FELLOW TRAVELERS

1. *Pravda,* 13 February (31 January), 1918.

2. Tsentralnyi gosudarstvennyi arkhiv Moskovskoi oblasti (Central State Archive of the Moscow Oblast) (TsGAMO), f. 66, op. 25, d. 39, ll. 20, 22.

3. *Sbornik tsirkuliarnykh pisem VChK-OGPU* (Collected Circular Letters of the VChK-OGPU) (Moscow, 1935), vol. 3, part 1, p. 301.

4. *Izvestiya vsesoyuznogo tsentralnogo ispolnitelnogo komiteta* (Izvestiya of the All-Union Central Executive Committee) (VTsIK), 21 September 1919.

5. AP RF, f. 3, op. 59, d. 14, l. 79; d. 2, l. 38.

6. Rossiiskii gosudarstvennyi arkhiv sotsialnoi i politicheskoi istorii (Russian State Archive of Social and Political History) (RGASPI), f. 5, op. 1, d. 2558, l. 3. Kamenev and his confederates were subsequently done away with by the Chekists. I realize that historical parallels can be misleading, but the basic motivation of all counterintelligence agencies is more or less the same: revenge. No sooner did I raise

with Gorbachev, at the beginning of 1989, the need for dividing the KGB into separate sections—intelligence, counterintelligence, border units, liaison, and security—than the resistance of the secret services bubbled up. Since then, the campaign against me has only intensified. From what I can make out, the KGB activated its agents in the literary, journalistic, and military fields and elsewhere. Surveillance, both technical and physical, increased markedly. The harassment continues to this day.

7. AP RF, f. 3, op. 59, d. 2, ll. 36–39.

8. RGASPI, f. 17, op. 3, d. 150, l. 1.

9. AP RF, f. 3, op. 59, d. 18, l. 101.

10. *Novyi Den* (The New Day), 13 and 14 April 1918.

11. RGASPI, f. 17, op. 4, d. 41, l. 3.

12. Ibid., d. 25, l. 4.

13. Ibid., d. 43, l. 1. In these minutes of a Politburo meeting on 4 December 1919, Avanesov asks which representatives of the Social Democrats and the populist parties were to be allowed to attend.

14. Ibid., d. 58, ll. 28–28 ob.

15. Tsentralnyi arkhiv federalnoi sluzhby bezopasnosti russkoi federatsii (Central Archive of the Federal Security Service of the Russian Federation) (TsA FSB RF), d. N-8, t. 9. l. 77.

16. *Izvestiya Tambovskogo gubsoveta* (Izvestiya of the Tambov Provincial Soviet), 4 July (17 July) 1918.

17. TsA FSB RF, d. N-8, t. 13, ll. 244, 245.

18. Z. N. Gippius, *Zhivye litsa: Vospominaniye* (Living Faces: Recollections), book 11 (Tbilisi, 1991), p. 355.

19. A. S. Izgoyev, *Pyat let v sovetskoi Rossii (obryvki, vospominaniye i zametki)* (Five Years in Soviet Russia: Fragments, Recollections and Notes), Archive of the Russian Revolution, ed. I. V. Gessen (Berlin, 1923), vol. 10, pp. 31, 32.

20. M. Liber, *Krizis revoliutsii i zadachi demokratii* (The Crisis of the Revolution and the Problems of Democracy) (Yekaterinoslav, 1918), p. 3.

21. V. I. Lenin, *Polnoye sobraniye sochinenii* (Complete Collected Works), vol. 37, pp. 219, 222, 228.

22. Ibid., vol. 97, pp. 220, 229.

23. AP RF, f. 3, op. 59, d. 14, l. 10.

24. TsGAMO, f. 66, op. 20, l. 55.

25. AP RF, f. 3, op. 59, d. 15, l. 2.

26. *Iz istorii VChK* (From the History of the VChK), l. 227.

27. *Sbornik tsirkulyarnykh pisem VChK-OGPU*, vol. 3, part 1, pp. 13, 14.

28. See, for example, the synopsis of a speech by Spiridonova at a meeting of the workers at the Duks factory on 6 February 1919 (TsA FSB RF, General Investigative File, d. N-685, t. 6, l. 12).

29. Ibid., l. 2.

30. *Sbornik tsirkulyarnykh pisem VChK-OGPU*, vol. 3, part 1, p. 48.

31. Ibid., p. 95.

32. TsA FSB RF, f. 1, op. 6, d. 331, l. 9.

33. RGASPI, f. 17, op. 112, d. 309, l. 40.

34. Ibid., f. 5, op. 1, d. 2558, l. 50.

35. TsA FSB RF. Osobyi fond (Special File), d. N-8, t. 1a, ll. 64–64 ob.

36. *Sbornik tsirkuliarov i rasporiazhenii VChK-OGPU, 1919–1924* (Collected Circulars and Directives of the VChK-OGPU, 1919–24), vol. 3, part 1, p. 32.

37. Ibid., pp. 60–61.

38. AP RF, f. 3, op. 59, d. 15, l. 6.

39. TsA FSB, f. 1, op. 5, d. 334, l. 3.

40. *Sbornik zakonodatelnykh i normativnykh aktov o repressiakh i reabilitatsii zhertv repressii* (Compilation of Legal and Normative Acts on the Arrest and Rehabilitation of Victims of Political Repression) (Moscow, 1993), p. 12.

41. RGASPI, f. 17, op. 112, d. 310, l. 3.

42. Ibid., f. 5, op. 1, d. 2576, ll. 11, 38.

43. Ibid., f. 17, op. 84, d. 273, l. 85; f. 5, op. 1, d. 2578, l. 15.

44. AP RF, f. 3, op. 59, d. 29, ll. 44–47.

45. Ibid., f. 3, op. 59, d. 16, ll. 4, 1, 2.

46. RGASPI, f. 5, op. 1, d. 2558, ll. 41–45.

47. Ibid., f. 17, op. 84, d. 546, ll. 1–1 ob.

48. AP RF, f. 3, op. 59, d. 29, ll. 223, 224.

49. Ibid., d. 14, l. 53; d. 18, l. 58.

50. Ibid., d. 2, ll. 30, 26, 55.

51. Ibid., l. 80.

52. RGASPI, f. 17, op. 112, d. 564, ll. 65, 76–77, 135, 237.

53. TsA FSB RF, f. 2, op. 1, d. 611, l. 124.

54. TsA FSB, f. 1, op. 6, d. 323, l. 18. The man in need of being neutralized was a Jewish worker barely able to speak Russian.

55. AP RF, f. 3, op. 59, d. 27, ll. 1–23.

56. Ibid., d. 16, l. 1.

57. RGASPI, f. 17, op. 60, d. 31, l. 3.

58. AP RF, f. 5, op. 1, d. 2558, l. 52.

59. Lenin, *Polnoye sobraniye sochinenii,* vol. 54, p. 144.

60. Ibid., vol. 45, p. 50.

61. AP RF, f. 34, op. 59, d. 15, l. 14.

62. Lenin, *Polnoye sobraniye sochinenii,* vol. 45, pp. 140–45.

63. Ibid., vol. 45, pp. 149, 534.

64. Ibid., vol. 54, p. 279.

65. RGASPI, f. 17, op. 60, d. 139, l. 58.

66. Ibid., op. 112, d. 439, ll. 101; d. 728, l. 30.

67. *VKP(b) v rezoliutsiyakh i resheniyakh s'ezdov, konferentsii i plenumov TsK* (The VKP(b) in Resolutions and Decisions at Congresses, Conferences, and Plenums of the CC) (Moscow, 1936), part 1, p. 475.

68. TsGAMO, f. 66, op. 25, d. 39, ll. 25, 26.

69. F. I. Dan, *Dva goda skitanii* (Two Years of Wandering) (Berlin, 1922), p. 58.

70. RGASPI, f. 17, op. 84, d. 42, ll. 7–13.

71. *Pisma Yu. O. Martova* (The Letters of Yu. O. Martov) (Benson, 1990), pp. 29–32.

72. *Izvestiya TsK KPSS* (Izvestiya of the CC of the CPSU), no. 7, 1989, p. 157.

73. *Pisma Yu. O. Martova,* pp. 55, 56.

74. Lenin, *Polnoye sobraniye sochinenii,* vol. 51, p. 150.

75. RGASPI, f. 17, op. 3, d. 84, l. 1.

76. Lenin, *Polnoye sobraniye sochinenii,* vol. 54, pp. 130–31.

77. RGASPI, f. 5, op. 1, d. 2578, l. 23.

78. AP RF, f. 3, op. 59, d. 2, ll. 94, 125.

79. Lenin, *Polnoye sobraniye sochinenii,* vol. 45, pp. 89, 189.

80. *Sbornik zakonodatelnykh i normativnykh aktov o repressiakh,* pp. 13, 14.

81. AP RF, f. 3, op. 59, d. 3, ll. 56, 78.

82. Ibid., f. 3, op. 58, d. 166, ll. 104, 105, 108.

83. Ibid., f. 3, op. 59, d. 21, ll. 1, 16, 19, 57, 58, 87, 100, 103, 104; d. 22, l. 2.

84. Ibid., d. 22, l. 1; d. 23, l. 1.

85. Ibid., op. 58, d. 168, l. 128.

86. Ibid., d. 169, l. 4.

Peasants

1. *Leninskii sbornik* (Anthology of Lenin's Works), vol. 18, pp. 93, 94.

2. V. I. Lenin, *Polnoye sobraniye sochinenii* (Complete Collected Works), vol. 50, p. 86.

3. 6th All-Russian Extraordinary Congress of Soviets, stenographic record (Moscow, 1919), p. 17.

4. 8th Congress of the RKP(b), stenographic record, p. 407.

5. Lenin, *Polnoye sobraniye sochinenii,* vol. 37, p. 41; vol. 50, pp. 137, 142–44, 145.

6. GARF, f. 8415, op. 1, d. 128, l. 5.

7. Russkii gosudarstvennyi voyennyi arkhiv (Russian State Military Archive) (RGVA), f. 6, op. 12, d. 194, l. 6.

8. RGASPI, f. 17, op. 84, d. 114, l. 81.

9. M. Ya. Latsis, *Dva goda borby* (Two Years of Struggle) (Moscow, 1920), p. 71.

10. *Revoliutsionnaya Rossiya* (Revolutionary Russia), no. 7, May 1921, p. 30.

11. Ibid., April 1921, no. 6, p. 30.

12. RGVA, f. 24380, op. 3, d. 70, l. 346.

13. Ibid., f. 34228, op. 1, d. 3, l. 1.

14. GARF, f. 8415, op. 1, d. 114, l. 62.

15. Tomskii oblastnoi tsentr dokumentatsii noveishei istorii (Tomsk Oblast Center for the Documentation of Current History), f. 1, op. 3, d. 2, l. 218; *Gosudarstvennyi arkhiv obshchestvenno-politicheskoi dokumentatsii Kurganskoi oblasti* (State Archive of Social-Political Documentation of Kurgan Oblast), f. 1, op. 1, d. 6a, l. 85.

16. Rossiiskii gosudarstvennyi arkhiv ekonomiki (Russian State Archive of Economics) (RGAE), f. 7486, op. 37, ed. khr. 78, ll. 43, 44 ob.

17. Ibid., ll. 96, 97.

18. *Pisma Stalina Molotovu, 1925–1936* (Stalin's Letters to Molotov, 1925–1936) (Moscow, 1995), p. 194.

19. Ibid., pp. 217, 218.

20. RGAE, f. 7486, op. 37, d. 78, l. 95.

21. GARF, f. 1235, op. 2, d. 463, l. 9.

22. RGASPI, f. 17, op. 20, d. 26, ll. 216, 217, 165.

23. Lenin, *Polnoye sobraniye sochinenii,* vol. 38, p. 69; vol. 39, pp. 31ff.

24. *Izvestiya TsK KPSS* (Izvestiya of the CC of the CPSU), no. 6, 1989, p. 178.

25. Ibid., no. 8, 1989, p. 163.

26. Ibid., no. 2, 1990, p. 171.

The Intelligentsia

1. V. I. Lenin, *Polnoye sobraniye sochinenii* (Complete Collected Works), vol. 47, p. 133.

2. Ibid., vol. 51, p. 48.

3. Yu. P. Annenkov, *Dnevnik moikh vstrech: Tsikl tragedii* (Diary of My Encounters: A Cycle of Tragedies) (Moscow, 1991), vol. 2, p. 270.

4. TsA FSB RF, f. 2, op. 4, d. 465.

5. Rossiiskii gosudarstvennyi arkhiv istorii i literatury (Russian State Archive of History and Literature [RGALI]), f. 656, op. 6, d. 28, l. 99.

6. AP RF, f. 3, op. 59, d.3, ll. 62, 63. Lenin's note to Stalin is not dated but was probably written in the summer of 1922. The question of exiling a large group of the Russian "counterrevolutionary" intelligentsia was first raised by Lenin in May 1922 in a note to Dzerzhinsky (*Polnoye sobraniye sochinenii,* vol. 54, pp. 265, 266). Judging from that note, the matter had been discussed in principle even earlier, but in May it was still under consideration.

7. Lenin, *Polnoye sobraniye sochinenii,* vol. 54, p. 270.

8. RGASPI, f. 17, op. 3, d. 296, ll. 3, 7.

9. I. A. Ilyin, *Sobranie sochinenii* (Collected Works) (Moscow, 1993), vol. 1, p. 26.

10. AP RF, f. 3, op. 35, d. 35, ll. 1–11.

11. TsA FSB RF, f. 1, op. 6, d. 26, l. 22.

12. Ibid., f. 3, op. 1, d. 56, ll. 160–63.

13. Nadezhda Mandelstam, *Hope against Hope: A Memoir,* trans. Max Hayward (Harmondsworth: Penguin, 1975), p. 13.

14. AP RF, f. 3, op. 35, d. 4, l. 13 ob.

15. Ibid., d. 45, ll. 26–29.

16. Ibid., f. 3, op. 34, d. 187, ll. 109–12.

17. Ibid, ll. 107, 108.

18. RGASPI, f. 17, op. 125, d. 212, ll. 1–3; d. 232, l. 9.

19. Tsentr khraneniya sovremennoi dokumentatsii (Center for the Preservation of Contemporary Documents) (TsKhSD), f. 5, op. 36, d. 37, ll. 24, 25.

20. D. A. Polikarpov headed the cultural department of the CC of the CPSU from 1955 to 1962. A. A. Surkov, the Soviet poet, was first secretary of the Writers Union of the USSR from 1953 to 1959.

21. In February 1957 Pasternak and Goslitizdat asked Feltrinelli to postpone publication of the novel until its appearance in the USSR. Feltrinelli agreed to wait

until September. On 21 August and 23 October, Pasternak signed the texts of a telegram and letter to Feltrinelli proposed to him by the cultural department of the CC of the CPSU, in which he objected to the novel's publication in the version in the publisher's hands and demanded that the manuscript be returned to him for revisions. These communications were unavailing, as work on publication was already far along and as Feltrinelli simply did not trust them, having reached a private agreement with Pasternak to correspond only in French.

22. On 23 October 1958, the day Pasternak was awarded the Nobel Prize, a proposal that the 1956 letter of the editors of *Novy Mir* be published in *Literaturnaya Gazeta* and *Novy Mir* was placed by M. A. Suslov before the Presidium of the CC of the CPSU. It was included as a separate clause in a decree passed that day, "On Pasternak's Slanderous Novel."

23. TsKhSD, f. 5, op. 36, d. 61, ll. 39, 40. The document was received by the CC of the CPSU on 17 September. The letter bears these notations: "To Comrade Yarustovsky, B. M. Comrade Furtseva requests that the department's proposal be prepared on an urgent basis. 19/9. N. Kalinin"; "CC of the CPSU. The cultural department of the CC of the CPSU has taken the necessary steps in regard to the campaign of the reactionary foreign press around the novel of B. Pasternak and the award to him of the Nobel Prize. Section head of the cultural department of the CC of the CPSU B. Yarustovsky. 10/11/58"; "Comrade Furtseva, E. A. is aware of the steps taken by the cultural department of the CPSU and the Soviet Writers Union and approves. N. Kalinin 12/11/58" N. S. Kalinin was assistant to the secretary of the CC of the CPSU, E. A. Furtseva.

24. TsKhSD, f. 5, op. 36, d. 61, ll. 64, 65.

25. AP RF, f. 3, op. 34, d. 269, ll. 53–57.

26. E. L. Lann (1896–1958), a Soviet writer and translator. He and his wife committed suicide.

27. TsKhSD, f. 5, op. 36, d. 59, ll. 200, 201.

28. Ibid., f. 5, op. 36, d. 93, ll. 25, 26.

29. Ibid., f. 5, op. 36, d. 61, l. 139.

30. *Ogonyok*, no. 3, 1969. The editor in chief was A. Sofronov.

31. TsKhSD, f. 89, d. 22, l. 24.

32. *Izvestiya*, 20 May 1992.

33. AP RF, Rabochaya zapis zasedaniya Politburo ot 7 ianvaria 1974 goda (Minutes of the Politburo meeting of 7 January 1974), ll. 19–33.

34. AP RF, minutes of Politburo meeting no. 117 (3 January 1980).

35. AP RF, op. 113, no. P-1240, ll. 1–5.

THE CLERGY

1. *Za Khrista postradavshiye: Goneniya na Russkuyu Pravoslavnuyu Tserkov, 1917–1956* (Martyrs for Christ: Persecution of the Russian Orthodox Church, 1917–1956) (Moscow: Orthodox Holy Tikhon Theological Institute, 1997). Work on the subject is continuing at a specialized Internet database, http://www.pstbi.ccas.ru. This site contains an article by N. E. Yemelyanov, "Otsenka statistiki gonenii na Russkuyu Pravoslavnoyu Tserkov, 1917–1952" (Assessment of Statistics

on the Persecution of the Russian Orthodox Church, 1917–1952). Another important source is a book by Father Damaskin (Orlovsky), *Mucheniki, ispovedniki and podvizhniki blagochestiya Russkoi Pravoslavnoi Tserkvi XX stoletia* (Martyrs, Father Confessors, and Defenders of the Piety of the Russian Orthodox Church in the Twentieth Century) (Tver, 1992).

2. RGASPI, f. 2, op. 12, d. 12176, l. 1.

3. *Izvestiya TsK KPSS* (Izvestiya of the CC of the CPSU), no. 4, 1990, ll. 192, 193.

4. TsKhSD, f. 89, op. 49, d. 1, ll. 6, 7.

5. *K kanonizatsii novomuchennikov rossiiskikh* (On the Canonization of New Russian Martyrs) (Moscow, 1991), pp. 29, 30.

6. TsA FSB RF, *Katalog sudebno-sledstvennykh del* (Catalog of Judicial-Investigative Cases).

7. GARF, f. 393, op. 2, d. 1799, ll. 65, 66.

8. TsA FSB RF, *Arkhivno-sledstvennoye delo* (Archival-Investigative Case) no. 4444, l. 85

9. Arkhiv upravleniya FSB po Yaroslavskoi oblasti. Spravka (Archive of the Administration of the FSB on Yaroslavl Oblast. Memorandum) ll. 12, 19.

10. GARF, f. 5263, op. 1, d. 145, l. 1; d. 97, ll. 4, 5.

11. Ibid., f. 6991, op. 4, d. 173, l. 187

12. TsKhSD, f. 5, op. 62, d. 37, l. 31.

TWICE BETRAYED

1. AP RF, f. 3, op. 50, d. 507, ll. 76–81.

2. Ibid., ll. 120, 121.

3. TsA FSB RF, f. 66, op. 1, k. 601, ll. 314–43.

4. AP RF, f. 3, op. 50, d. 506, ll. 9, 10.

5. AGSh VS RF, op. 37820, d. 1, ll. 1–3, 37–39.

6. AP RF, f. 3, op. 50, d. 507, ll. 44–52.

7. Ibid., op. 58, d. 179, ll. 28, 29, 30–34.

8. Ibid., op. 50, d. 509, ll. 96–100.

9. Ibid., d. 511, ll. 23–32.

10. Ibid.

11. Ibid., ll. 17–22.

FOREVER SLANDERED

1. GARF, f. R-5446, op. 12, d. 209, ll. 30–34.

2. Ibid., f. R-9479, op. 1, d. 641, l. 89.

3. Ibid., f. R-5446, op. 29, d. 48, l. 17.

4. *Prostor,* no. 2, 1987, ll. 59, 60.

5. GARF, f. R-9479, op. 1, d. 83, ll. 1–3.

6. Ibid.

7. *Literaturnaya gazeta,* 11 October 1989.

8. GARF, f. R-9479, op. 1, d. 768, l. 129.

9. Ibid., f. R-374, op. 28, d. 4055, l. 47.

10. Ibid., f. R-9401, op. 2, d. 64, l. 167.

11. Ibid., ll. 165, 162.

12. *Istoriya SSSR* (History of the USSR), no. 1, 1992, p. 134.

13. GARF, f. R-9478, op. 1, d. 137, ll. 15, 16.

14. Ibid., d. 32, l. 237; d. 41, l. 244.

15. *Konferentsiya repressirovannykh narodov Rossiiskoi Federatsii (1991– 1992). Dokumenty i materialy* (Conference of Repressed Peoples of the Russian Federation, 1991–1992. Documents and Materials) (Moscow, 1993), p. 46.

16. *Repressirovannyie narody Rossii: chechentsy i ingushi. Dokumenty, fakty, kommentarii* (Repressed Peoples of Russia: Chechens and Ingush. Documents, Facts, Commentary) (Moscow, 1994), pp. 11, 12.

17. GARF, f. R-9479, op. 1, d. 925, l. 127.

18. Ibid., f. R-9401, op. 1, d. 480, ll. 358, 359.

ANTI-SEMITISM

1. Izvestiya of the CC of the CPSU, no. 3, 1989, p. 179.

2. There is no archival source for what Stalin said in this conversation; Stalin was extremely cautious in recording his words. There are, however, notes taken by the translator or translators at this meeting, and these are reflected in the book *Zastolnyie razgovory Gitlera* (Hitler's Table-Talk), by Henry Picker (Smolensk, 1993).

3. TsA FSB RF, *Arkhivno sledstvennoye delo N-3215. Dopros Ryumina, M. D., 24 iyunya 1953 g.* (Archival Case N-3215, Investigation and Evidence. Interrogation of M. D. Ryumin, 24 June 1953).

4. TsA FSB RF, R-3208. Komarov's letter to Stalin is dated 18 February 1953.

5. TsA FSB RF, d. 2354, ll. 227–39.

6. Recounted by Yu. Stetsovsky in *Istoriya sovetskikh repressii* (History of Soviet Repressions) (Moscow, 1997), p. 494.

7. TsA FSB RF, R-3208. *Materialy proverki Glavnoi voyennoy prokuratury po delu Lozovskogo, S. A., Fefera, I. S., Markisha, P. D., i dr.* (Materials for Verification by the Chief Military Prosecutor's Office in the Case of S. A. Lozovsky, I. S. Fefer, P. D. Markish, and Others).

8. Arkhiv Patriarkha/*Sovietskaya kultura* (Patriarch's Archive/*Soviet Culture*), 25 January 1991.

FROM KRONSTADT TO NOVOCHERKASSK

1. RGASPI, f. 17, op. 3, d. 136, ll. 1, 2.

2. Izvestiya of the Provisional Revolutionary Committee of Sailors, Red Army Men, and Workers, Kronstadt, 3 March 1921.

3. TsA FSB RF, f. 114728, t. 3, l. 30.

4. RGVA, f. 33988, op. 2, d. 324, l. 505.

5. Ibid., l. 16.

6. Ibid., d. 367, l. 40.

7. TsA FSB RF, f. 114728, t. 74, ll. 2–4 ob.

8. Ibid., f. 114728: *Materialy po kronshtadskomu myatyozhu* (Materials on the Kronstadt Mutiny), l. 24.

9. Ibid., f. 114728, t. 82, l. 436; t. 83, ll. 1, 2.

10. Ibid., f. 114728: *Materialy po kronshtadskomu myatyozhu*, l. 25.

11. Ibid., l. 1.

12. Ibid., f. 114728, t. 206, l. 18.

13. RGASPI, f. 17, op. 3, d. 153, ll. 2, 3.

14. Ibid., l. 98.

15. Ibid., ll. 142–44.

16. Ibid., l. 103.

17. AP RF, f. 3, op. 58, d. 211, l. 146.

Index